ROSSLYN

COUNTRY OF PAINTER AND POET

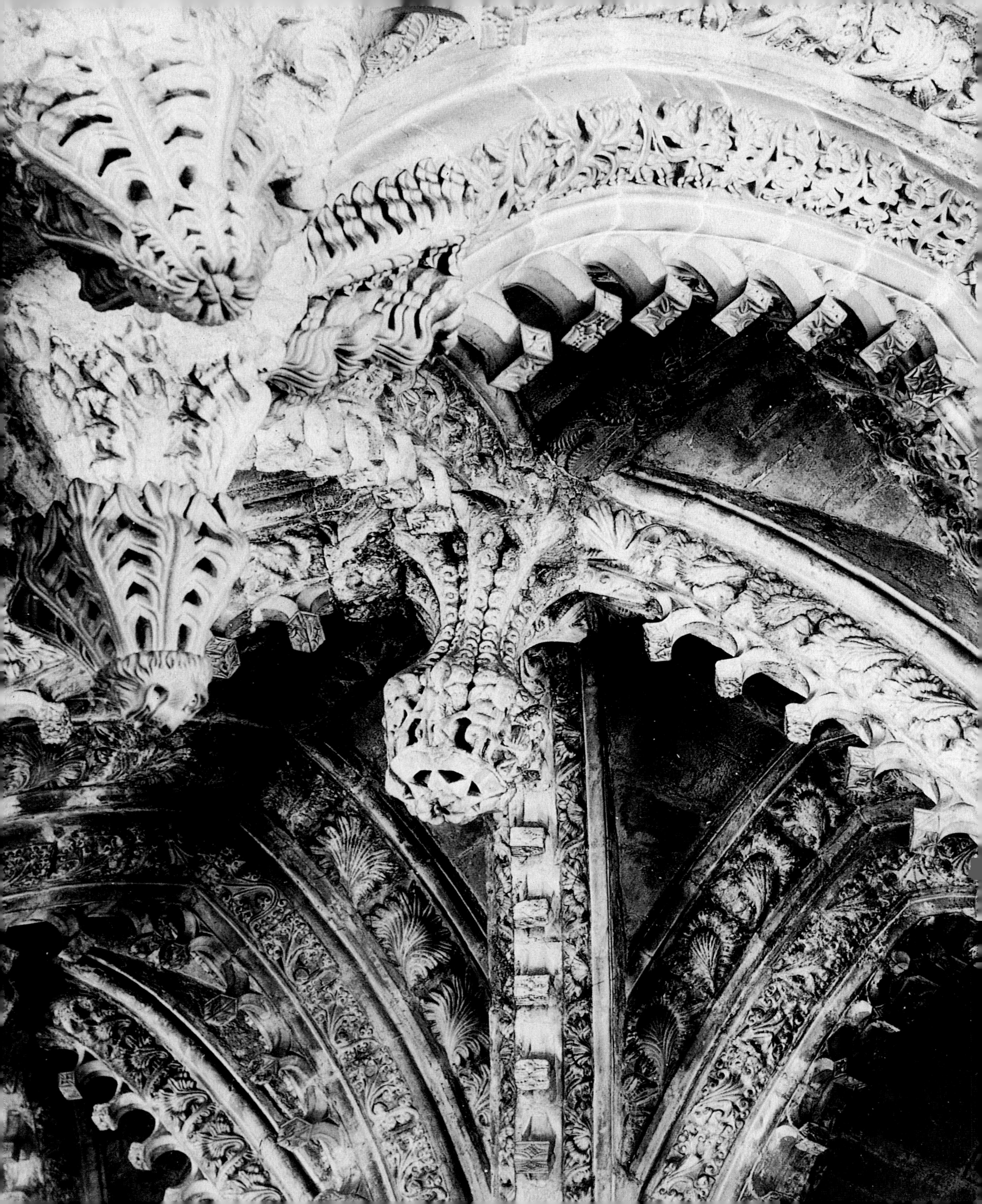

HELEN ROSSLYN & ANGELO MAGGI

ROSSLYN
Country of Painter and Poet

NATIONAL GALLERY OF SCOTLAND
EDINBURGH · 2002

Published by the Trustees of the
National Galleries of Scotland to accompany
the exhibition *Rosslyn: Country of Painter and Poet*
held at the National Gallery of Scotland, Edinburgh
from 11 April to 7 July 2002.

ISBN 1 903278 30 9 *hardback*
ISBN 1 903278 29 5 *paperback*

Designed by Dalrymple
Typeset in Haarlemmer and Rialto by Brian Young
Printed by Snoeck-Ducaju & Zoon, Belgium

Front cover illustration: detail from
Alexander Nasmyth *Rosslyn Castle with Rosslyn Chapel*, *c.*1789
Collection of E. Derricott

Back cover illustration: William Delacour
A Perspective View of the Outside of Rosslyn Chapel, *c.*1761
British Library Board, London

Frontispiece: George Washington Wilson
Detail of the Ceiling of the Lady Chapel, Rosslyn Chapel, *c.*1880
Private Collection

SPONSORED BY

Lindsays
WS
Solicitors

Foreword

The picturesque and romantic locality of Rosslyn lies near the Pentland Hills, seven miles from the city of Edinburgh. The mystique of Rosslyn Chapel as the presumed repository of the lost scrolls of Solomon's Temple and the Holy Grail, and its association with the Knights Templar and the origins of Scottish Freemasonry have attracted countless artists, writers and antiquaries for over two hundred years. By the mid-nineteenth century, Rosslyn Chapel, Castle and Glen were firmly established upon the popular tourist itinerary of Scotland, and in 1842 the controversial preservation of the exquisite fifteenth-century Chapel drew the attention of Queen Victoria and the Scottish painter, David Roberts. It is remarkable then, that the present exhibition, and the book that accompanies it, should be the first to explore the fascinating pictorial and literary traditions of Rosslyn.

In collaboration with the National Gallery of Scotland, the exhibition has been selected by two guest curators with a deep interest in, and personal commitment to, this subject: Helen Rosslyn, Countess of Rosslyn, whose knowledge and enthusiasm have been invaluable, and Dr Angelo Maggi, whose postgraduate research has been dedicated to the architectural history and development of Rosslyn. Their work has been supported by the vital contributions made by the administrative and academic skills of Katrina Thomson, former Senior Curator of Prints and Drawings at the National Gallery of Scotland, and her colleagues Helen Smailes, Senior Curator of British Art, and Valerie Hunter, Curator of Prints and Drawings. As always, we are deeply indebted to all our colleagues in the National Galleries of Scotland.

Our greatest debt, however, is to the generosity and enthusiasm of the many private and institutional lenders without whom this pioneering exhibition could not have been realised. We are especially grateful to the curatorial and administrative staff of the British Library in London and the National Library of Scotland for their patience and resourcefulness.

Finally, we are delighted to welcome as our exhibition sponsor the Edinburgh legal firm Lindsays WS. We hope that Lindsays' first venture in sponsorship with the National Galleries of Scotland will prove to be one of many mutually rewarding collaborations in the future.

MICHAEL CLARKE
Acting Director-General, National Galleries of Scotland

JULIA LLOYD WILLIAMS
Acting Director, National Gallery of Scotland

Acknowledgements

Our first thanks are due to Sir Timothy Clifford and Michael Clarke of the National Galleries of Scotland, without whom this exhibition would not have taken place. We acknowledge the tremendous support which has been given to us by all the staff of the National Galleries of Scotland, but must mention in particular Julia Lloyd Williams, Helen Smailes, our in-house curator, Valerie Hunter, Agnes Valencak-Kruger and Lesley Stevenson. Katrina Thomson deserves recognition for her contribution to this project in its infancy. We also owe a particular vote of thanks to Tim Pethick for his speedy efficiency in designing the show, and to James Simpson for his endless support during the last few years. We are enormously grateful to both Janis Adams and Christine Thompson for their guidance and tireless work on this book and would also like to record our gratitude to the Rosslyn Chapel Trust, in particular to the project director, Stuart Beattie, for its support of this publication.

To others we are indebted in various ways: James Holloway, Susanna Kerr, Sara Stevenson and Helen Watson, Scottish National Portrait Gallery; Dr Iain Gordon Brown and Kenneth Dunn, National Library of Scotland; Joanna Soden, Royal Scottish Academy; Sheila Millar, Midlothian Local Studies: Robert Cooper, Grand Lodge of Scotland; Graeme Munro, Historic Scotland; Clara Young, McManus Galleries, Dundee; Dr Katharine Lochnan, Art Gallery of Ontario; Martin Krause, Indianapolis Museum of Art; staff at the School of Architecture, Edinburgh College of Art; Patrick Bourne, Bourne Fine Art, Edinburgh; Antony Griffiths and Kim Sloan, British Museum, London; Peter Barber, British Library, London; Margaret Richardson, Susan Palmer and Stephen Astley, Sir John Soane's Museum, London; Charles Hind, the British Architectural Library, Royal Institute of British Architects, London; Janet Skidmore, Victoria & Albert Museum, London; Jane Cunningham, Witt Library, London; James Mitchell, Mitchell & Sons, London; James Holland-Hibbert and Sarah Hobrough, Spink-Leger Gallery, London; Stephen Wildman, Ruskin Library, University of Lancaster; Julie Milne, Mappin Art Gallery, Sheffield; Henry Wemyss and Henrietta Pattinson, Sotheby's, London; Jeremy Rex-Parkes and Lynda McLeod, Christie's Archives, London; Alice Lynne, *Country Life*; Gordon Cooke and Simon Edsor, The Fine Art Society, London; Anna Doni and Silvana Prosdocimo, the Italian Cultural Institute, London; Dante Marianacci and Luisa Matera, the Italian Cultural Institute, Edinburgh; the Duke and Duchess of Buccleuch; the Countess of Sutherland; the Earl and Countess of Wemyss; the Earl and Countess of Crawford and Balcarres; Sir Howard Colvin; Margaret Stewart; John G. Fleming; Francina Irwin; the Hon. Christopher Gibbs; Dr Ian Gregg; Krystyna Matyjaszkiewicz; Anna Quaranta; Sabrina and Paul Watts; Sallie Ashworth; P.A. Campbell Fraser; Joan B. Taylor; David P. Hemmings; Robert Brydon; Roc Sanford and George and Marcelle Blancett. Our particular thanks go to Shirley Watters and Professor Alistair Rowan for their constructive criticism of the text.

An exhibition such as this relies heavily on private loans. Our thanks are due to all our generous lenders and also to those whose pictures we were ultimately unable to include, but whose hospitality and enthusiasm added so much to the enjoyment of our search for material.

Finally, we would like to pay tribute to those whose domestic support and forbearance have enabled this exhibition to take place. Peter, Jamie, Alice, Lucia and Harry in England and Bianca in Italy have been patient and understanding and it is to them that we dedicate this book.

HELEN ROSSLYN AND ANGELO MAGGI

Introduction

The emergence of landscape as a dominant genre in eighteenth-century Scottish painting has been recognised as a major cultural phenomenon. For the first time, Scottish painters began to explore their indigenous landscape, and visiting English painters plotted their own itinerary of picturesque places. One such place was Rosslyn, a small and scenic spot nestling in its own glen just seven miles from the centre of Edinburgh.

The Chapel, Castle and Earldom use the spelling Rosslyn, the village, however, is spelt Roslin. Both derive from the Celtic words *Ross*, a rocky promontory, and *lynn*, a waterfall, features of the scenery in the glen below the Castle, through which passes one of Scotland's romantic rivers, the Esk. Without pretensions to grandeur of character or greatness of dimension, Rosslyn offers a simple picturesque beauty to the sensitive spirit: the ancient trees spreading their branches across the rushing stream; the steep and overhanging cliffs covered with hazels and brushwood; and the rivulet that precipitates itself into a dark den, reverberating from the opposite rocks. More than just an aesthetic landscape, the legendary Castle and Chapel, built by the St Clair family in the Middle Ages, are cultural icons of a glorious period in Scottish history.

A fortuitous meeting in 1997 cemented plans for this exhibition. The iconography of Rosslyn Chapel and Castle had been charted from two different perspectives, that of the architectural historian and that of the enthusiast for the painted landscape. The title, *Country of Painter and Poet*, pays tribute to a nineteenth-century artist, David Roberts, whose lifelong affection for Rosslyn renders him a fitting spokesman. Roberts knew the place from childhood and revisited it throughout his life as a source of constant inspiration. His Rosslyn oil paintings and watercolours have been borrowed from diverse collections and are exhibited together for the first time. But David Roberts is only one of a number of artists whose works have been influenced by Rosslyn, from the celebrated visions of Joseph Michael Gandy, to the minutely detailed etchings of the talented amateur John Clerk of Eldin. Rich in artistic fantasy, the Chapel won international fame as the subject of Daguerre's renowned diorama in London and Paris, while the Castle became a favourite haunt for the practice of sketching *en plein air* advocated by Alexander Nasmyth and Julius Caesar Ibbetson to their lady amateurs. Roberts's own words, 'It is unquestionably the country of the painter as well as the poet', acknowledge the contribution of fellow painters such as William Delacour, Paul Sandby, Thomas Hearne, Hugh William Williams, John Thomson, J.M.W. Turner, and the poets, William Drummond, Robert Burns, Walter Scott and William Wordsworth, all of whom were inspired to record the essence of Rosslyn.

This exhibition represents only one of the ways in which such a theme could have been developed. There are many other fine oil paintings, watercolours, drawings, prints, and photographs of historical value and documentary interest that we have been unable to include. Had space allowed, we would have liked to venture along the glen to include Hawthornden, the castle of the poet, William Drummond, now preserved as a writers' retreat by the Hawthornden Trust, thus continuing the tradition of painter and poet on the banks of the Esk. Nevertheless, our journey through Rosslyn's cultural history has been a delightful one and we hope that our selection will afford the same pleasure to the viewer as it has to the curators.

HELEN ROSSLYN AND ANGELO MAGGI

NOTE: ROSSLYN OR ROSLIN ?

In preparing this exhibition, it became apparent that during the eighteenth and nineteenth centuries there was little consistency in the spelling of the name Rosslyn. Artists, amongst whom David Roberts is a notable example, variously inscribed different works with different spellings and used different spellings again in correspondence. In the following essays, we have opted for consistency and used the ancient spelling of Rosslyn, except in quoted material or where the village of Roslin is being discussed.

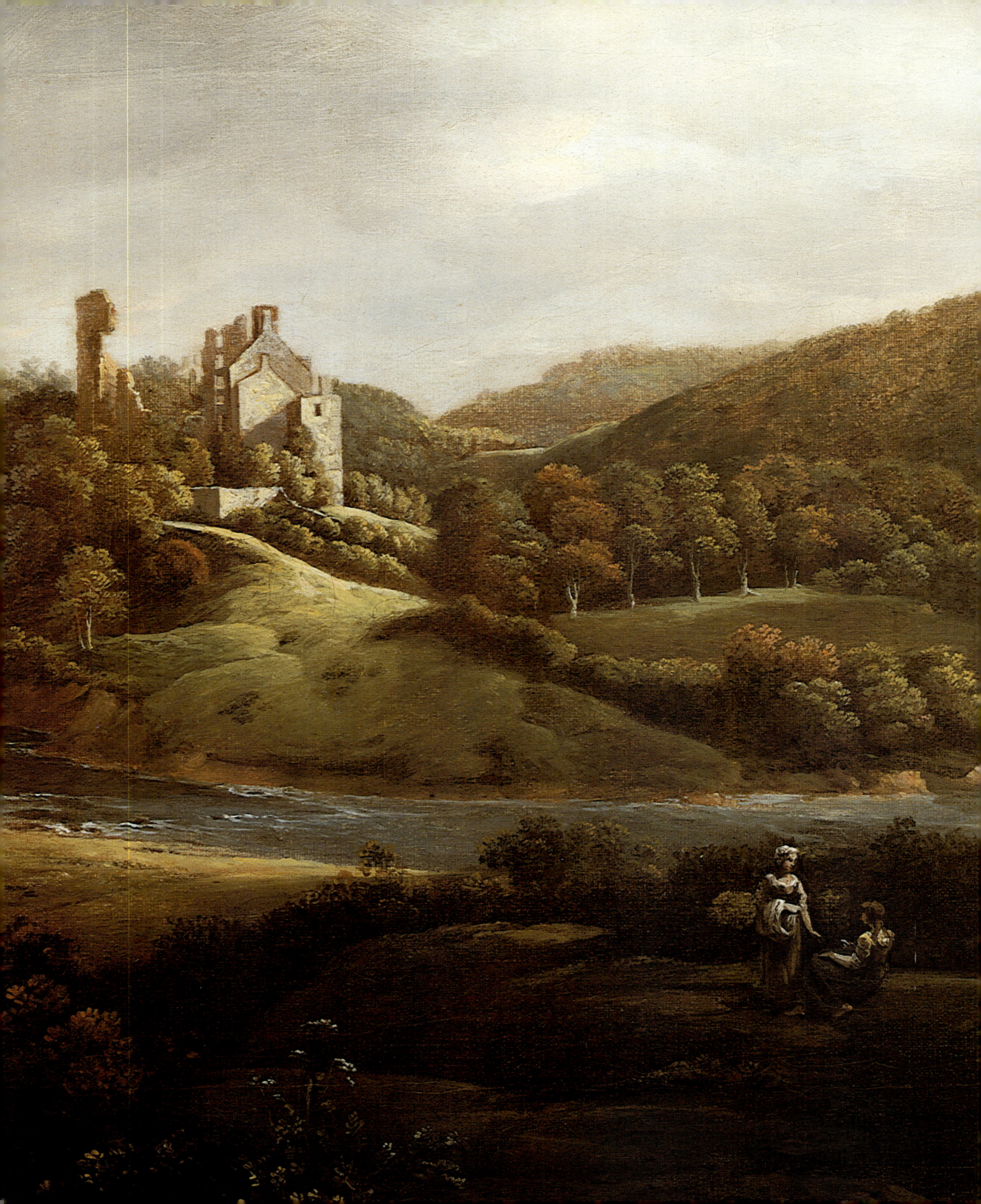

HELEN ROSSLYN

The Living Tradition

Romance and real history have the same common origin … and indeed the traditional memorials of all earlier ages … may be termed either romantic histories, or historical romances.[1]

In the days of King Robert the Bruce, in the Age of Chivalry, the knights St Clair of Rosslyn stood centre stage in the pageant of Scottish history and legend.

In 1066, William St Clair came to Britain from France with his cousin, William the Conqueror. Like many other Anglo-Norman families, the St Clairs were drawn to Scotland by the offer of land from King Malcolm Canmore. William soon became a favourite of the king, who called him 'the Seemly St Clair' and entrusted him with the vital task of escorting his future queen, the Saxon Princess Margaret, from the court of Hungary. As Cup Bearer to Queen Margaret, William was then granted the barony of Rosslyn. His son, Henry St Clair, was knighted by King Malcolm for his military prowess in defending Scotland against the English and thus were created the knights St Clair of Rosslyn.[2]

There are various accounts of when the first Castle was built at Rosslyn. The probable founder of the original building was 'the Seemly St Clair', on receipt of the barony of Rosslyn in around 1070.[3] This seems most likely, as the land was described by Father Hay in his *Genealogie of the Sainteclaires of Rosslyn* as 'a great Forrest'. It has also been suggested by various sources that the original Castle was built on a different site from that of the present one. Oliver & Boyd's *Scottish Tourist*, published in 1852, makes this claim: 'The first castle of Roslin was called the Maiden castle, some vestiges of the foundation of which can be traced within a bend of the Esk at a short distance.' Father Hay also recorded how a later St Clair founded the present Castle on his return from the Battle of Roslin in 1302. He chose a new location on the advice of an English prisoner '… who, because he saw the Castle of Rosline not to be strong enough, he advised him to build it upon the rock where it now standeth; which councell he embraced, and builded the Wall Tower with other buildings, and there he dwelt'.[4] The earliest part of the Castle surviving today is the lantern-tower to the north-east of the entrance, dating from 1304.

Annals record the continuation of 'the lordly line of high St Clair'[5] throughout the twelfth and thirteenth centuries and it is noted that, 'While at the zenith of their glory, they stood in the foremost ranks of Scotia's nobility'.[6] The advent of the fourteenth century saw the St Clair family holding court at a newly fortified Rosslyn Castle and closely allied to King Robert the Bruce. Sir Henry St Clair (1297–1331) and his two sons, John and William, fought with the king at the Battle of Bannockburn. He was rewarded for his bravery with the gift of Pentland Moor, the Charter for which, dated 12 April 1316, still remains in the family archives. Tales are told of a magnificent feast held at Rosslyn in 1314 before the Battle of Bannockburn, when St Clair invited the fifteen thousand Scottish troops to meet on his land and prepare to march to Stirling together to face the English. Victory for the Scots heralded a time of peace, during which one of the king's favourite pastimes was the sport of 'the chase'. The valour and skill of the young Sir William St Clair, ally of King Robert at the Battle of Bannockburn, are recalled as follows in the legend of the *Royal Hunt of Roslin.*[7]

The nearby Pentland Hills were home to one particular white faunch deer, which consistently refused to be caught by the royal hounds. Sir William St Clair, responding to a challenge from the king, wagered his own life that his two hounds, Help and Hold, could catch the deer before it reached the safety of the March Burn. In a dramatic contest, the hounds caught hold of the deer just as it crossed the burn. The two hounds are henceforth part of the iconography of Rosslyn, appearing in the engraving of the Chapel in John Slezer's *Theatrum Scotiae* [plate 2], and gracing both Sir William's tombstone in the Chapel and a prize cup presented in 1844 at Ascot by the Royal Hunt of England, in tribute to the 'Master of her Majesty's Buckhounds' of the day, the 3rd Earl of Rosslyn. The presence of the two dogs in David Roberts's *The Interior of Rosslyn Chapel* alludes to the same legend [plate 3].

On the death of Robert the Bruce in 1329, Sir William was one of the knights chosen to accompany his heart to Jerusalem where he had wished it to be buried. The knights were killed fighting against the Moors in Spain in 1330 and their bodies, together with the heart of Bruce, were brought back to Scotland. William was succeeded by

OPPOSITE
Detail from Alexander Nasmyth *Rosslyn Castle with Rosslyn Chapel*, *c.*1789, plate 34

his grandson, also called William, who married Isabella de Strathearn, daughter of Malise, Earl of Caithness, Strathearn and Orkney. As Malise had no male heir, Henry St Clair, William and Isabella's son, became first Prince of Orkney. Throughout the fourteenth and fifteenth centuries, the St Clair family continued to reside in great style at Rosslyn Castle. In 1390, Sir Henry, second Prince of Orkney '… builded the great dungeon of Rosslyn, and other walls thereabout, together with parks for red and fallow deer'.[8] On his death in 1420, his son Sir William St Clair became third and last Prince of Orkney, resigning this title to the King of Scotland in 1470 in exchange for lands at Ravenscraig. He has been described as the 'most brilliant of all the St Clairs',[9] and with good reason, as he was to become the founder of Rosslyn Chapel in 1446. He also made many additions to the Castle on his succession to the estate and lived in great splendour with his princess: 'In his house he was royally served in gold and silver vessels, in most princely manner … He had his halls and his chambers richly hung with embroidered hangings, &c.'[10]

Unfortunately, though life was lived on a flamboyant scale, domestic setbacks had grave consequences. In 1447, according to the writings of Father Hay, the princess, 'who tooke great delight in little dogs', sent one of her ladies to look under her bed with a lighted candle for a litter of puppies. Predictably, 'the fire rose and burnt the bed, and then passed to the seeling of the great chamber in which the Princess was'.[11] The Castle was severely damaged through fire. Repair was swift, however, and Sir William turned his attention once again to the building of his beloved Rosslyn Chapel.

At this point the St Clair family split into three branches. Sir William, founder of the Chapel, had six sons and divided his estates between the eldest three: William, by his first marriage; and Oliver and William by his second.

1

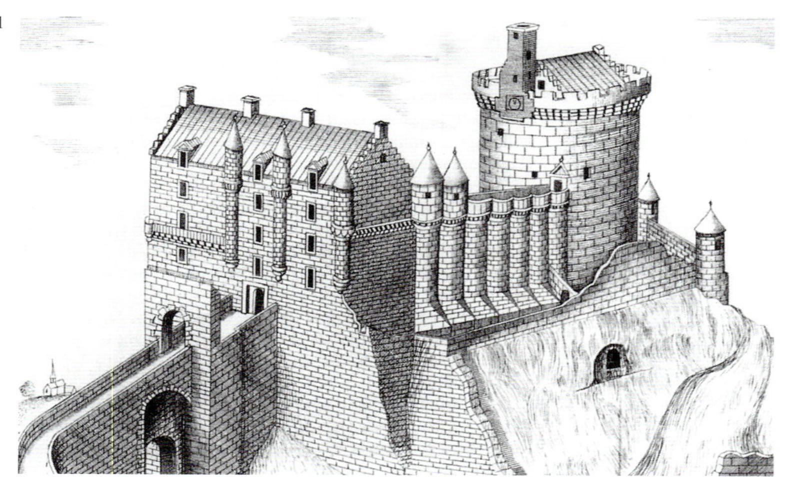

2

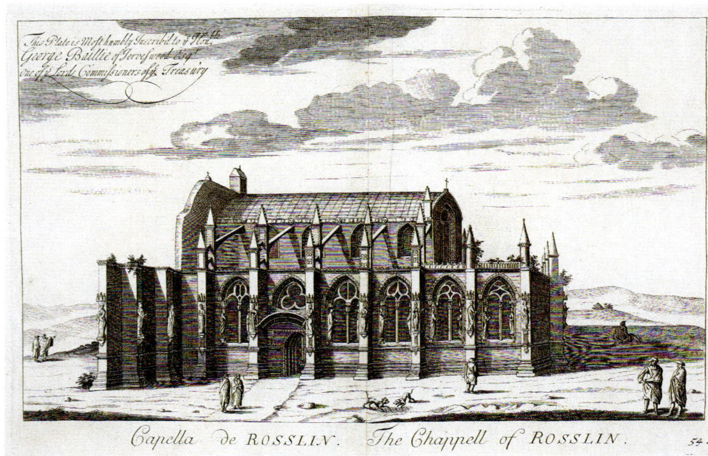

The eldest son, known as 'William the Waster' was effectively disinherited and was bequeathed only the lands of Dysart and Ravenscraig in Fife; the second son, Oliver, inherited the majority of the estate, including the lands at Rosslyn; and the third son, also called William, was given the earldom of Caithness. So it was that the powerful family of the St Clairs, with its extensive lands amassed over generations, was divided in the mid-fifteenth century into three separate lines: the lords St Clair of Dysart; the St Clairs of Rosslyn; and the Sinclairs of Caithness.

The St Clairs of Rosslyn continued to live at the Castle. It was almost totally destroyed in 1544, during the rupture between England and Scotland over Henry VIII's attempt to unite the two kingdoms through marriage. His planned union between his son Edward, still a child, and the infant Mary, Queen of Scots, known as the 'Rough Wooing', was strongly opposed by many of the leading Scottish nobility, including Sir William St Clair, who were staunch supporters of the pre-Reformation church. Henry's plot failed and the Earl of Hertford was sent to Scotland in May 1544 to take vengeance on behalf of the king. Rosslyn Castle was attacked and burnt, but was once again rebuilt. This Sir William St Clair, 'a man of brilliant parts',[12] was then made Lord Justice-General of Scotland in 1559. He was a fair-minded man and once saved a gypsy from the gallows, '… upon which accoumpt [sic] the whole body of gypsies were, of old, accustomed to gather in the Stanks of Rosslyn every year, where they acted severall plays'.[13] They were permitted to reside in two of the Castle towers, known thenceforth as Robin Hood and Little John, after one of the most famous May-tide plays in Scotland during the fifteenth and sixteenth centuries. This ancient custom of welcoming travelling players to Rosslyn forms an early part of its cultural heritage, to which later reference is often made [plate 4]. It has been suggested that the many carvings of the Green Man in Rosslyn Chapel also bear relation to the legendary

3

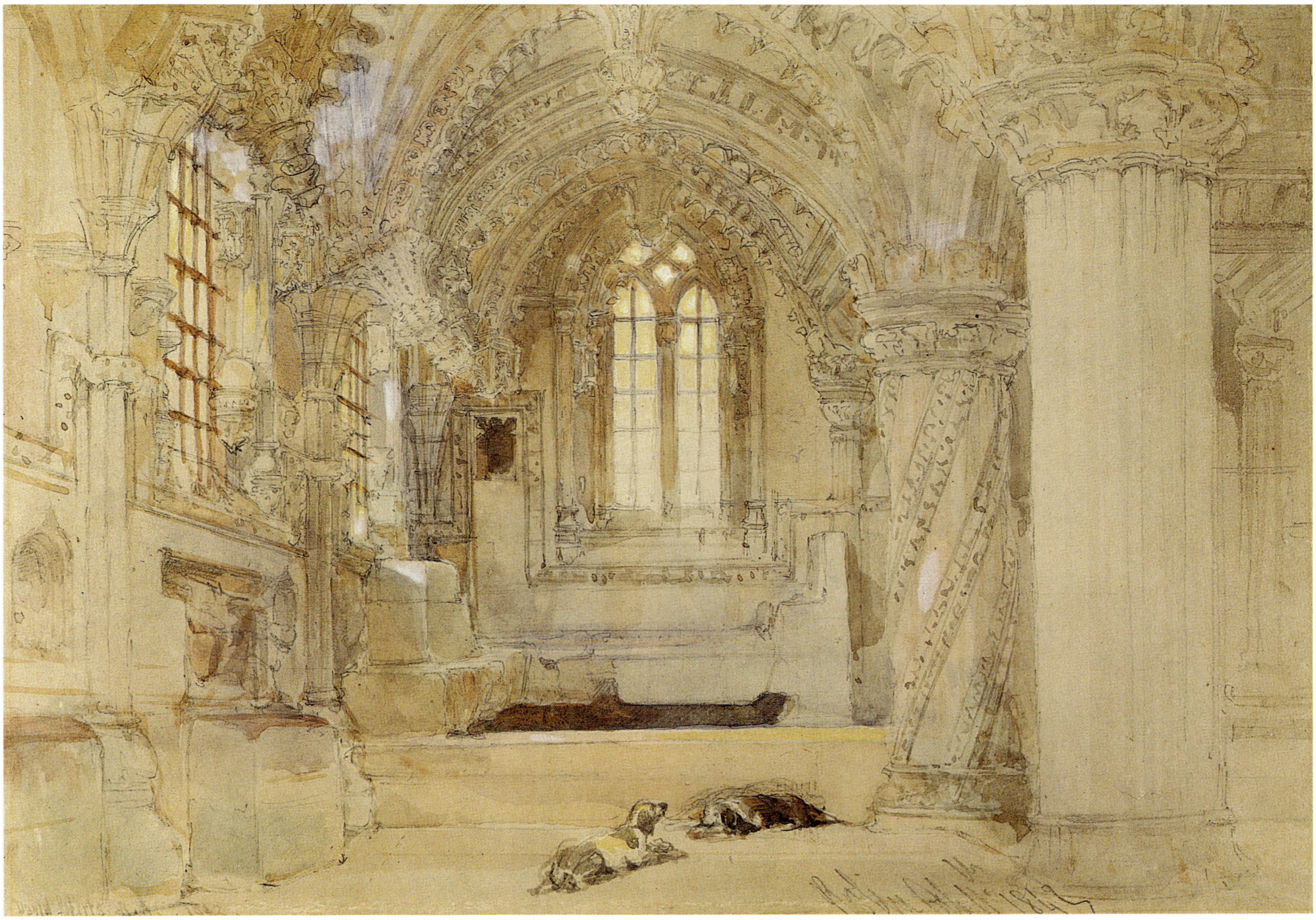

PLATE 1

J. Gellatly

Rosslyn Castle, before 1700

Private Collection

PLATE 2

Captain John Slezer

The Chapel of Rosslyn, from *Theatrum Scotiae*, 1693

Private Collection

PLATE 3

David Roberts

The Interior of Rosslyn Chapel, 1842

National Gallery of Scotland, Edinburgh

PLATE 4

Julius Caesar Ibbetson

Harvest Field, Roslin

Private Collection

4

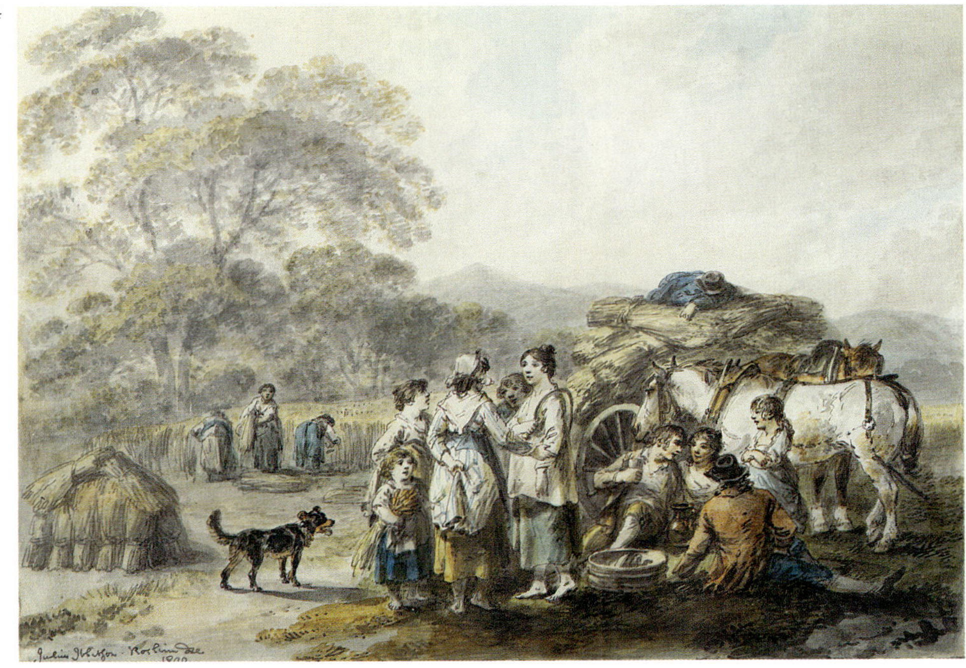

5

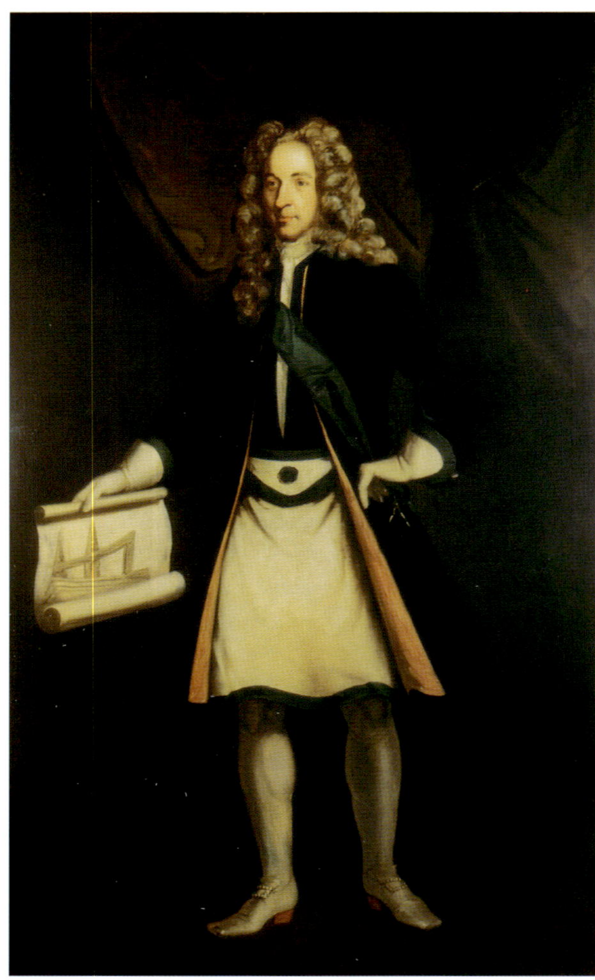

figure of Robin Hood.[14] It is said that this Sir William St Clair was responsible for collecting together a huge number of valuable manuscripts that had been taken from monasteries at the time of the Reformation.[15]

The next Sir William St Clair, who succeeded to the estate in 1582, also made many additions to the building: 'He built the vaults and great turnpike of Roslin … He builded one of the arches of the Drawbridge, and a fine house near the Milne [mill] and the Tower of the Dungeon where the clock was kept …'[16] He also built the Great Hall. The fireplace from the Great Hall still stands today, bearing the date 1596. His son, also Sir William, finished building over the vaults to the level of the courtyard. His initials, with the date 1622, remain over the door of the Castle, as does the ornate plaster ceiling of the same date in the Great Room. This Sir William St Clair died in 1650 and was succeeded by his son John.

It was at this period that the Castle must have stood at its most complete, for in 1650 it was attacked by Cromwell's troops under General Monck. The Chapel was spared to provide stabling for their horses, but the Castle was ransacked. It was again pillaged and burnt in 1688, shortly after the Protestant William of Orange landed in England and displaced the Catholic James II & VII. On the night of 11 December, a mob from Edinburgh, joined by villagers of Roslin, broke into the Chapel and destroyed furniture and vestments which were by then regarded as Popish and idolatrous. Sir John St Clair, occupant of the Castle at that time, was sent as a prisoner to Tynemouth Castle. On his death in 1690, the estate passed to his younger brother James.

By the end of the seventeenth century the glory of Rosslyn Castle and the noble family of St Clair had faded, to become the stuff of legend. John Slezer's *Theatrum Scotiae* of 1693 talks of 'The Sleeping Lady' of Rosslyn Castle. The story tells of a great treasure, buried beneath the vaults under the courtyard and guarded by a sleeping lady of the ancient house of St Clair, who was only to be woken by the sound of a trumpet coming from one of the lower dungeons. Once wakened, she would point to the treasure, upon which Rosslyn Castle might rise from the ruins and become the majestic place that once it was. But legend it was to remain, and William St Clair, grandson of Sir James, became the last male heir of the Rosslyn branch of the St Clairs in 1706. He was known as 'the last Rosslyn' [plate 5] and died in 1778, having settled the derelict estate of Rosslyn in 1735 upon General James St Clair, who was descended from the Dysart branch of the St Clair family.

6

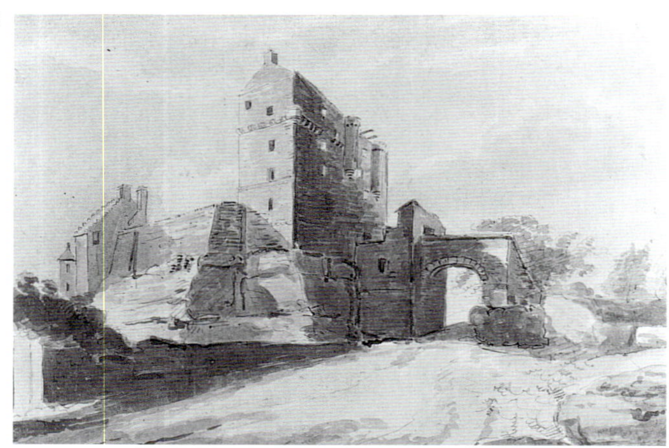

8

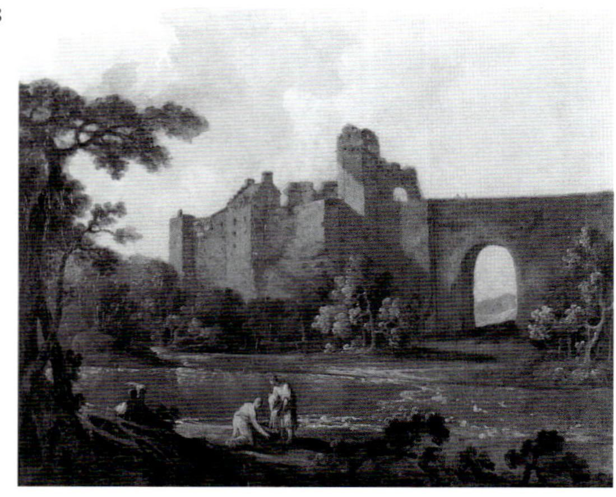

PLATE 5
Attributed to Edward Miller
Sir William St Clair of Rosslyn, 1736
The Grand Lodge of Antient, Free and Accepted Masons of Scotland

PLATE 6
Attributed to Paul Sandby
Rosslyn Castle from the South-East, showing the Tower and the Gateway, c.1750s
Collection of Dr D. Groghan

PLATE 7A&B
William Delacour
Prospect of Rosslyn Castle and Chapel from the South-East and from the North-West, 1761
British Library Board, London

PLATE 8
Jacob More *Rosslyn Castle from the South*, c.1771
Collection of the Earl of Wemyss and March KT

7A

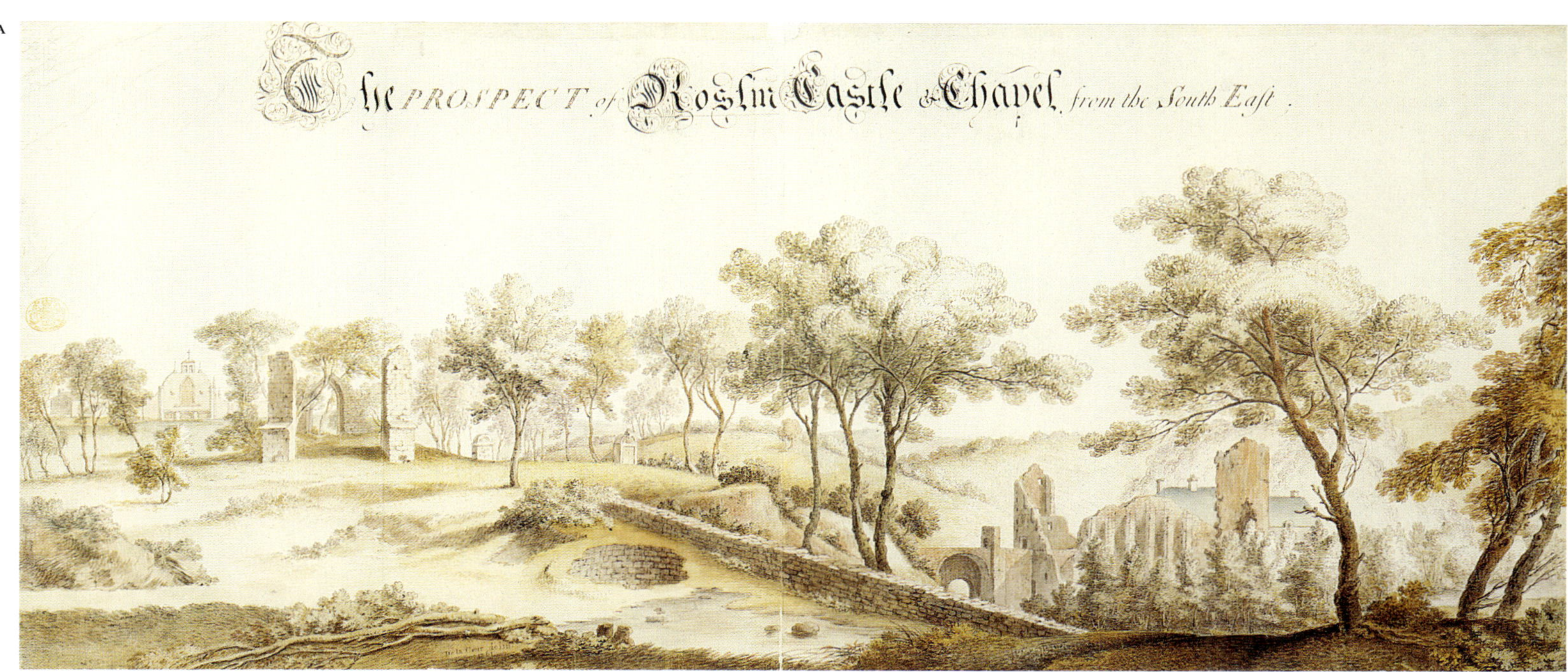

7B

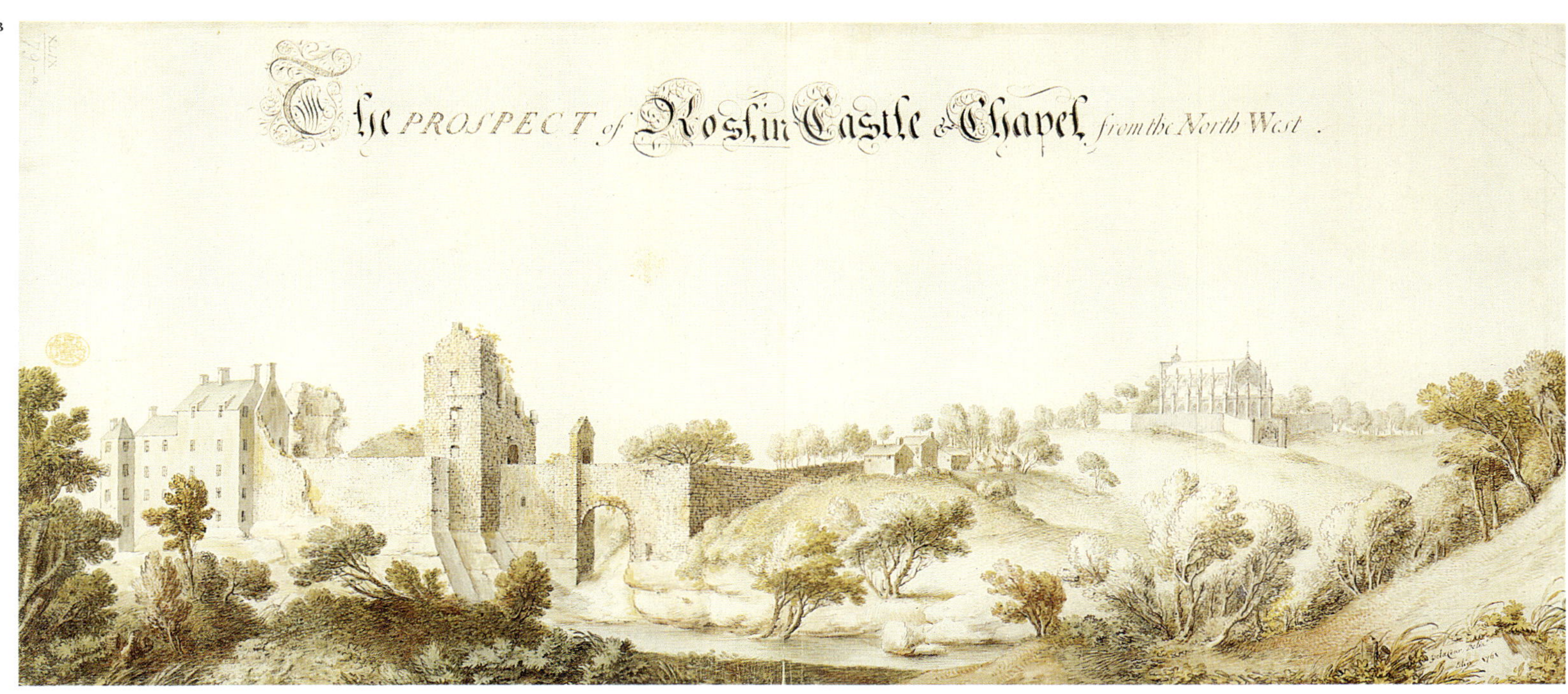

So, for some years during the latter part of the eighteenth century, the ruined Castle lay abandoned in its glen, at a time when interest in local picturesque landscape was growing. The curtailment of Grand Tours in Europe during the Anglo-French wars was encouraging antiquarians and artists to explore Britain. Little was done towards the upkeep of the Castle during this period and there are few papers relating to estate matters. It is, therefore, difficult to date the deterioration of particular parts of the building. The pictures painted of Rosslyn at the turn of the century offer us the best means of revisiting the place as it was then. The pen and wash drawing attributed to Paul Sandby (1731–1809), possibly executed in the late 1740s during visits he made as draughtsman for the Scottish Ordnance Survey, shows a complete section of the Castle still standing over the entrance bridge, with a second, smaller gateway in front [plate 6]. By 1761, it is clear from the panoramic *Prospect of Rosslyn Castle and Chapel from the North-West* by William Delacour (d.1767) [plate 7b] that this significant wing of the Castle had lost

9

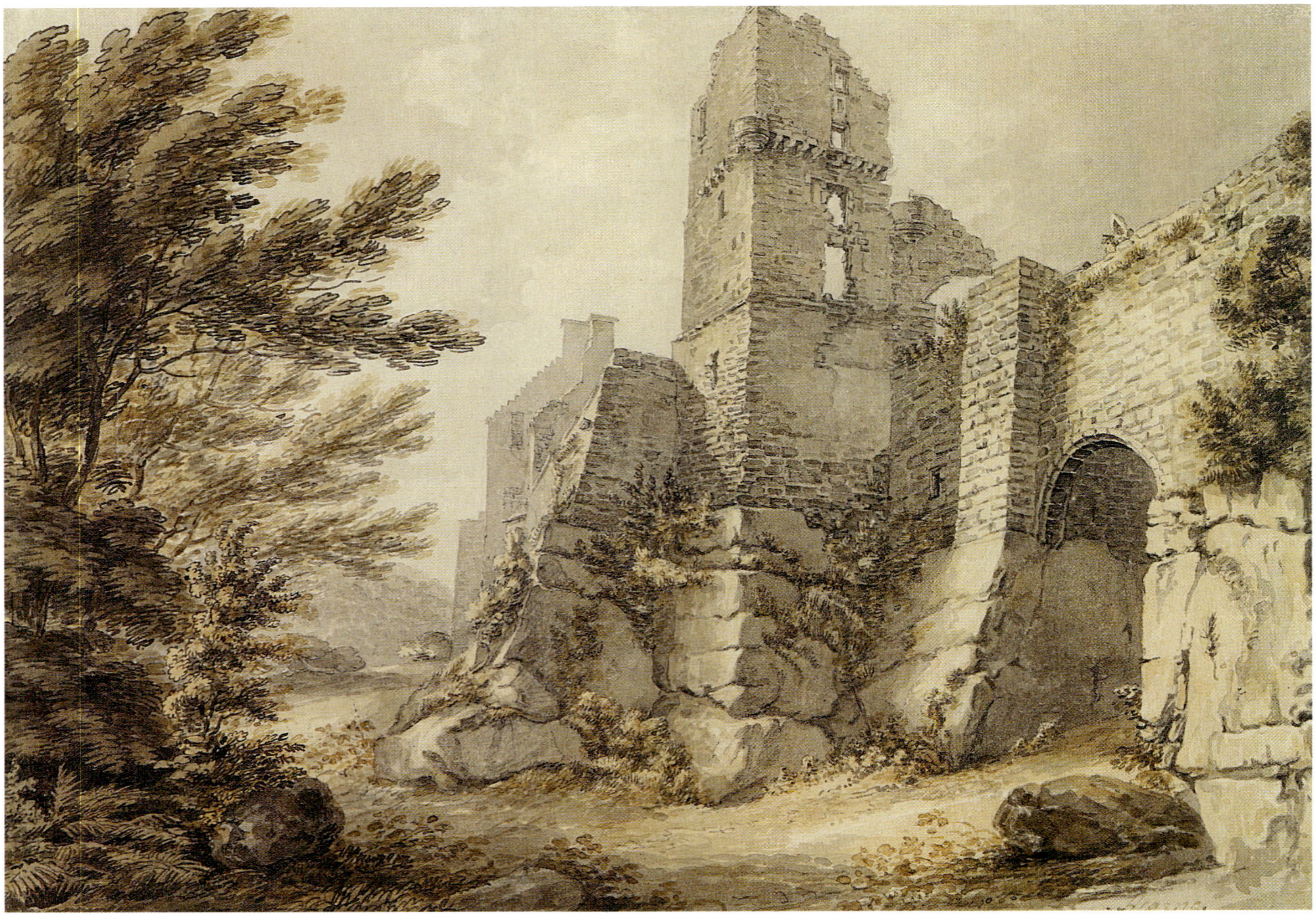

10

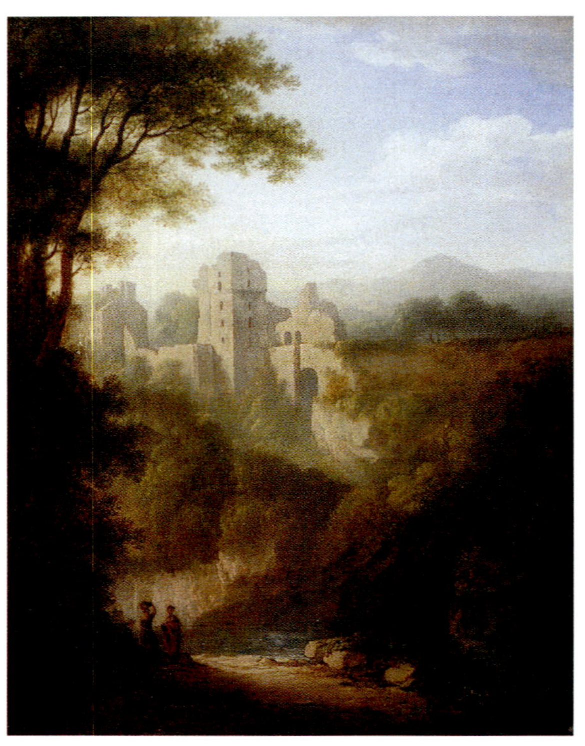

its roof and turrets and had been reduced to a ruined archway over the bridge, though still with its entrance gate. This smaller gateway is no longer evident ten years later, in the view of the Castle from the same angle [plate 8], dated 1771, by Jacob More (1740–1793). The tower, however, seems largely unchanged, still retaining a complete arch over the bridge. This is reaffirmed in an engraving made for Thomas Pennant's *Tour of Scotland* by Moses Griffiths, published in the following year.

By 1778, according to the detailed architectural drawing by Thomas Hearne (1744–1817), the arch over the bridge had largely fallen, though the tower remained [plate 9]. Whether there was further slight deterioration of this arch or not over the next two decades is subject for conjecture, but the tower seems to have stood intact with windows for some time. Joseph Farington (1747–1821) made a pen and wash study of the ruins in 1788 [plate 42]; Alexander Nasmyth (1758–1840) used the same view in his oil, *Rosslyn Castle with the Esk* [plate 10]; and this distinctive tower is still visible in the paintings of Julius Caesar Ibbetson (1759–1817), which date from his stay in the village of Roslin in 1800.[17]

PLATE 9
Thomas Hearne
Rosslyn Castle, 1778
Art Gallery of Ontario, Toronto

PLATE 10
Alexander Nasmyth
Rosslyn Castle with the Esk, c.1789
Private Collection

PLATE 11
Samuel Dukinfield Swarbreck
Rosslyn Castle and Glen, 1837
Private Collection

A significant deterioration of the tower is first apparent in the watercolour, *View of Rosslyn Castle from the River*, by John 'Old Jock' Wilson (1774–1855), dated 1808, which suggests that the tower fell sometime between 1800 and 1808. This is how it appears in *Sketches in Scotland*, published in 1837 [plate 11], by Samuel Dukinfield Swarbreck (active 1830–1865) and indeed is largely how it is today. Views of the Castle from all sides show that the low-lying land at the foot of the Castle, known as 'the Stanks',[18] still existed in the eighteenth century.

While the physical remains of the Castle were crumbling, the fortunes of the family were changing once again. In 1801 the earldom of Rosslyn was created and joined with the estate in 1805, in the following manner. General James St Clair, having no children, left the estate to the son of his sister, Grizel, eldest daughter of Henry, 10th Lord St Clair. This son, James Paterson, assumed his uncle's name of St Clair on inheriting the estate, but also had no male heir. He, therefore, left the estate of Rosslyn, together with the estate of Dysart, to James Erskine, grandson of his aunt Katherine, second daughter of Henry, 10th Lord St Clair. Katherine had married Sir John Erskine of Alva, and their son, Sir Henry Erskine, married Janet Wedderburn. Their son James [plate 12], also took the name of St Clair on inheriting the estate, thus becoming Sir James St Clair-Erskine, which remains the family name of the Earls of Rosslyn to this day.

11

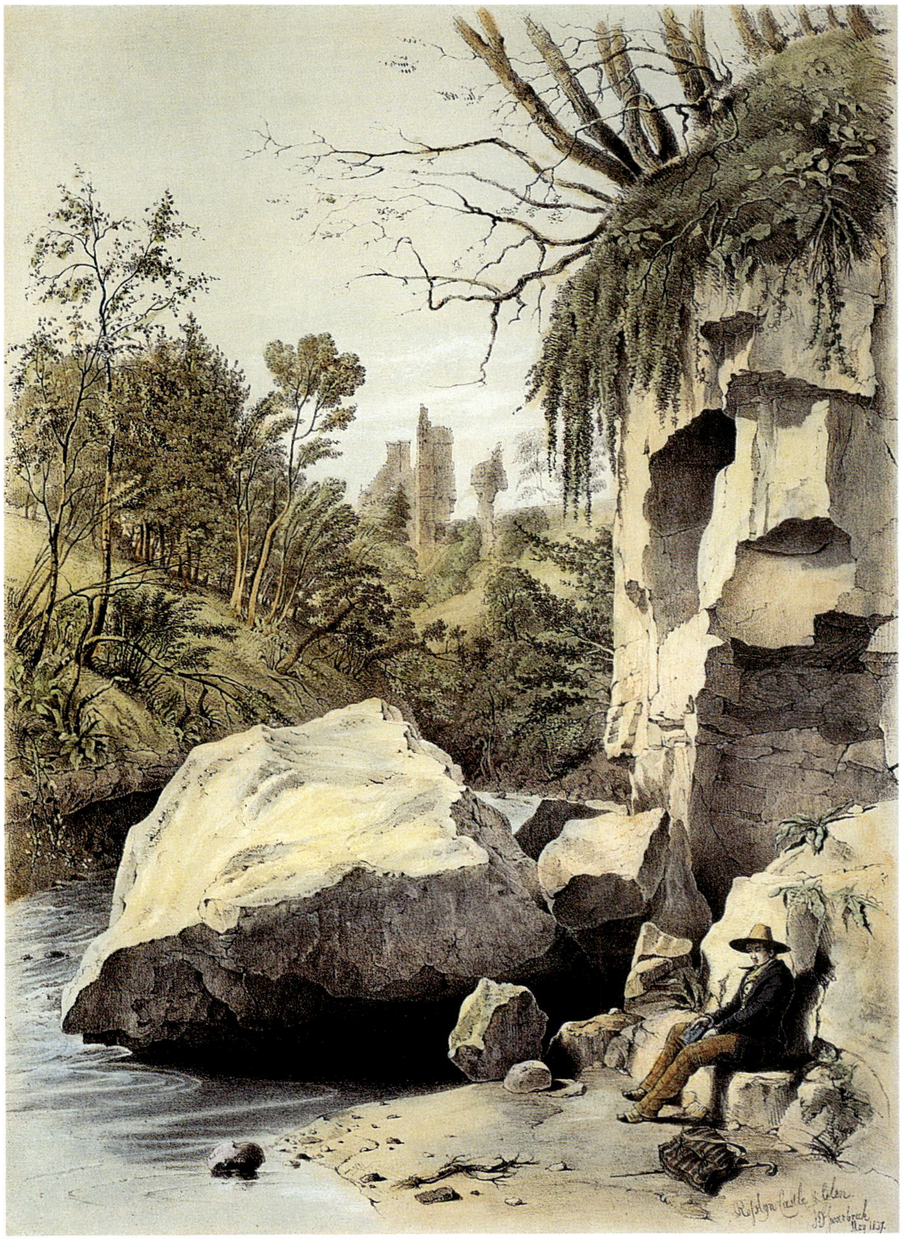

Through another line, the title Earl of Rosslyn was inherited by the same Sir James St Clair-Erskine, as described below. 'The last Rosslyn', the William St Clair mentioned above, had only one surviving daughter, Sarah, who married Sir Peter Wedderburn. They had two children, a son Alexander, and a daughter Janet, who married Sir Henry Erskine. During his lifetime, Alexander Wedderburn was made Lord Chancellor and was created Baron Loughborough in 1795 and 1st Earl of Rosslyn in 1801, with provision for both titles to be passed to his nephew, as he had no children himself. His sister's son, James St Clair-Erskine, therefore became the 2nd Earl of Rosslyn in 1805. From this point onwards, title and estate have passed together through the male line.

There also exists an historical link between the St Clair family and Scottish Freemasonry which is often quoted in connection with Rosslyn Chapel. The preface to a recent edition of *An Account of the Chapel of Roslin 1778* contains the following: 'This small volume, written more than 200 years ago, shows that Freemasons of the time were fascinated by Rosslyn Chapel.'[19] The history of Scottish Freemasonry is well documented from 1598 and two documents survive from *c.*1601 and *c.*1628, known respectively, as the First and Second St Clair Charters, in which the Masons of Scotland petitioned the current head of the St Clair family to resume the position of their 'patron and protector'. This implies an earlier association between the St Clairs and the Scottish Masons, which may have begun in the mid-fifteenth century, during the building of Rosslyn Chapel.

Legend has it that Sir William St Clair, who founded the Chapel, was granted the privilege of Grand Master of the Scottish Masons by James II & VII and that this honour became hereditary in his family. This was a position of some importance, as the Grand Master acted as a mediator in disputes between fellow Masons, thus assuming the role of Grand Judge. That the honour might have been bestowed on the family is possible, considering the prominence of the St Clairs in the fifteenth century. The ornate Rosslyn Chapel, to which Sir William dedicated his life, is indeed a celebration of the craft of stonemasons and many masons' marks are to be found carved into the walls. Sir William brought in his artisans 'from other regions and forraigne kingdoms', so intent was he on producing a building of the highest quality. He treated his workmen well: 'Because he thought the [stone] masons had not a convenient place to lodge in … he made them build the town of Rosline that now is extant and gave everyone a house and lands'.[20]

The family connection with the craft lasted until 1736, the date of the foundation of the Grand Lodge of Scotland. At this point the title of Grand Master was held by William St Clair, 'the last Rosslyn'. He tendered the resignation of his hereditary office, only to be voted back as Scotland's first elected Grand Master. He was also Master Mason in the Canongate-Kilwinning Lodge, where his portrait still hangs. In more recent times, two Earls of Rosslyn are numbered amongst the Grand Master Masons of the Grand Lodge of Scotland: James St Clair-Erskine, 2nd earl (1810–12); and Francis Robert, 4th earl (1870–3).

In this way, the beginning of the nineteenth century witnessed the reunion of the estate and family line and marked the start of the gradual regeneration of Rosslyn. General James St Clair, whose nephew was to become the 2nd earl, has been credited with saving the Chapel from destitution. Francis Grose in his *Antiquities of Scotland* states: 'Of late years, this beautiful edifice was in great danger of becoming quite ruinous: but to the great honour of the late General Sinclair, then proprietor, he prevented it, by putting new flagstones on the roof: and new wooden casements, with glass, into all the windows.'[21] There was also a groundsman in residence who tended to the estate at the time of Francis Grose's visit to Rosslyn in 1788, as he remarked on 'a dwelling house … inhabited by the family of a gardener'.[22] Indeed, by 1801, the date of John Stoddart's *Remarks on Local Scenery and Manners in Scotland*, we learn that Rosslyn was already famous for its fruit gardens and remarkable strawberries: 'To go to Roslin and eat strawberries was one of the proper things to be achieved by an inhabitant of Edinburgh during the summer months.'[23]

General James was descended from the Dysart line of St Clairs and it was at Dysart House that the 2nd Earl of Rosslyn (1805–1837) lived with his wife Henrietta, daughter of the Hon. Edward Bouverie. He was at various times a Member of Parliament for Castle Rising, Morpeth and Kirkcaldy, Director-General of Chancery in Scotland and Lord President of the Council. On his death he was succeeded by his son James Alexander, who became the 3rd Earl of Rosslyn (1837–1866). He married Frances, daughter of Lt General Wemyss of Wemyss Castle in Fife and, like his father, lived at Dysart House. The 3rd earl became more closely involved than either of his predecessors in the maintenance and upkeep of the Chapel, instructing work to be carried out on both the exterior and interior of the building over a period of two decades. It was acknowledged even by his vociferous opponents in 'the restoration controversy' that 'Lord Roslin has admirably preserved the chapel'.[24]

His son, Francis Robert, the 4th earl (1866–1890), showed a similar dedication to the building. He was by all accounts a kind and well-respected member of the Dysart community who took a personal interest in the welfare of his tenants and workers. Despite continuing to live at Dysart House, he was closely involved with the estate at Rosslyn, corresponding on a regular basis with the factor of the estate and Chapel custodian, John Thomson, who lived at College Hill House from 1851 until his death in 1881. It was during the lifetime of the 4th earl that the apse and organ loft of the chapel were designed and built in the early 1880s by the architect, Andrew Kerr.

The 5th Earl of Rosslyn (1890–1939) has often been described as the most colourful of the recent 'St Clairs of Rosslyn'. Inheriting the title at the age of just twenty-one, he moved to Dysart House with his young bride, Violet. He was a close friend of the Prince of Wales, later Edward VII, who proposed the toast at his wedding, and he was part of the prince's wild and glamorous set. His love of the high life and his penchant for gambling were to be his undoing; by 1896 he had lost most of the fortune he had inherited from his father, including Dysart House. He moved south and continued to live a life of adventure, which he later chronicled in his autobiography *My Gamble with Life*. He outlived his son and was succeeded by his

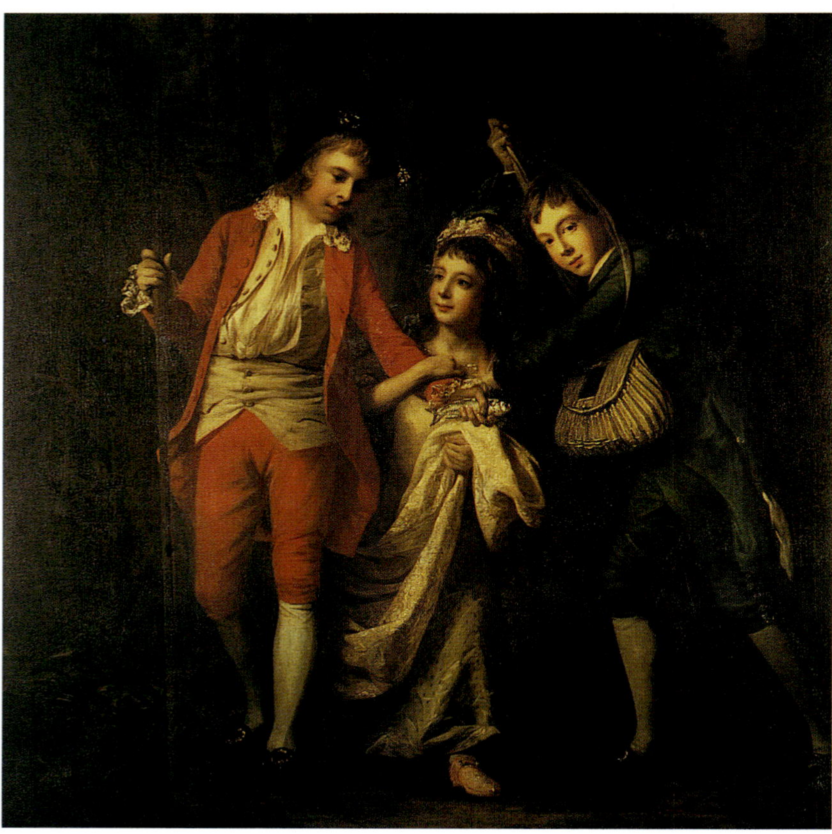
12

13

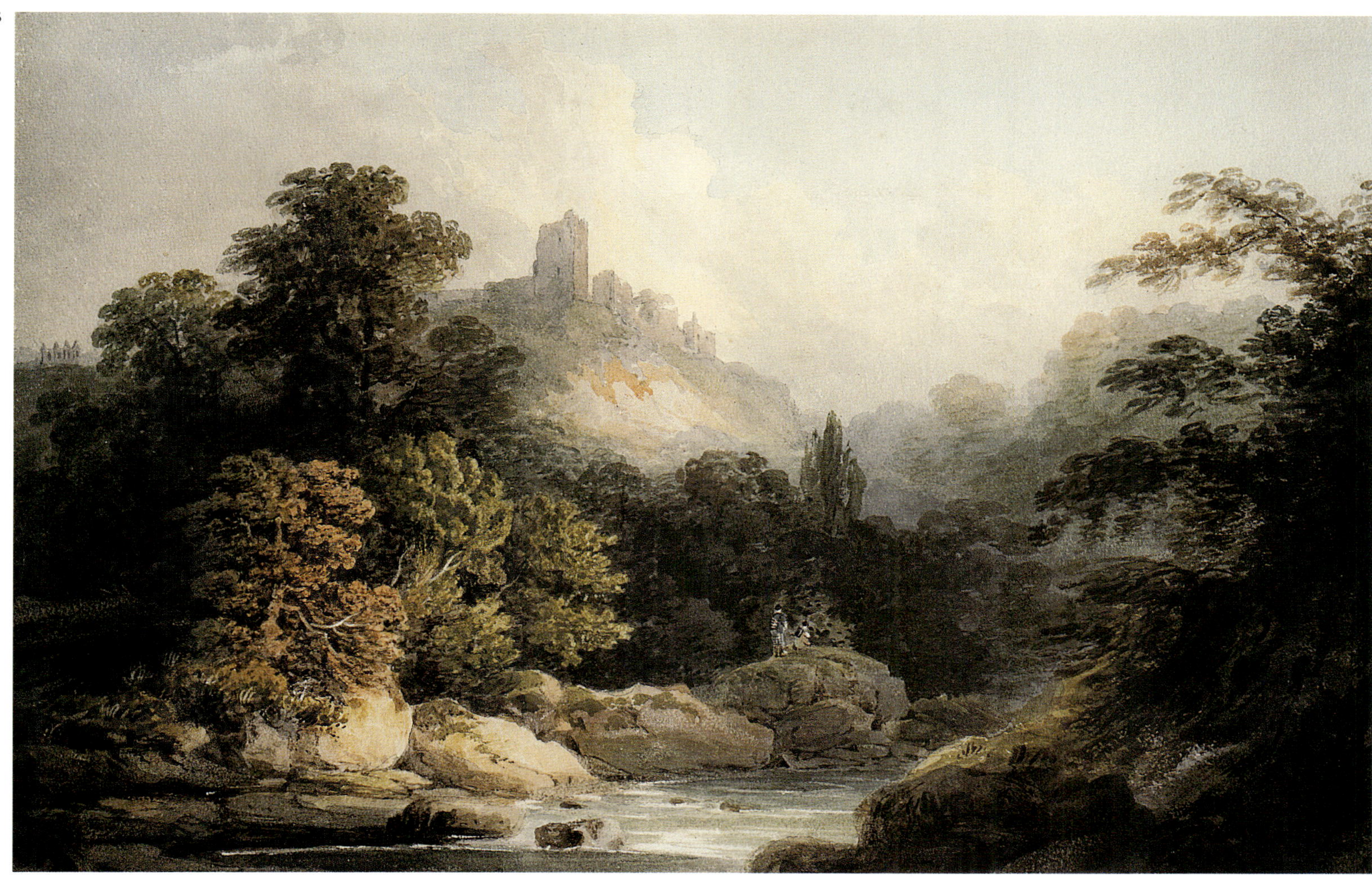

grandson, Anthony Hugh Francis Harry, the 6th earl (1939–1977), who commissioned conservation work and the cleaning of the Chapel interior in the 1950s and added the stained-glass windows in the baptistery.

This commitment continues today. Communications pass between earl and architect much in the manner of the well-documented correspondence between the 4th earl and his architect, Andrew Kerr, though thankfully more harmoniously than in his Lordship's letter of 5 October 1880: 'I did not altogether like the sketch for the top of the stone cope … The drawing did not quite come up to my idea and the price seemed disproportionately high.'[25] In 1996, a charitable trust, of which the present Earl of Rosslyn is chairman, was established to oversee a continuing programme of conservation at the Chapel.

It is only in recent years that attention has been paid to the regeneration of the Castle. Less than thirty years ago, it lay completely empty and open to the elements. The picturesque ruin had at last reached a point where it must crumble or be saved. Since succeeding to the title and inheriting the estate in 1977, my husband has initiated and overseen an extensive programme of restoration at the Castle. The ruined walls have been stabilised, the windows and roof repaired or replaced and the panelling in the Great Room restored, under the guidance of our architect, James Simpson. For the first time in three hundred years the family is now able to stay at Rosslyn Castle, which is also open to others through the Landmark Trust, whose founder, Sir John Smith, has given us great support. The plaster ceiling of 1622, conserved in the Great Room, looks down once more upon feasting and revelry, albeit of a different order from its former days. In restoring the fabric of the building, great care has been taken to leave its exterior looking as it has over the last three centuries [plate 13]:

> *… in its isolated and precipitous site – greatly enhanced by the romantic scenery of which it forms the centre – one of the most beautiful and picturesque ruins in Scotland … a landscape over which the genius of poetry and romance has shed its hereditary charms.*[26]

PLATE 12
Nathaniel Dance
The Erskine Children (James St Clair-Erskine is on the left)
The National Trust for Scotland (Fyvie Castle Collection)

PLATE 13
Francis Nicholson
Rosslyn Castle from the South-West, *c.*1812
Private Collection

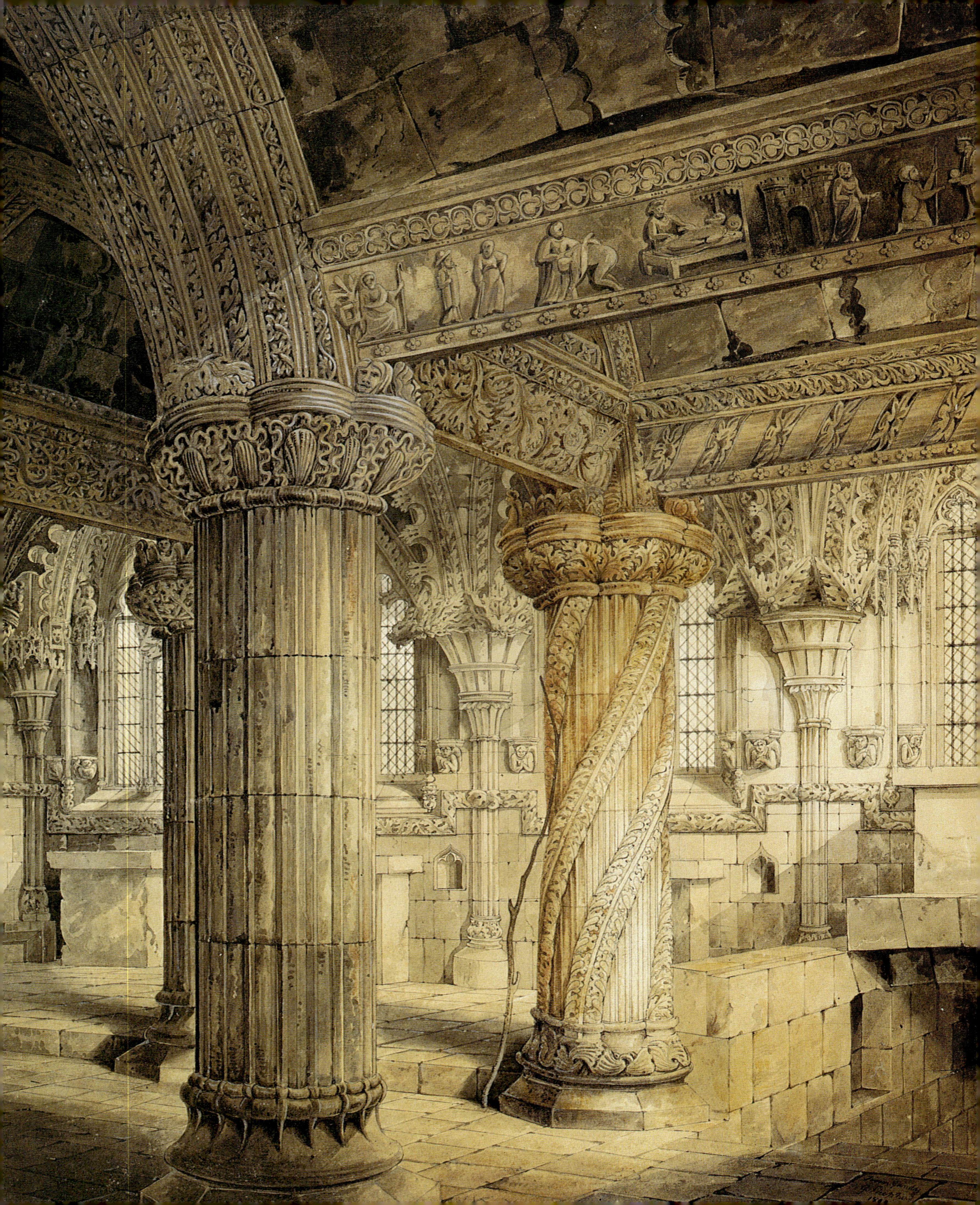

ANGELO MAGGI

Rosslyn Chapel: a Pocket Cathedral in an Earthly Paradise

The Chapel of Roslin … is situated on a rising ground charmingly beautified with wood, water, and rocks; the Esk gliding along the west and south foot of the hill, some trees below rustling their boughs across the purling stream, others aloft weaving their curling tops in the clouds, and the flinty rocks jutting out here and there between the trees, shew their rugged forms and depending heads, and serve to complete the delightfully variegated landscape. – A place formed by Nature for heavenly contemplation.[1]

This evocative description of the location of the Collegiate Church of St Matthew the Apostle, commonly called Rosslyn Chapel, was published in *The Edinburgh Magazine* in 1761 by the Episcopalian Bishop of Caithness, Robert Forbes (1708–1775). The Chapel is situated at a short distance from Rosslyn Castle on a high bank overlooking the valley of the River Esk. It is said to have originally been called *Roskelyn*, a Gaelic or Erse word signifying 'a hill in a glen', which describes exactly the position of the Chapel, and is easily recognisable in the modern Rosslyn.[2] According to the *Genealogie of the Sainteclaires of Rosslyn* compiled by Father Hay (1661–1736), the Chapel was commenced in the year 1446, by William St Clair, Prince of Orkney [plate 14a, b].[3] It was intended to combine a collegiate establishment with a place of interment for himself and his successors. St Clair, though a late-medieval employer, appears to have acted with unusual enlightenment towards those working on the Chapel. He is said to have assembled skilful workmen from all parts, and to have rewarded their work generously and 'with a munificence well calculated to give energy to their operations'.[4] As the building is evidently incomplete, and as there is no record of the demolition of any part of it, it is most probable that work ceased at the death of the earl in 1484. At that time, only the choir, or east end, was finished, and the transept existed simply as an external wall. Once stopped, the work was never resumed. The whole building is remarkable for the peculiarities of its style, and for the richness of its ornament. This led Forbes to write that 'no person can enter into it, who has the smallest degree of solid thinking, without being struck with reverential awe at its august appearance'.[5]

Rosslyn Chapel possesses a breathtaking concentration of architectural embellishment and a startling richness of carving. The entire ceiling, bosses of the vaults, capitals, architraves – indeed the whole interior – are covered with sculptures representing flowers, leaves, passages of sacred history, texts of scripture and grotesque figures, all executed with astonishing precision. The effect is rich and bizarre. Its most renowned feature stands at the south-east angle of the Chapel – a column wreathed with ascending spirals of foliage, known as the Apprentice Pillar. According to legend, the master-mason of the Chapel was unable to execute a complex design of this pier from the plans furnished to him and had to go to Rome to take an accurate drawing of a similar one there. On his return, he found that his apprentice had, in his absence, overcome all difficulties and that the work was already finished. Instead of being delighted at having trained such

OPPOSITE
Detail from George Shepherd after Joseph Michael Gandy
The Apprentice Pillar, Rosslyn Chapel, 1809, plate 16

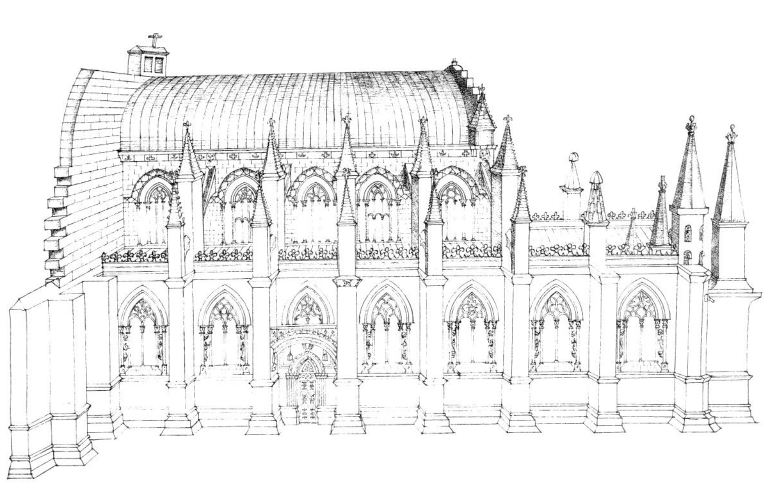

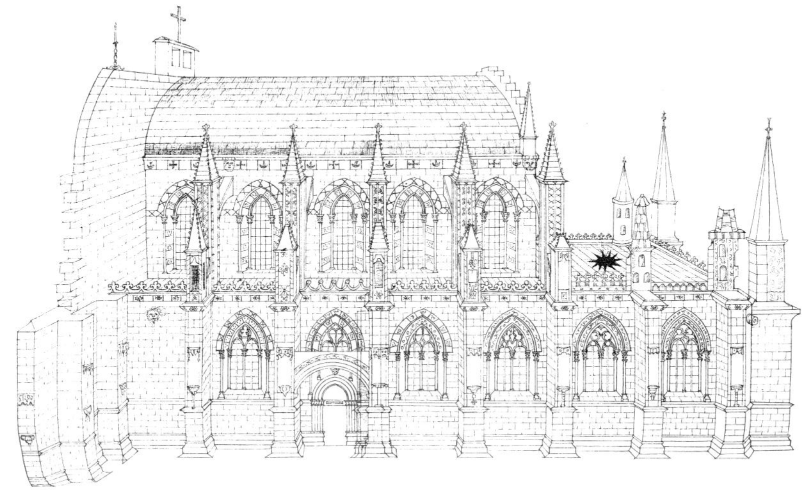

PLATE 14A&B
Father Richard Augustine Hay
Outline Drawings of Rosslyn Chapel, c.1700 from *Hay's Memoirs*
National Library of Scotland, Edinburgh

a workman, the mason was so overcome by jealousy that he immediately killed the apprentice with a blow of his hammer, and thereafter paid the penalty of death by hanging for his own misdeed.[6]

In this legend are to be found all the ingredients which continued to draw literary visitors, inspire poets and attract 'visionary architects', one of whom was Joseph Michael Gandy (1771–1843). Gandy, one of the most favoured draughtsmen in Sir John Soane's atelier, travelled from London in order to prepare a complete survey of the building in 1806.[7] It was Rosslyn's evanescent and mysterious air that inspired his idealised architectural compositions. In the summer of 1809 Gandy exhibited at the Royal Academy in London a large watercolour depicting a corner of the choir and Lady Chapel, with the stair leading to the crypt. This painting includes a reminder of an old woman called Annie Wilson [plate 15] – a 'venerable damsel of Caledonian nativity'[8] – who guided visitors around Rosslyn Chapel, pointing out the prominent enrichments with the aid of a long mysterious divining-rod which Gandy shows leaning against the Apprentice Pillar.[9] Unfortunately Gandy's painting has disappeared, but a copy of it made in the same year by George Shepherd (fl.1800–1830) shows the extent to which he was intrigued by the decoration [plate 16]. The massive pillars and vaulted arches, with a variety of foliate mouldings and chevrons, emerge from the darkness as various sources of light illuminate them to create an ethereal atmosphere.[10]

It seems probable that the fame which Gandy achieved with this painting brought him to the attention of the antiquarian and publisher, John Britton (1771–1857), who invited him to draw the fifteen plates of Rosslyn Chapel for the third volume of *The Architectural Antiquities of Great Britain*, published in 1812.[11] Britton's historical exegesis of Rosslyn Chapel dwelt on the building's anachronistic style, which he thought was manifest in its unclassifiable combination of overcharged ornament and primitive solidity. He also discussed the Masonic lore surrounding the building: the story of the jealous master-mason and the hallowed lineage of the lords of Rosslyn in Scottish Freemasonry.

According to Britton, the Chapel 'awakened the enthusiasm' of Gandy's genius; and it was 'highly credit-

15

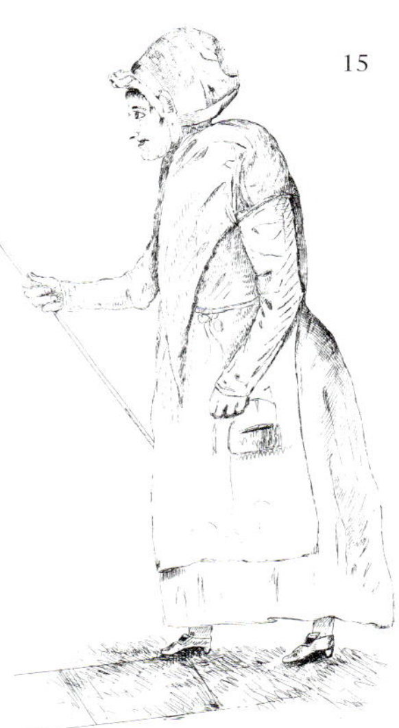

16

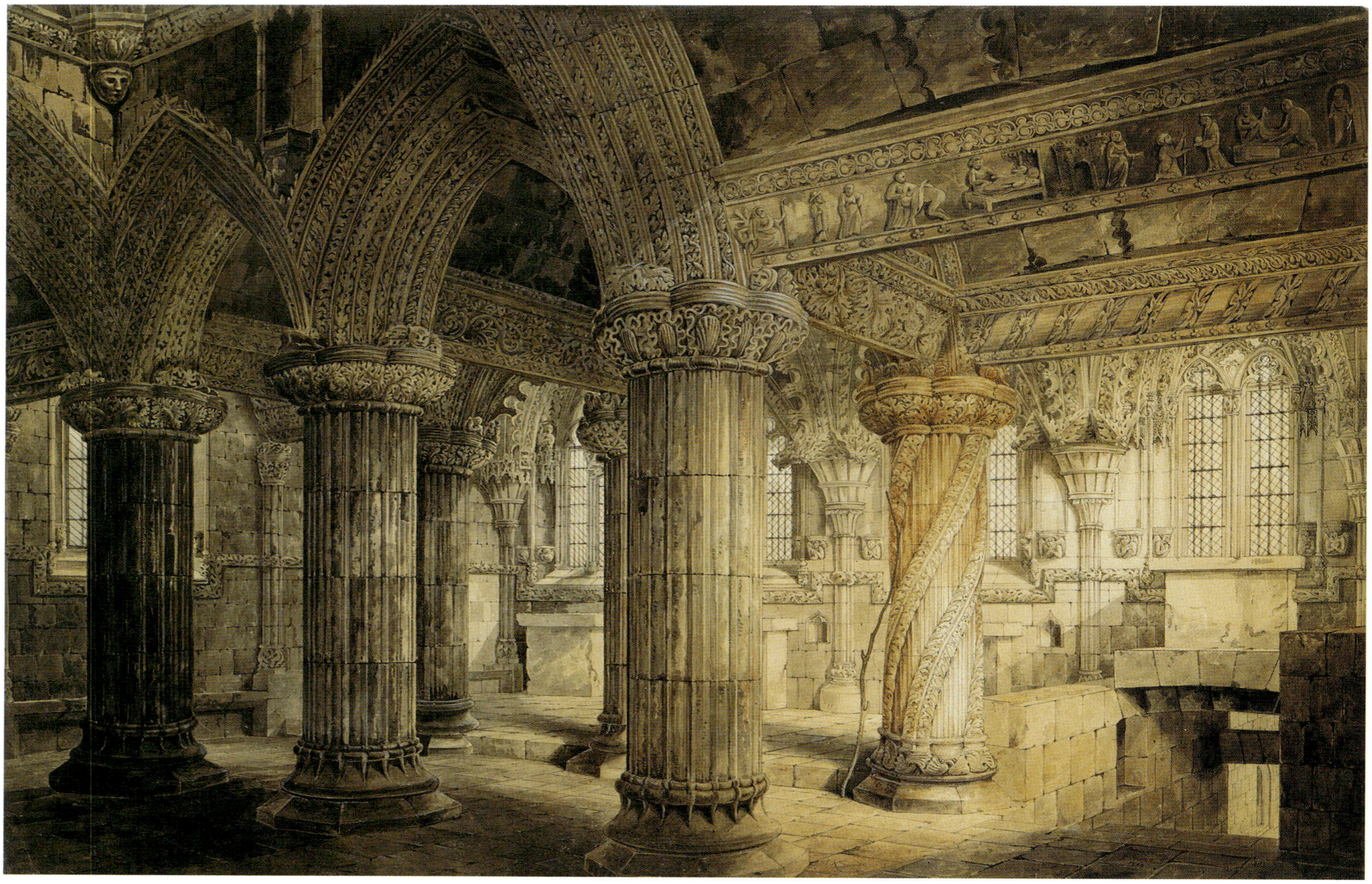

PLATE 15
Annie Wilson, from *The Gentleman's Magazine*, September 1817
National Library of Scotland, Edinburgh

PLATE 16
George Shepherd after Joseph Michael Gandy
The Apprentice Pillar, Rosslyn Chapel, 1809
Victoria & Albert Museum, London

PLATE 17
J. Burnett after Joseph Michael Gandy
Elevation of Part of the South Side, Rosslyn Chapel, 1812
Private Collection

PLATE 18
Joseph Michael Gandy
Rosslyn Chapel from a sketchbook, 1806
Sir John Soane's Museum, London

able to this artist, that he did not leave the spot till he had stored his sketch book with all the architectural parts of the chapel, as well as general views of the surrounding scenery'.[12] If we think of the difficulty of executing a detailed representation of a building which is so rich in its ornament, the comment seems more than justified. For Gandy, the need to revisit the sacred and mystical traditions of this building provoked a patient search for authoritative references for his visionary works. It is exactly this visionary style which affects his exterior views. Here, the result is that the artist decides to concentrate in one single illustration the most striking parts of the Chapel. Thus the observer is made to appreciate the splendour of the work even if it does not correspond precisely to the truth. The plates, in fact, are ambiguous and cannot answer modern ideas of architectural accuracy. We should not blame Gandy, however, for over-embellishing his prints of the building or for having changed part of its essence, especially when we consider the taste of the collectors for whom the plates were intended. It is the genius of Gandy that the whole process of embellishment, or fakery, remains almost imperceptible. Only the closest attention to detail can allow us to unravel his manipulation of the architectural features. As a good architect, Gandy studies every single detail, fusing all together with a taste which, with a gratifying logic, respects the historic identity of the building. The ambiguity of his approach is shown in the view entitled *Elevation of Part of the South Side, Rosslyn Chapel* [plate 17], where he inserts a small window that interrupts the base course in order to show us an interesting architectural feature that appears three bays further on. Also in the same view, he chooses to crown the south wall with architectural finishes: a delicate stone cresting and cusp and arched battlements, each of which comes from a different location on the east end walls.

17

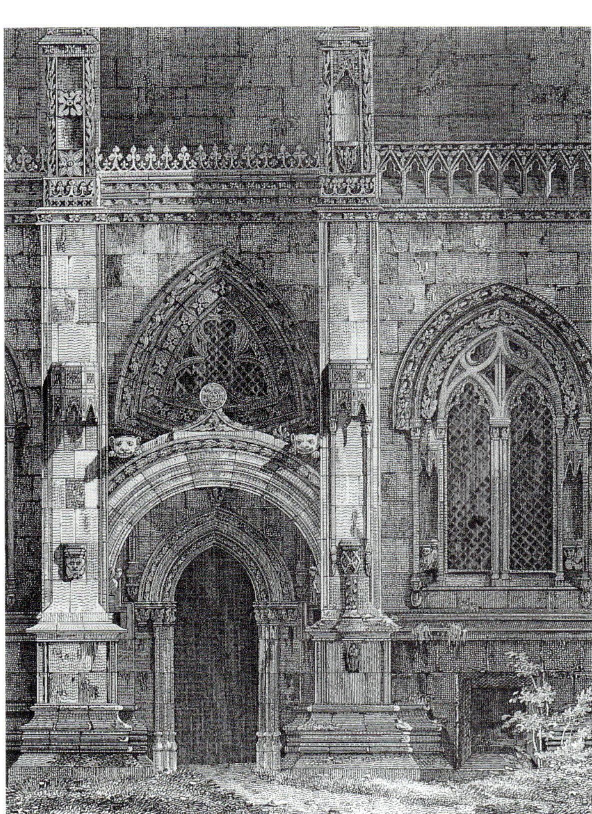

18

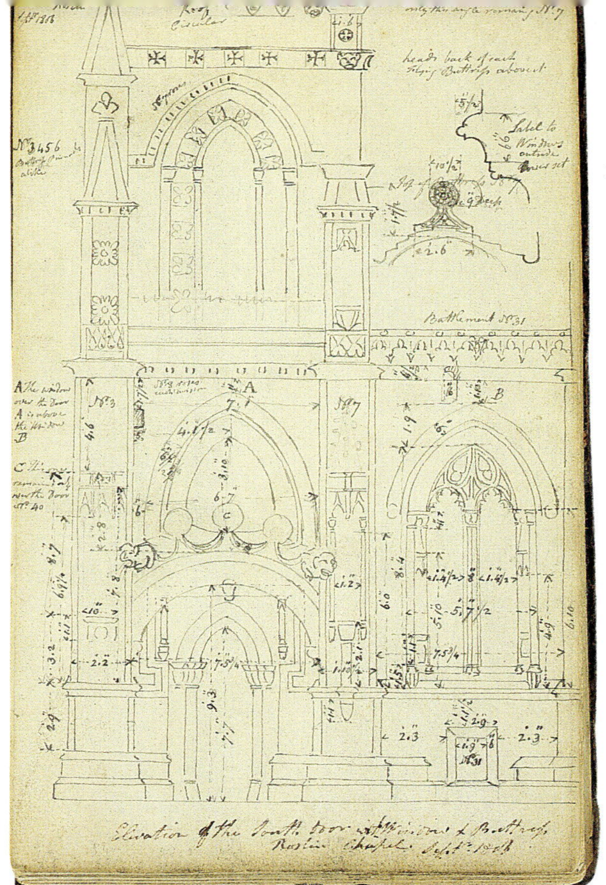

The measured drawings in Gandy's sketchbook show the same architectural collage in which, guided by the refinement of the most elaborately carved parts of the Chapel, he sketches different details that were to be reassembled later on. One of the most interesting elements with which he seems to play is that of the circular finial; there are three of them on the north wall of the Chapel. In the published view only one is shown and this is positioned by Gandy on the arch over the south door.[13] In the sketchbook, however, this motif is accompanied by two others in a single crowning decorative element [plate 18]. Once again the composition of the details on paper does not correspond with the reality in stone; rather, this *capriccio* helps us to understand the overall context of the Chapel.

Gandy was not the only architect to distort the original appearance of the building and the functionality of all its parts. George Meikle Kemp (1794–1844), the architect of the Scott Monument, made frequent journeys in order to inspect and 'reinvent' Rosslyn Chapel.[14] He prepared drawings for a planned volume of Scottish ecclesiastical remains. These took several years and were not completed at the time of Kemp's premature death. Nevertheless, his watercolour view of the Apprentice Pillar reveals more than an imaginative competence in his approach to the Gothic style [plate 19]. The image that he presents goes well beyond the architectural truth: a panelled loggia, for which there is, and never has been, any evidence, is inserted in the final part of the choir. The whole design resembles a theatre. The two columns and the architrave in the foreground are in darkness and they seem to be intended to frame the drawing. The result is a delimitation of the representation with a remarkable architectonic frame.

Another architectural fantasist, enthralled by the medieval beauties at Rosslyn, is the English painter George Cattermole (1800–1868), who worked for the antiquarian John Britton, producing finely worked views of many extant British churches. His oil painting, *Rosslyn Chapel* [plate 20], engraved by Thomas Higham (1796–1844) for a work titled *Scott and Scotland* (1835),[15] provides a new hypothesis, not previously noted in the history of the building, for the existence of some form of screening between the nave and the aisle.[16] The masonry wall on which the artist adds a piscina, taken either from the transept or from one of the entrances to the Chapel, is part of his fictional depiction. Thus the poetic manipulation of masonry celebrated by Gandy, becomes in Cattermole's work an extraordinary assemblage where every object and episode is organised inside a balanced visual composition that captures both the appearance of the medieval church and the pre-Victorian state of restoration.

When Gandy described the building as a 'combination of Egyptian, Grecian, Roman, and Saracenic styles',[17] he did not intend to reduce Rosslyn Chapel to a bizarre, eclectic agglomeration of parts, but rather to extol it as one of the most astonishing architectural compositions ever realised. And it is in the same spirit that he depicts the architecture in one of his finest watercolour perspectives, *The Tomb of Merlin* [plate 21]. Gandy's interior view of Rosslyn Chapel, exhibited at the Royal Academy, has many key elements that were to be reworked in his representation of 'Merlin's Tomb Chamber'. These are the same viewpoint, the definition of the architectural details and the pervasive luminosity. [18]

The Tomb of Merlin – painted in 1815 and subsequently donated by the artist to his patron Sir John Soane (1753–1837) – represents a passage from the chivalric poem, *Orlando Furioso* (1516), written by Ludovico Ariosto, according to whom Merlin had been imprisoned and killed by the Witch of the Lake, who had stolen his magic powers. Merlin's body and spirit, the latter being still alive, were kept inside a cavern where 'The very marble was so clear and bright, / That though the sun no light unto it gave, / The tomb itself did lighten all the cave.'[19]

The similarities between the painting and Rosslyn Chapel are not only obvious in some of the architectural aspects, like the evident reminiscence of the Apprentice Pillar, but also in their legendary associations. In fact, the imaginary burial chamber which Gandy portrayed has a noteworthy source. There is a local legend that the night before a lord of Rosslyn died, the Chapel appeared to burn, but without sustaining any injury. What was believed to be an unconsuming fire, a supernatural radiance prescient of life beyond death, must have been associated in Gandy's mind with the spectral glow from Merlin's tomb.[20]

The superstition, as with so many others, was developed by the fascinating pen of Sir Walter Scott (1771–1832), who, in *The Lay of the Last Minstrel* (1805), recounts in poetic tones how Rosslyn Chapel seemed to be on fire when death drew near for a member of the St Clair family:

Seem'd all on fire that chapel proud,
Where Roslin's chiefs uncoffin'd lie;
Each baron, for a sable shroud,
Sheathed in his iron panoply.

Seem'd all on fire within, around,
Deep sacristy and altars pale;
Shone every pillar foliage bound,
And glimmer'd all the dead men's mail.

Blaz'd battlement, and pinnet high,
Blaz'd every rose-carved buttress fair
So still they blaze, when fate is nigh,
The lordly line of high St Clair.[21]

A later text by Robert William Billings (1813–1874), which accompanied the plates of Rosslyn in *The Baronial and Ecclesiastical Antiquities of Scotland* (1845), gives us a logical explanation for this eerie effect. Billings explains how he was rendered speechless 'by the appearance, through the branches of the trees, of what seemed a row of bright-red smokeless furnaces',[22] but which was only 'a fine setting sun shining straight through the double windows of the chapel. The phenomenon had a powerful effect on the vision; but it was more that of ignition than of sunlight, from the rich red which often attends Scottish sunsets.'[23] It is probable, then, that this remarkable 'supernatural' effect was determined by the position of the building which Billings claimed was 'the most appropriate that could be chosen, had its builder desired to produce this effect'.[24] Although the Chapel is located halfway down the side of a hill, there are no obstacles to interrupt the lowest rays of the setting sun.

It was a combination of such phantasmagorical light effects, the richness of the carved forms, and the legendary events in its history, which captured the public's

PLATE 19
George Meikle Kemp
The Apprentice Pillar, Rosslyn Chapel, 1824
Royal Scottish Academy, Edinburgh

PLATE 20
George Cattermole
Rosslyn Chapel, c.1835
Sheffield Galleries and Museums Trust

PLATE 21
Joseph Michael Gandy
The Tomb of Merlin, 1815
Library Drawings Collection, Royal Institute of British Architects, London

19

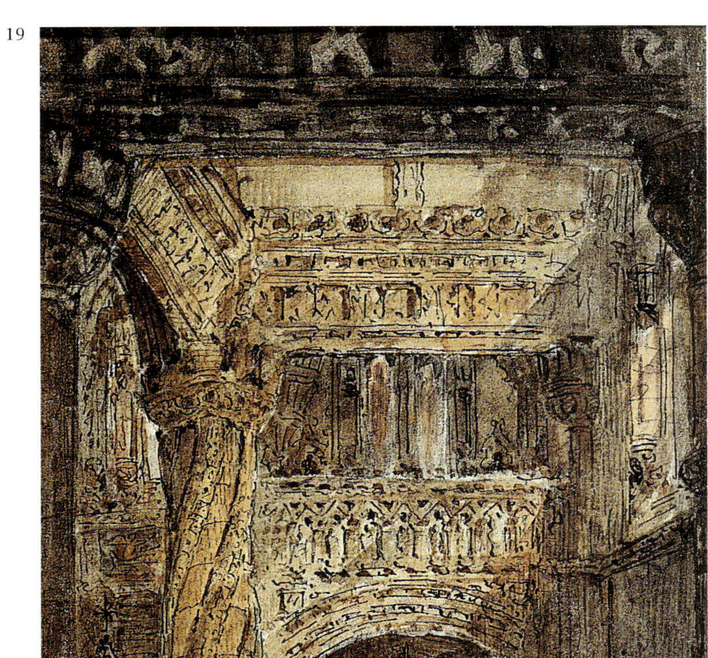

20

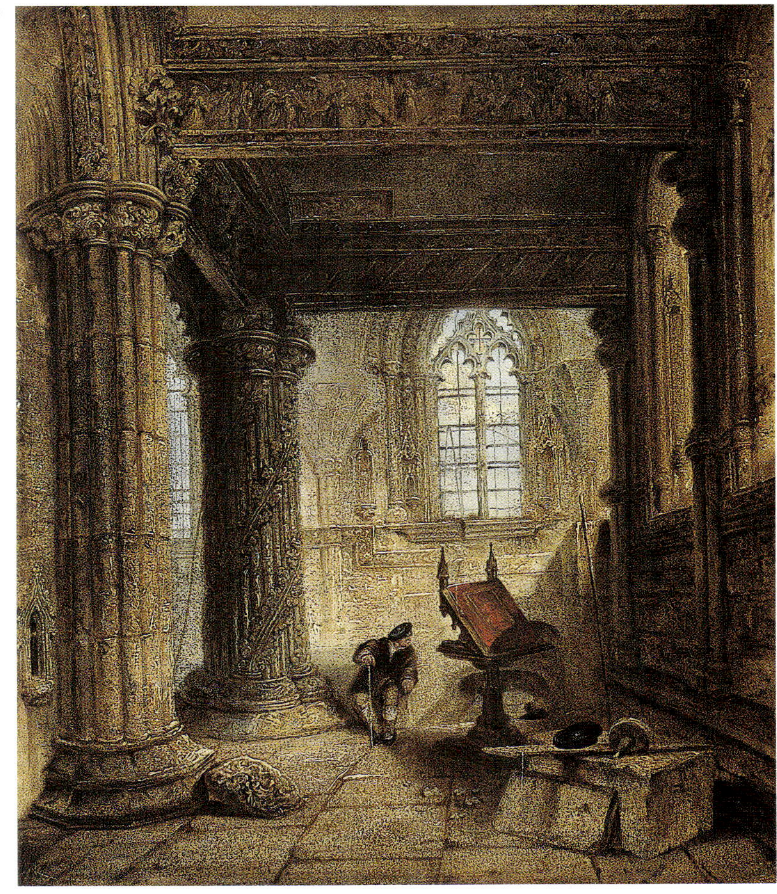

21

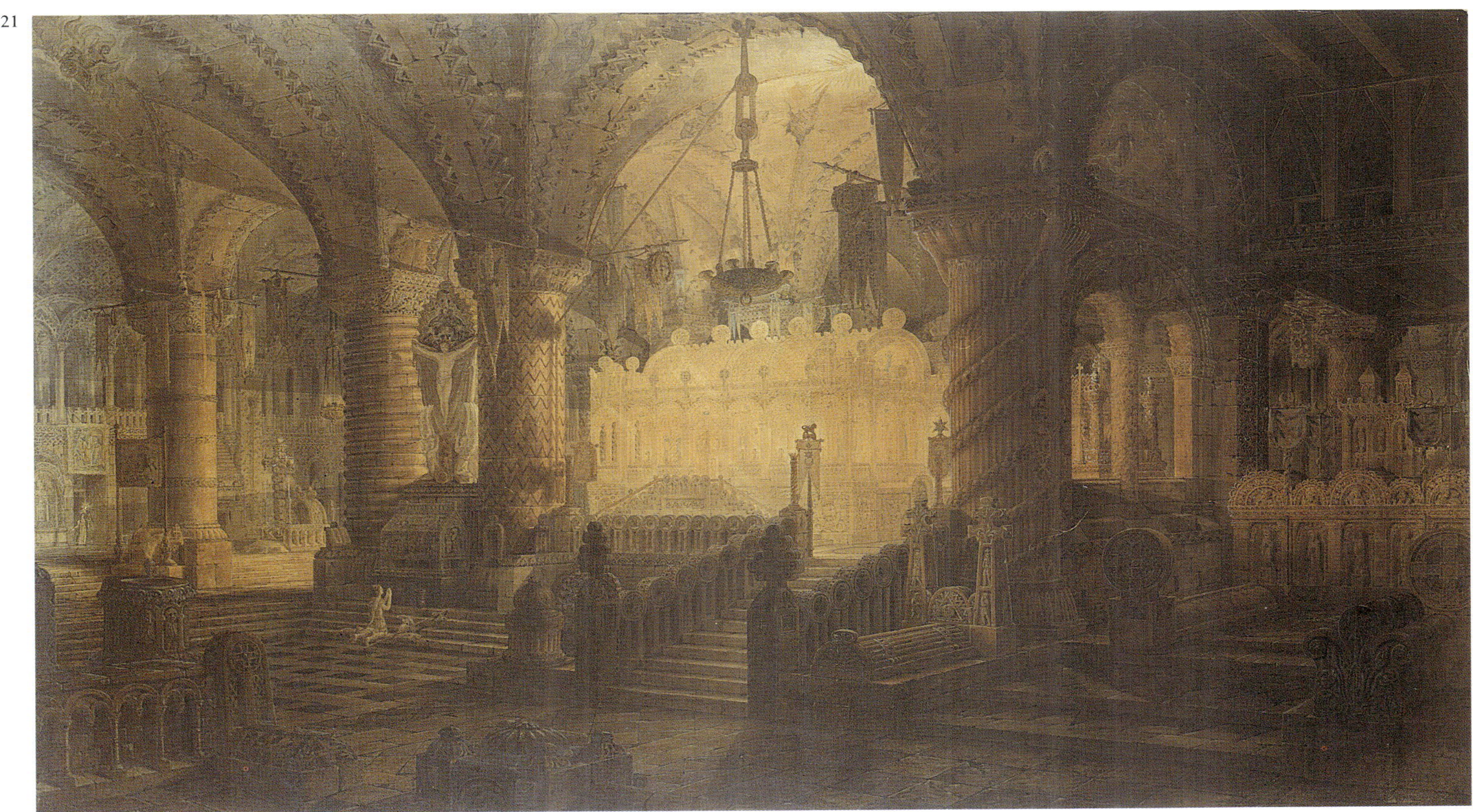

imagination and transformed Rosslyn and its surroundings into one of the most important tourist attractions in nineteenth-century Scotland. Contemporary improvements in transport also contributed greatly to the rediscovery of the building, encouraging antiquarians, artists, poets and tourists from all parts of the country to visit the Chapel. Inspired by his visit in 1838, John Ruskin (1819–1900) in his *Praeterita* (1885) titled one of the chapters *Roslyn Chapel* and made clear reference to Scott's words when describing the strength of his response: '... lurid, like the vaults of Roslyn, when weird fire gleamed on its pillars, foliage-bound, and far in the depth of twilight, *blazed every rose-carved buttress fair*'.[25] He even made two extraordinary drawings of the interior of the Chapel in the style of Samuel Prout (1783–1852) showing his splendid powers of draughtsmanship at an early age.[26] One of these is a view taken from just within the ambulatory at the east end with most of the picture area taken up by the deeply projecting nave [plate 22]. Although Ruskin gave careful attention to light and shade, his primary intention was to emphasise the verticality of the complex grouping of Gothic details against the horizontal elements of the structure. His purpose was thus to combine Romanticism with accurate recording.

According to Britton, Rosslyn Chapel was certainly 'calculated to amaze the illiterate, and intimidate the weak'.[27] Exactly these sentiments might be said to have inspired Louis-Jacques-Mandé Daguerre (1789–1851), another person who was to promote the extraordinary interest in Rosslyn, when contriving his celebrated and popular tour de force, the diorama of Rosslyn Chapel. Daguerre was famous for his stage sets and especially for his lighting effects, long before he was to be immortalised for his experiments with photography and the invention of the daguerreotype. He believed that the Chapel, with its phantasmagorical effects, offered an ideal subject for a dioramic illusion and that the legends linked to the Chapel would be sure to attract large numbers of visitors.[28]

The diorama was a form of public entertainment that reached the peak of its popularity in Britain in the late Regency period.[29] It was an ideal medium for dramatic visual presentations and depicted scenes applied to a large transparent screen which was lit from a variety of sources. The illusion of reality and of a changing spectacle was produced by changing the lighting.[30] One of its most interesting features, apart from the complicated lighting arrangements, was the proximity of the audience to the enormous screen which was twenty-two metres wide by fourteen metres high. The pictures remained stationary while the auditorium, a cylindrical room with a single opening in the wall like the proscenium of a stage, was slowly revolved from one picture to another.[31]

Daguerre's diorama of the interior of Rosslyn Chapel, entitled *L'Abbaye de Roslyn, effet de soleil*, was exhibited in Paris in 1824 and in London in 1826.[32] Press comment in France was highly evocative: *Monsieur Daguerre nous donne un effet de soleil ravissant ..., les rayons du soleil qui paraissent par intervalles en dessinant sur le corps les ombres portées, le reflet qui règne dans l'intérieur, sont si justes que nous avons cru un moment qu'ils étaient produits par la nature.*[33] The first mention of the Rosslyn diorama in a Scottish publication was in *Blackwood's Edinburgh Magazine*, where a correspondent from London describes its impact:

The Diorama pictures, opened only about a week since, are interesting. One of them – a view of the interior of Roslin Chapel, by Daguerre – is decidedly the best that has been exhibited. Independent, indeed, of any aid from mechanical contrivance, it is a most finished and extraordinary painting. The effect of the trees, seen through the windows on the right hand of the Chapel, sparkling when the sun bursts out upon them, is absolutely magical. And yet, perhaps, this is inferior as a work of art – as every thing I ever recollect to have seen is in execution – except Rembrandt. To the side opposite, where the building is in shade, the eye absolutely, upon deliberation, seems to penetrate into darkness, and to discover objects, after a time, which at first were not visible. From your acquaintance with the reality, I am sure you will be delighted when you see it.[34]

An important surviving visual record of the diorama is an engraving [plate 23] in a magazine of the time, *The Mirror of Literature, Amusement and Instruction*. The article that accompanies the illustration contains a detailed description of the Chapel and is written in tones of high praise:

The view of Roslyn Chapel was painted by Daguerre, and surpasses every representation of an architectural structure we ever saw. A Scotchman would drop on his knees before it,

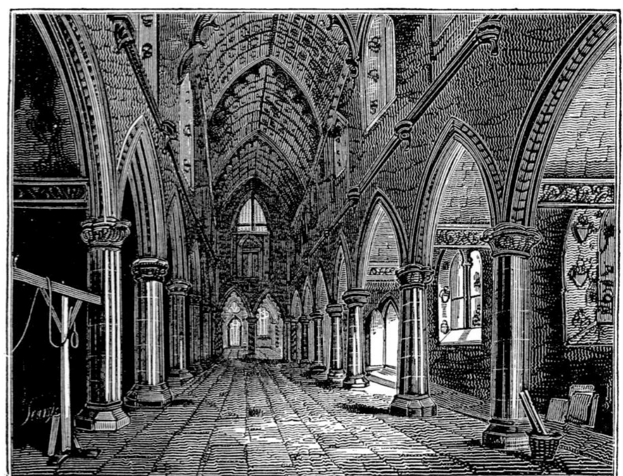
The Mirror
OF
LITERATURE, AMUSEMENT, AND INSTRUCTION.
No. CLXXXV.] SATURDAY, MARCH 4, 1826. [Price 2d.
View of Roslyn Chapel, at the Diorama.

23

PLATE 22
John Ruskin
Rosslyn Chapel, 1838
Ruskin Foundation, Ruskin Library, University of Lancaster

PLATE 23
Anonymous after Louis-Jacques-Mandé Daguerre
View of Rosslyn Chapel at the Diorama from *The Mirror of Literature, Amusement and Instruction*, 1826
British Library Board, London

22

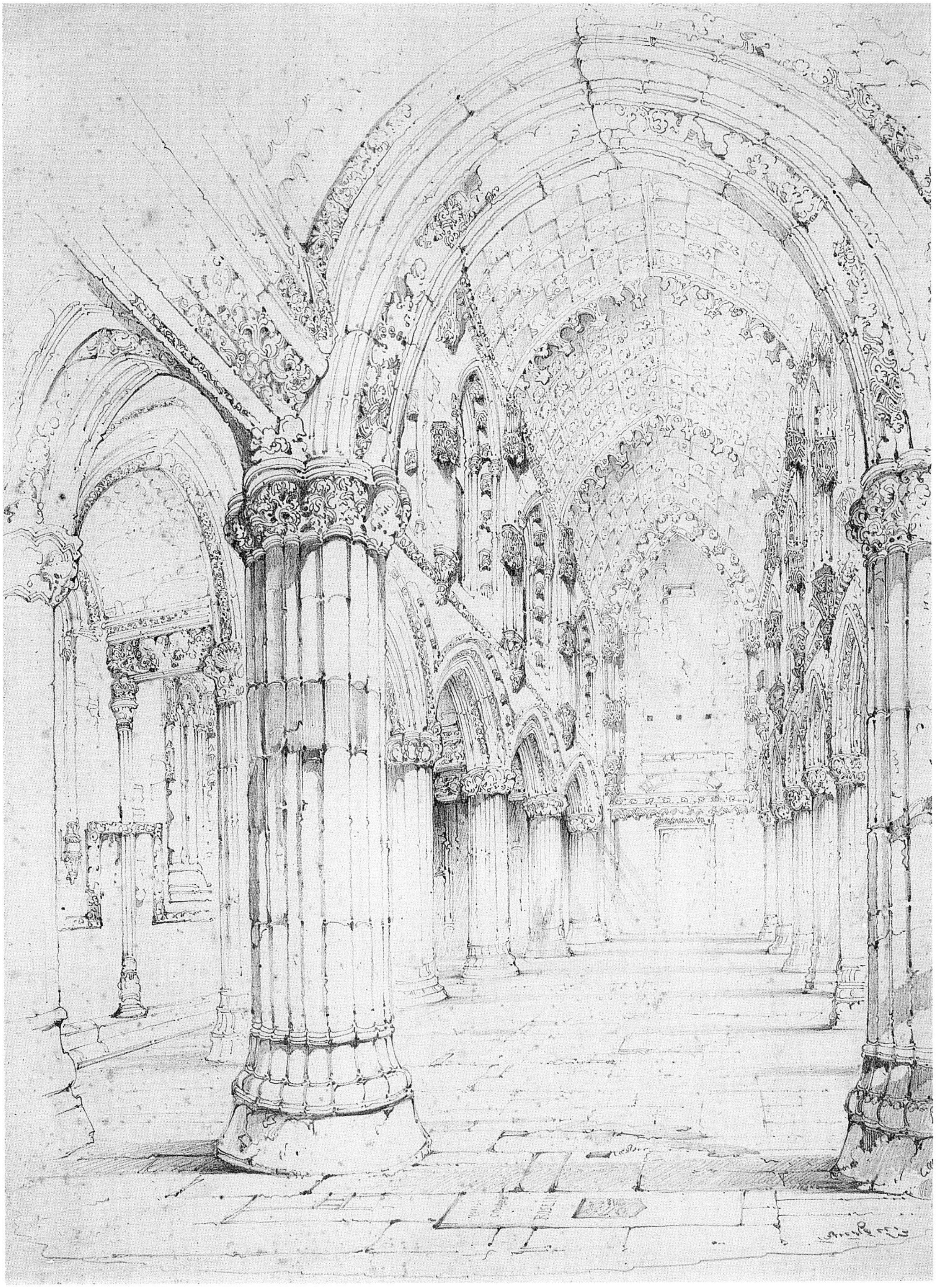

and no person would believe that the variety of light and shade – the management of the rays of the sun reflected through a half opened door, the cobweb tinge of the window – the beam of timber and the loose cord, together with the mixture of light and shade which it displays are mere effect of art; yet such is the case, and we are sure it requires no prophetic ken to say, that Roslyn Chapel will be one of the most attractive features of the most fascinating exhibition ever opened in London within our knowledge.[35]

What caused most amazement and interest was the extraordinary illusion and brilliant illumination of the show: the building, flooded by intense sunlight, appeared suddenly in the dark hall, the diorama being accompanied by an ancient Scottish tune played on bagpipes.[36]

A diorama building opened in Edinburgh on Lothian Road at the end of 1827. The building, which also housed a lithographic establishment, was designed for programmes showing only one diorama picture at a time. Scottish people, however, had to wait almost ten years before the Rosslyn entertainment reached Edinburgh. Even then it has never been confirmed that the Lothian Road diorama of Rosslyn was the one painted by Daguerre in Paris and exhibited in London.[37] Indeed, in 1825 a reviewer in the *Caledonian Mercury* reported that an unnamed 'young artist' of Edinburgh, who 'has not to boast of the borrowed name of a French artist,'[38] was 'engaged in bringing out a View of … the Interior of Rosslyn Chapel; for the exhibition of which an appropriate building will be erected'.[39] According to the historian R. Derek Wood, the only Edinburgh artist involved in painting dioramas of the same subjects as those done in Paris was David Roberts (1796–1864). Roberts had probably been commissioned to produce copies to avoid the need of bringing the original from London. This 'rival version' of the Rosslyn diorama painting was also exhibited in Dublin in 1828 and in Liverpool at the end of May 1829.

Debate centres around the sources that influenced Daguerre's spectacular depiction of Rosslyn Chapel. It seems likely that he studied Gandy's views and measured drawings which had been published fifteen years earlier, and that in devising his own work he made use of their accuracy of detail and studied their lighting effects. Another source available to the artist was *A Perspective View of the Inside of Rosslyn Chapel* [plate 24] drawn by the engraver Andrew Bell (1726–1810) and published with Forbes's 'Account of the Chapel of Roslin' in 1761.[40] Daguerre could also have had access to a series of drawings, executed in the same year of the publication of Bell's engraving, by the French painter and scenographer, William Delacour (d.1767).

From 1760 to 1767 William Delacour held the first appointment as Master of the Trustees' Academy, the newly established school of drawing and design in Edinburgh.[41] After a period working in London, he had settled in Edinburgh in 1757 where he produced landscapes for use in stage scenery and architectural settings. Delacour's drawings of Rosslyn Chapel exhibit such a degree of simplification that every elaborate ornament in the original is eliminated. While this makes the architectural structure of the building clearer, the process of elimination has led to a number of errors. For instance, in the drawing titled *Elevation of the East End of Rosslyn Chapel* [plate 25] Delacour has eliminated the side buttresses together with their pinnacles, which reappear, incorrectly, in the North to South section [plate 26]. Delacour's pictorial approach becomes more topographically precise in his picturesque views of the Chapel and the Castle [plate 7a, b], and his graphic work contributed immeasurably to the image of the place. All the elements in the landscape are recorded accurately –

24

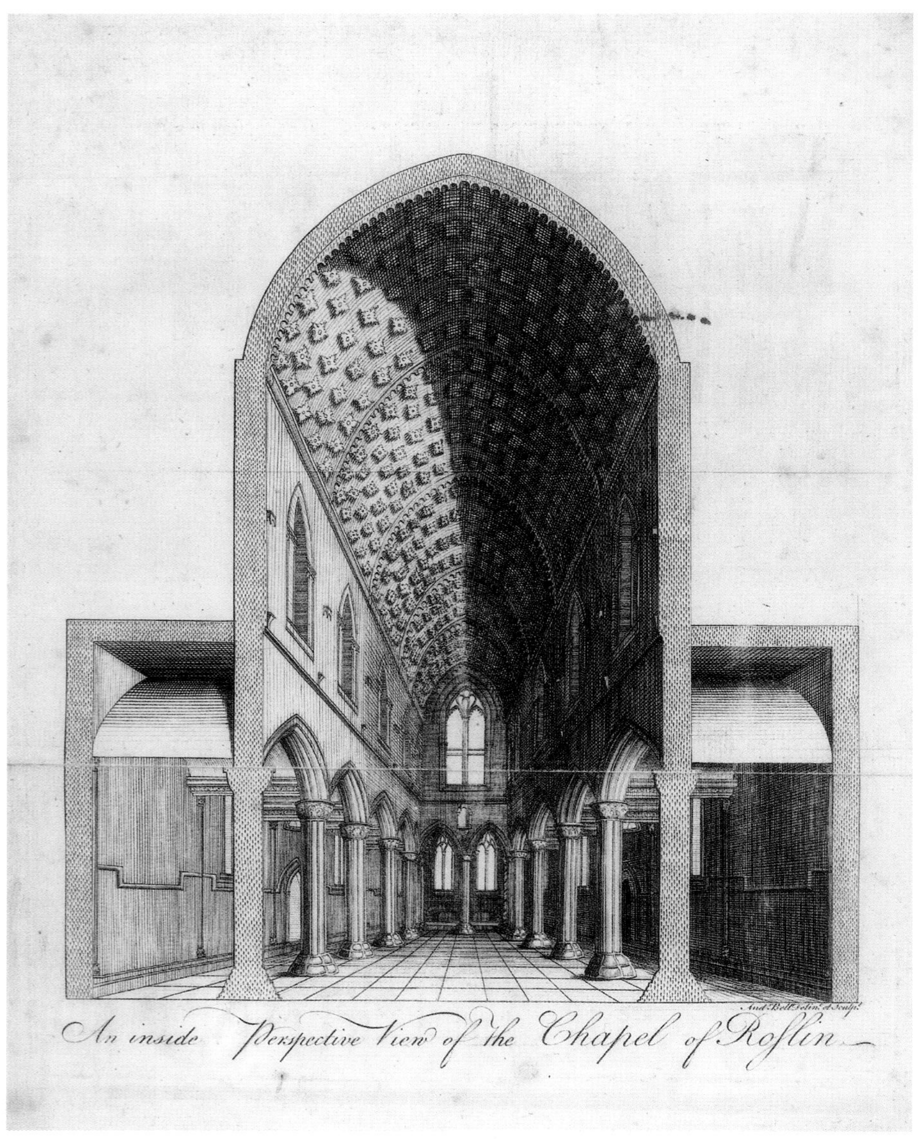

PLATE 24
Andrew Bell
A Perspective View of the Inside of Rosslyn Chapel, 1761
Scottish Library, Edinburgh City Libraries and Information Services

PLATES 25, 26 & 27
William Delacour
Elevation of the East End of Rosslyn Chapel, c.1761
Section of Rosslyn Chapel from North to South, c.1761
A Perspective View of the Inside of Rosslyn Chapel, c.1761
British Library Board, London

25

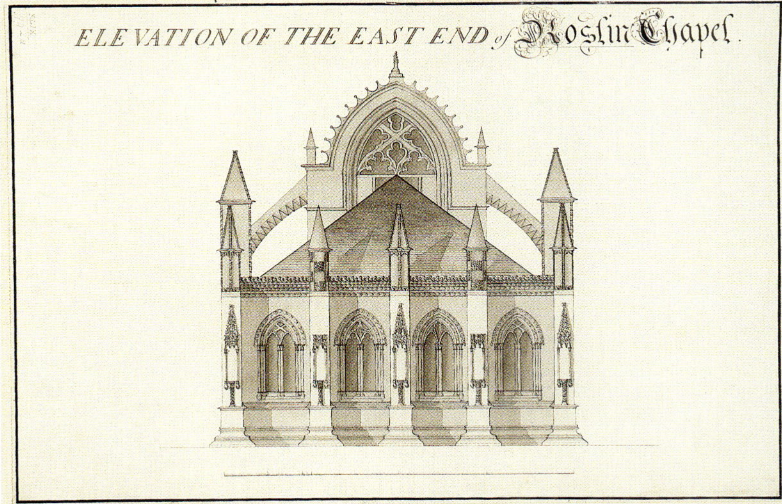

26

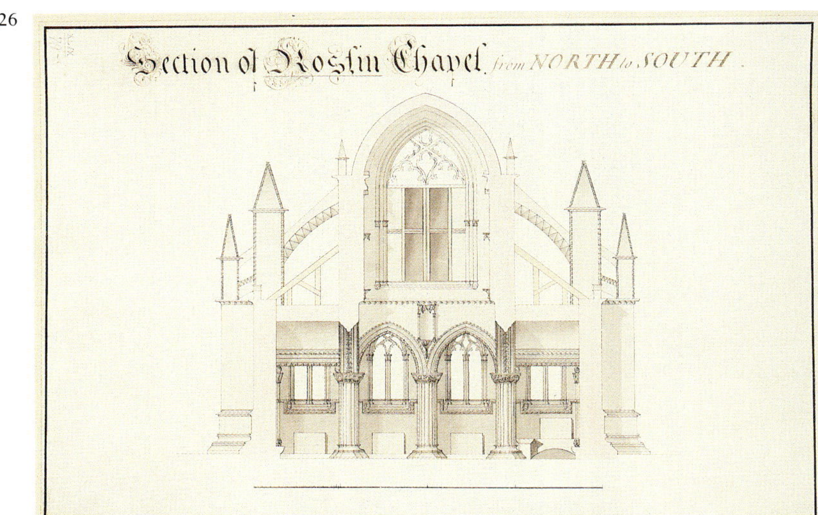

27

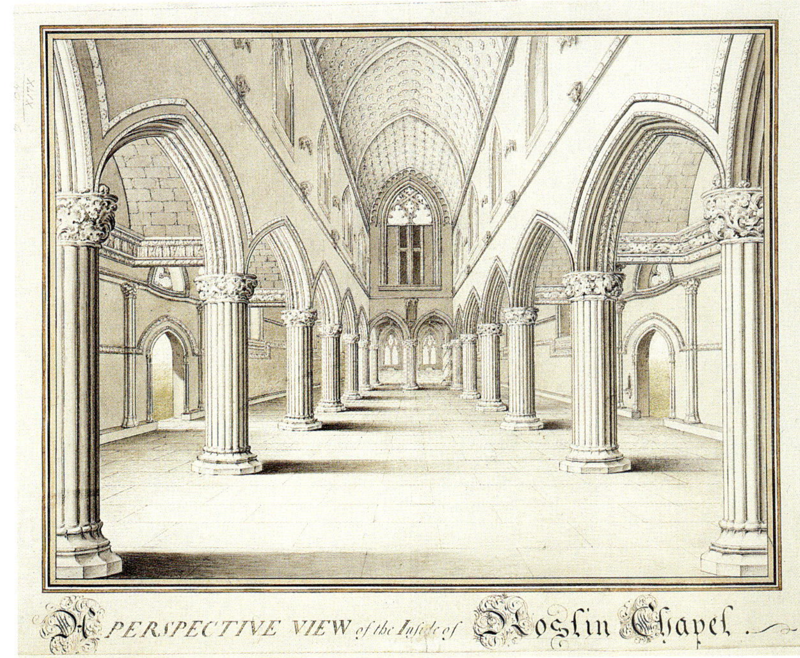

for example, the bridge of the Castle on the River Esk and the ruined arch in the distant view of the Chapel through the foliage are skilfully used by Delacour to create a significantly picturesque scene.

A comparison between Delacour's *A Perspective View of the Inside of Rosslyn Chapel* [plate 27] and the woodcut of the view of Rosslyn Chapel at the diorama [plate 21], reveals extraordinary similarities: both the engraver and Delacour show the interior of the Chapel in a perspective which greatly exaggerates its actual length. Since the drawing by Delacour was part of the collection of George III, transferred to the British Museum in 1820, it would seem likely that the anonymous London engraver had access to it and was able to base his design on it. This would go some way to explaining the interesting similarities in the two views. But this is not sufficient to prove that one is based on the other and that Daguerre had made use of Delacour's perspective view for his own representation. The diorama, being addressed to a mass audience, had the important and particularly effective function of arousing curiosity about the place itself, thanks to the new sense of stunning reality created by Daguerre, or someone working for him who had certainly seen and recorded the building.

Daguerre started his career as a painter of stage scenery. Although he also practised conventional easel painting, and achieved some success, he made only a few oil paintings representing diorama subjects. The oil painting, *The Interior of Rosslyn Chapel*, which was on display at the Salon of 1824, seems to have followed the diorama in Paris. This painting seems to have been part of an exercise in representing identical subjects in different techniques, purely for the artist's own interest. It is not even certain that these versions were sold in the wake of the success of the diorama pictures.

Helmut Gernsheim, in his *History of Photography*, has argued that the precise detail in the diorama and in Daguerre's painting of 1825, *The Ruins of Holyrood Chapel by Moonlight* [plate 28], is only to be explained by Daguerre's use of a camera obscura while actually working at Holyrood.[42] However, Daguerre is not recorded as ever visiting Scotland and by 1816 the tracery in the east window at Holyrood, which he shows ruined, had in fact been repaired. The writer of the pamphlet describing the diorama in Regent's Park, entitled *Two Views, Holyrood Chapel etc.*, observed that Daguerre deliberately showed the tracery unrepaired to give a more picturesque effect.[43] If Daguerre's visit to Holyrood is doubtful, the question arises as to how he could paint and create a diorama of the building. The same question can be posed about Rosslyn Chapel: how could Daguerre paint it in such detail and arouse such enthusiasm in his London audience, without ever visiting it or making a drawing of it?

28

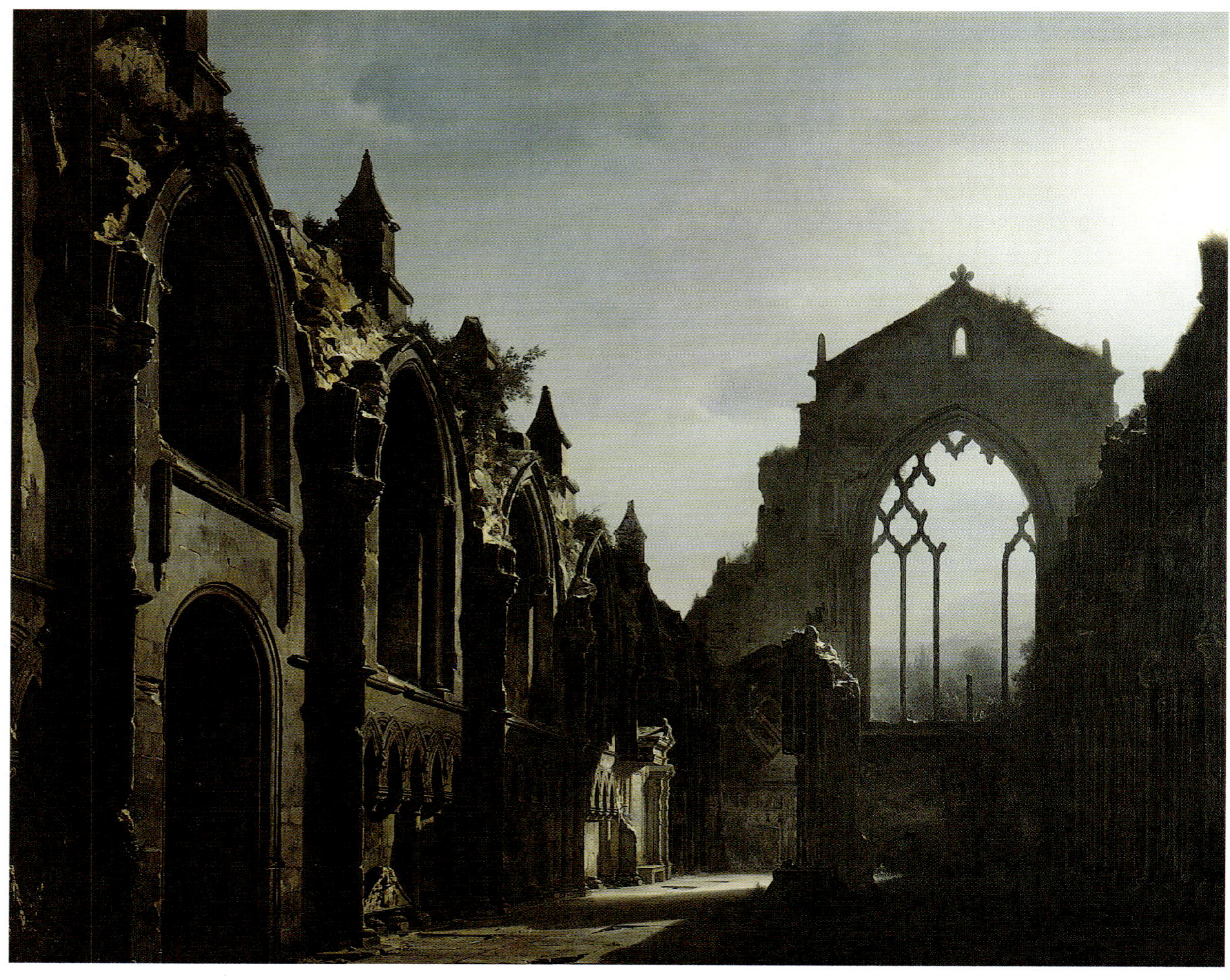

As already mentioned, the only visual evidence, until now, of the Rosslyn diorama was the engraving that appeared in *The Mirror of Literature* in 1826, where the differences in the image from the reality of the structure cannot prove Daguerre's presence at the Chapel. The answer may be found in the history of the painting by Daguerre, *The Interior of Rosslyn Chapel* [plate 29a]. This work, exhibited at the Salon in 1824 and for many years considered lost, has recently come to light. As Helmut Gernshiem might have said if he had known this painting, it is so 'remarkably realistic that in a reproduction it may at first sight be taken for an actual photograph'.[44] The canvas does indeed display astonishing 'photographic' detail, lighting, and treatment of perspective. Daguerre subtly manipulates the building's real dimensions to make the scale more impressive, raising the pointed arches in the foreground while making the distant arches lower and diminishing the scale of the figures. The resulting effect is to make the Chapel seem vast, dwarfing the three Knights Templar contemplating the stone flags laid by two workmen.[45]

The 'liberties' taken by Daguerre in his painting of the interior are determined by a dual concern for perspective – the convincing depiction of three dimensional space – on the one hand, and, on the other, the need to create an aesthetically satisfying composition. Each of the elements is persuasive, and in combination they provide an understanding of the building, though not one that is 'factually' accurate. Although wishing to record the salient features of the Chapel as well as capturing its subjective 'feel', Daguerre added to the composition a few imaginary architectural features which never existed. One of these is the open porch at the east end which, together with the cusped arches of the roof, gives added variety to the spatial patterns and effectively emphasises the awesome sense of height.

The Scottish Victorian photographer Thomas Vernon Begbie (1840–1915) compiled a large group of photographs of Rosslyn Chapel, taken before and during the building's restoration in the period 1860–1, under the guidance of the architect, David Bryce (1803–1876).[46] Begbie's photographs of the building, more than forty exposures, may have been of use in determining what, if any, damage occurred during the restoration works. It is

PLATE 28
Louis-Jacques-Mandé Daguerre
The Ruins of Holyrood Chapel by Moonlight
National Museums and Galleries on Merseyside (Walker Art Gallery, Liverpool)

PLATE 29A
Louis-Jacques-Mandé Daguerre
The Interior of Rosslyn Chapel, 1824
Private Collection

29A

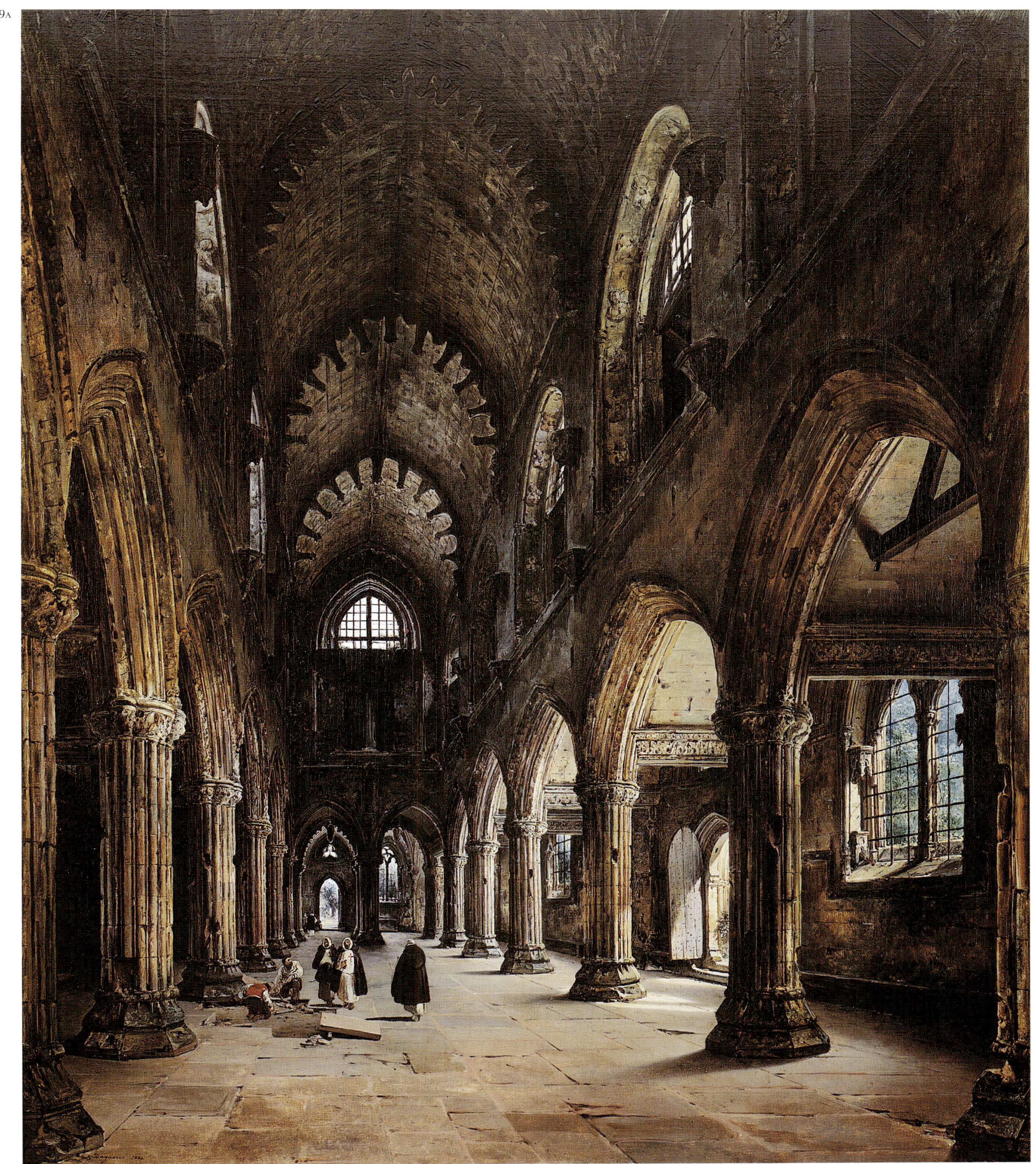

29B

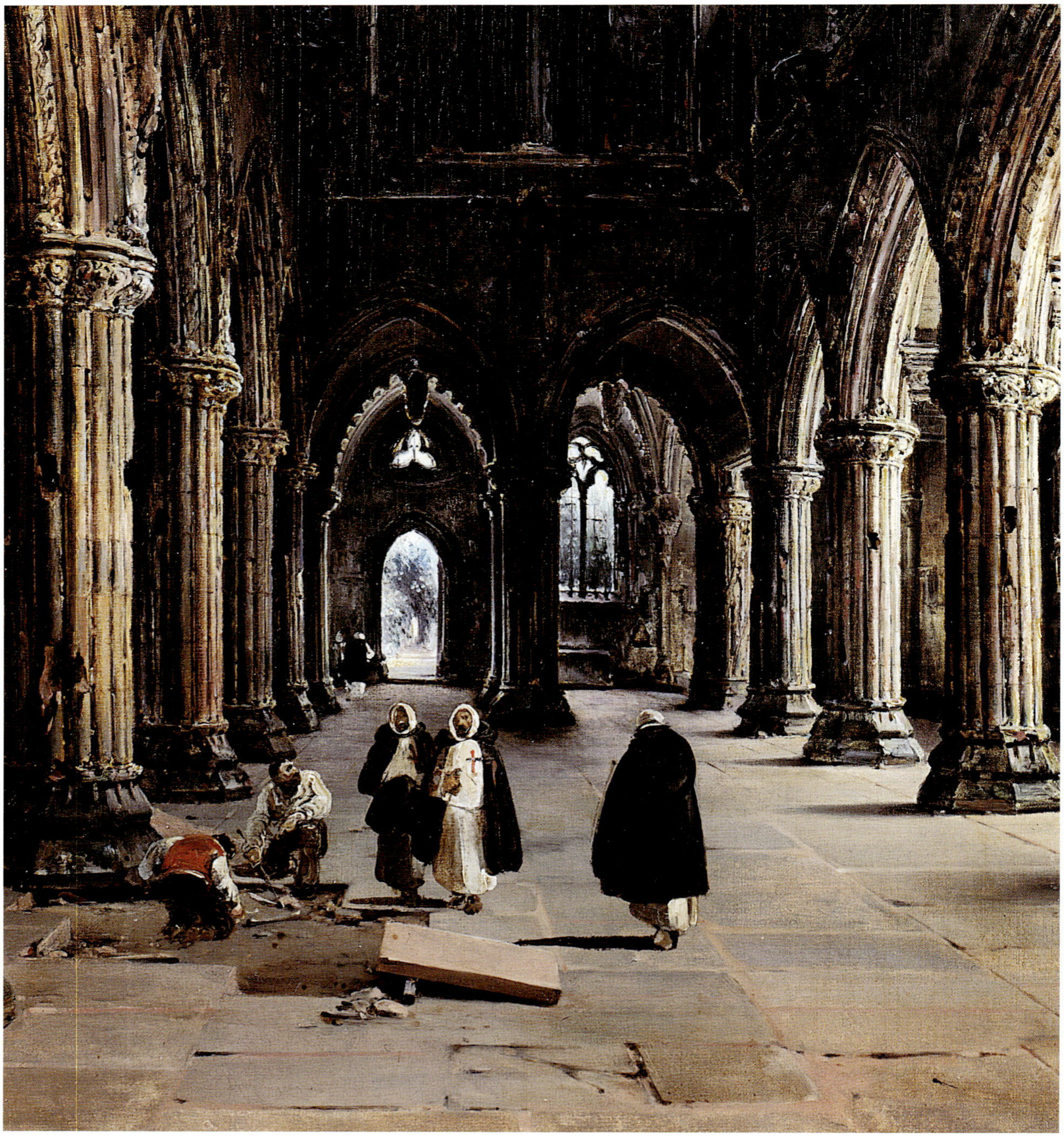

30

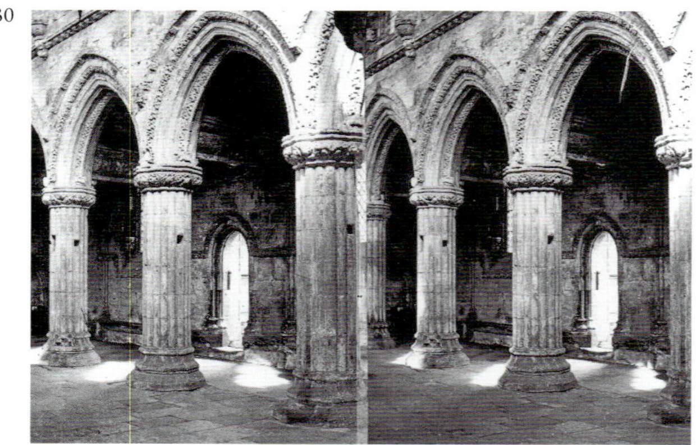

interesting to note that in some of these photographs, the piers have a series of holes at the same height [plate 30]. These photographs, taken before the holes were filled during the restoration, could possibly provide new evidence about Daguerre's presence at the Chapel. Daguerre's painting has these holes clearly marked in the piers of the right arcade, exactly as shown in the photographs taken a few years later. No artist before Daguerre had ever included this detail. So the question remains: is this a study of the sensual play of light within a mathematically realised space, or is it Daguerre revealing Rosslyn Chapel as a visual wonder of architecture?

From the beginning of the twentieth century the artists who depicted the Chapel started to experiment far more imaginatively with architectural ideas. Detailed plans and elevations of how this 'pocket cathedral' might have been, if ever completed, were prepared by the Scottish architect, Thomas Ross (1839–1930). He made a most charming perspective sketch of a finished nave and transept with a fine centre tower and spire [plate 31]. In perfect keeping with the existing parts of the building, his Rosslyn Chapel in its supposed finished state becomes one of the major themes discussed in a paper read at Rosslyn in 1914.[47] In this paper Ross loses nothing in comparison with Sir Walter Scott when he uses words like 'poem of stone', when he describes the vault of the Chapel as 'powdered with stars' in a new *Paradise Lost*, or when he defines the effect of the building as 'a fantastic fairy dream as no mortal ever dared to dream before'.[48]

The 'pocket proportions' of Rosslyn Chapel, its setting and its strange light effects, as well as the eerie tales associated with it, have captured the imagination of poets, writers and amateurs, and many others in the world of art and architecture. The analysis of the visual evidence amplifies our knowledge not only of the Chapel but also of the cultural tastes existing at different moments in English and Scottish society. Certainly, the Chapel as seen and depicted by John Slezer (*c*.1645–1717) towards the end of the seventeenth century has a very different meaning from the building recorded by Joseph Michael Gandy in 1806, or the idealised completed version of Thomas Ross. Rich in artistic fantasy and legend, Rosslyn Chapel was the perfect choice for a diorama show. Viewed in such a way, Rosslyn Chapel becomes a changing cultural icon for succeeding generations of architects, architectural critics and amateurs and a touchstone for essential value-judgements. This national and international perspective is encapsulated in the words of a journalist on *The Scotsman* newspaper who once wrote:

Roslin Chapel, of all buildings in the world, is one of the most remarkable. Setting the conventional and accepted rules of architecture at defiance by its bold and original beauty, and the exquisitely delicate and truthful tracery of its ornamentation, it is a wonder and a joy to all. Every one visits it, and no one ever forgets it; the very name calls up delightful, or, it may be, sad memories; and there is no land, however distant, where it is not spoken of with enthusiasm and affection.[49]

31

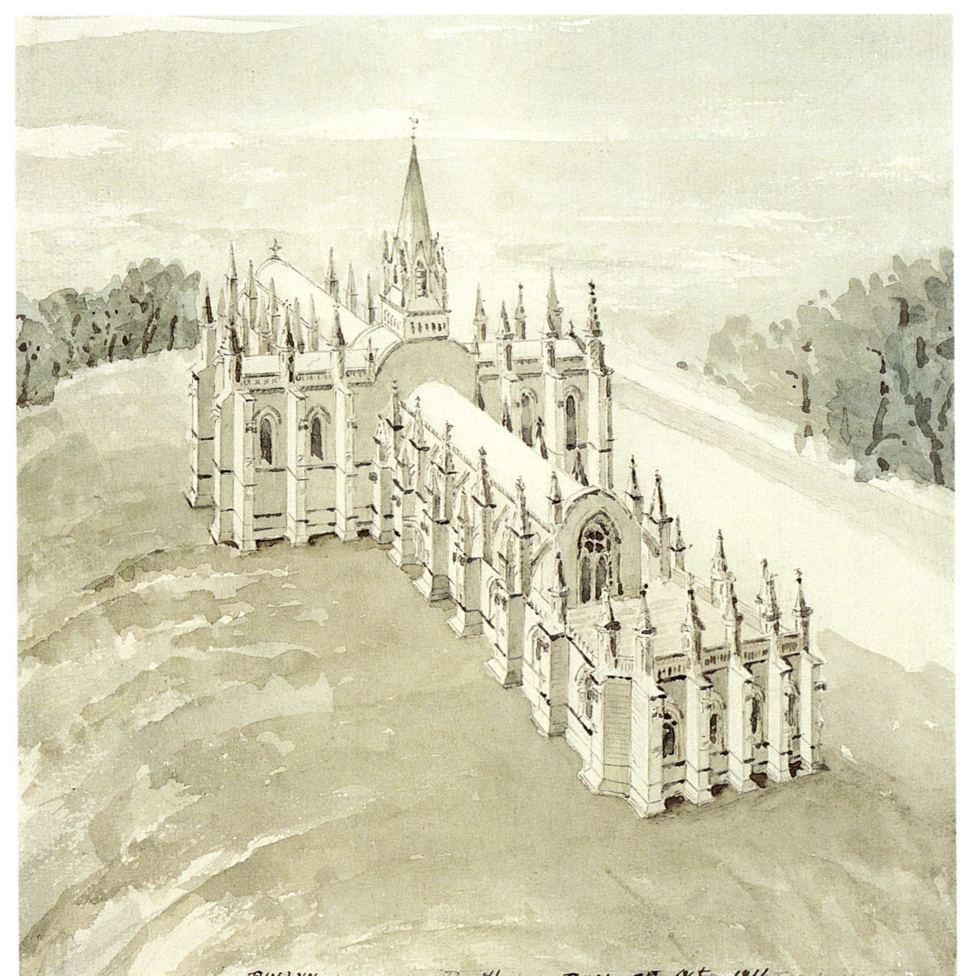

PLATE 29B
Detail from Louis-Jacques-Mandé Daguerre *The Interior of Rosslyn Chapel*, 1824, showing the holes in the piers.

PLATE 30
Thomas Vernon Begbie
Rosslyn Chapel
(stereo photograph)
The Cavaye Collection of Thomas Begbie Prints
City Art Centre: Edinburgh Museums and Galleries

PLATE 31
Thomas Ross
Rosslyn from the East, 1914
National Library of Scotland, Edinburgh

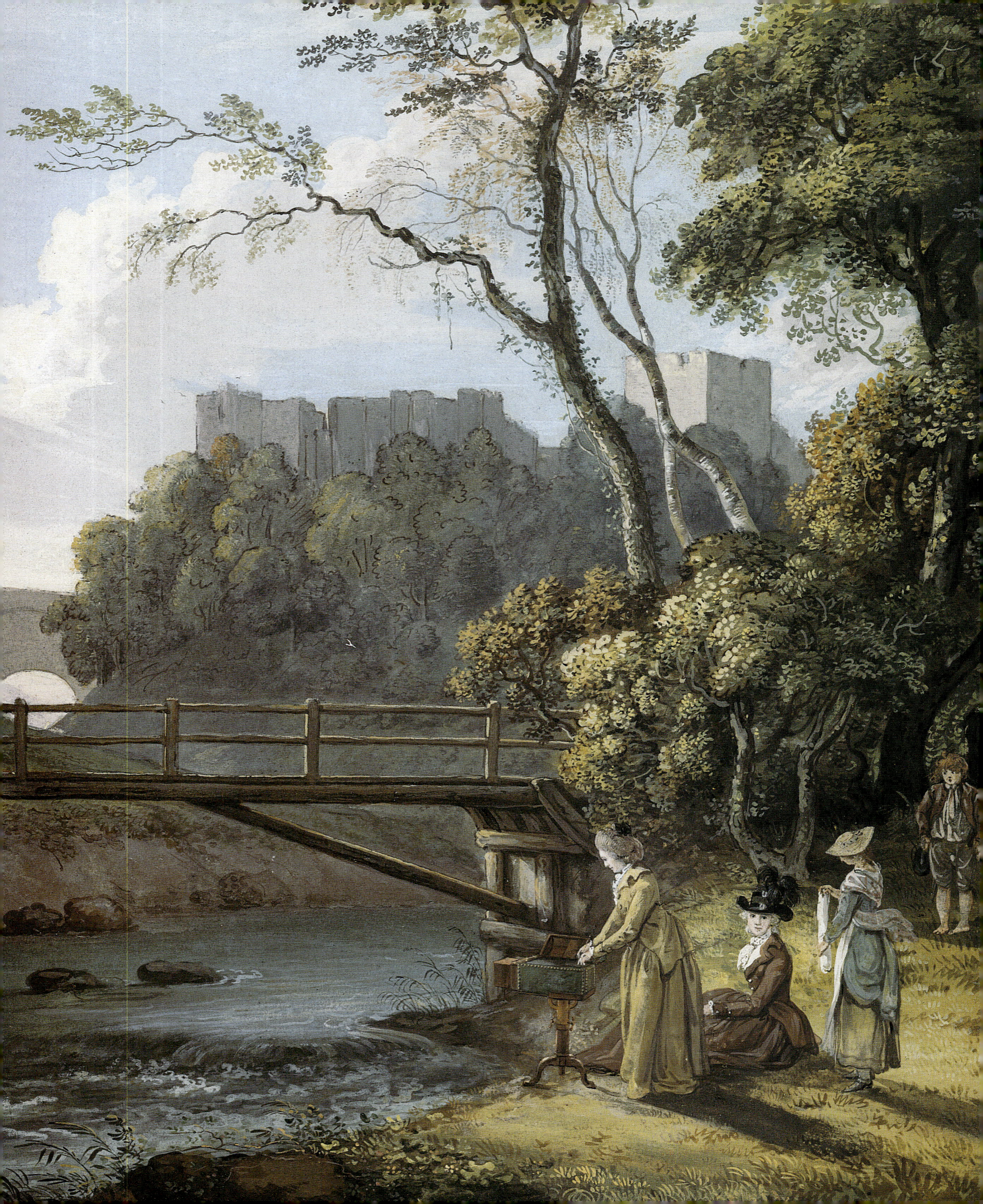

HELEN ROSSLYN

Rosslyn: 'That Romantic Spot'

In Roslin's wild and wooded glen
The clash of swords the shepherd hears
And from the groves of Hawthornden
Gleam forth ten thousand spears:...

St Clair! Thy princely halls
In ruin sink decay'd,
And moss now greens the chapel walls
Where thy proud line is laid![1]

The appeal of Rosslyn has two sources, which over time have become intermingled: the colourful history of the Castle, Chapel and the 'Lordly line of high St Clair';[2] and the picturesque beauty of the landscape. The publication of Sir Walter Scott's *The Lay of the Last Minstrel* in 1805 changed the volume and nature of visitors to Rosslyn, heralding the establishment of its own coach service from Princes Street in Edinburgh.[3] Until this time, the landscape was the domain of the discerning and intrepid painters and poets who recorded their thoughts with brush and pen, and it is to them that this chapter is dedicated.

The literary history of Rosslyn Glen has its origins in the seventeenth century, when the St Clair family was living in splendour at Rosslyn Castle, and the neighbouring Hawthornden Castle, just a mile along the River Esk, was home to William Drummond (1585–1649). Having lost his first wife shortly after their marriage, he retired to the gentle landscape of the Esk valley, from which he drew great comfort and to which he returned at various stages throughout his life. He was a poet of such renown that Ben Jonson (1572–1637) apparently made the journey from London to Drummond's 'romantic mansion of Hawthornden' in 1618 on foot. Their meeting was the occasion of a charming interchange between the two poets. Drummond was apparently sitting under a tree, and greeted his visitor with the words: 'Welcome, welcome, royal Ben', to which the other, not to be outdone in courtesy or craft, replied: 'Thank ye, thank ye, Hawthornden.'[4]

This was the glorious age recalled in Sir Walter Scott's *The Lay of the Last Minstrel.* Canto sixth introduces 'Harold, bard of brave St Clair' who tells the sad tale of Rosabelle, drowning in the stormy Firth of Forth on her way to Rosslyn Castle.[5] The ancient family tradition of burying the St Clair knights 'uncoffin'd' in their armour, and the legend that tells of the Chapel glowing as though aflame upon the death of a member of the St Clair family, were used by Scott to create a visual image that was long to be associated with the Chapel. His words were remembered by John Ruskin (1819–1900) in his *Praeterita*, of which the first volume ends with a chapter entitled 'Roslyn Chapel': '...and all the strength and framework of my mind, lurid, like the vaults of Roslyn, when weird fire gleamed on its pillars, foliage-bound, and far in the depth of twilight, *blazed every rose-carved buttress fair*'.[6]

But the growing awareness of landscape in eighteenth-century Scottish painting and poetry owed as much to the gentle pastoral tradition of the lowlands as to that of the grand historical legend. Painters and poets were beginning to celebrate their contemporary native scenery in addition to classical splendours or extravagant events of the past. Allan Ramsay (1686–1758) was one of the first to do this in his pastoral play, *The Gentle Shepherd.* First published in 1729, it was inspired by the Esk landscape: 'Such were the lays blithe Ramsay sweetly sung, / When on the banks of Esk his lyre was strung.'[7] It is interesting that the popular eighteenth-century Scottish ballad entitled 'Roslin Castle' does not sing of past glories as one might expect, but of the shepherd boy, serenading the object of his affections:

Of Celia's charms the shepherd sung,
The hills and dales with Celia rung,
While Roslin castle heard the swain,
And echoed back the chearful strain.[8]

Herein lay the versatility of the Esk landscape, which offered both history and romance to the observer. As we will see, it was primarily as a picturesque landscape that Rosslyn became so beloved of painters and poets at the turn of that century [plate 33].

Landscape painting in Scotland until the latter part of the eighteenth century had been restricted to the domain of decorative interiors or commissioned topographical works. The Edinburgh firm of interior painters run by James Norie (1684–1757) and his son Robert (d.1766) was one of the most fertile training grounds for many of the emerging Scottish landscape painters, including John 'Old Jock' Wilson (1774–1855), Jacob More (1740–1793)

OPPOSITE
Detail from Paul Sandby *Rosslyn Castle, Midlothian*, c.1780, plate 32

32

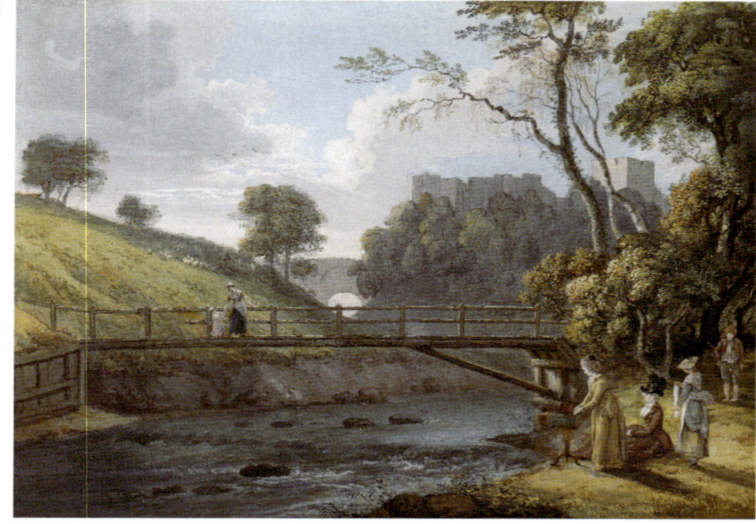

33

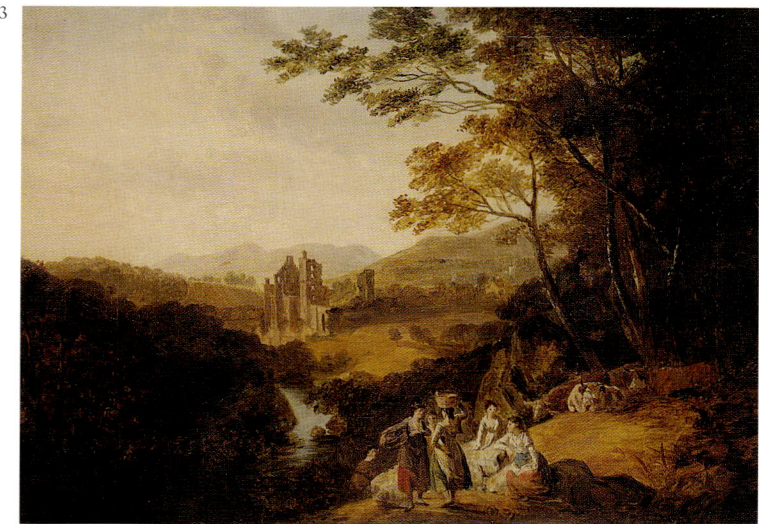

and Alexander Runciman (1736–1785). The Nories were highly skilled in producing accomplished pastoral scenes to set over doors and fireplaces, based largely on Italian and Dutch prints, and bearing little relation to the local landscape. The emergence of Scottish pride in its national heritage – the poetical works of Burns and Scott – coupled with the travelling English antiquaries' reverence of Scottish 'picturesque places' heralded a change in the approach to landscape, placing an emphasis on 'drawing on the spot' rather than working in the studio.

35

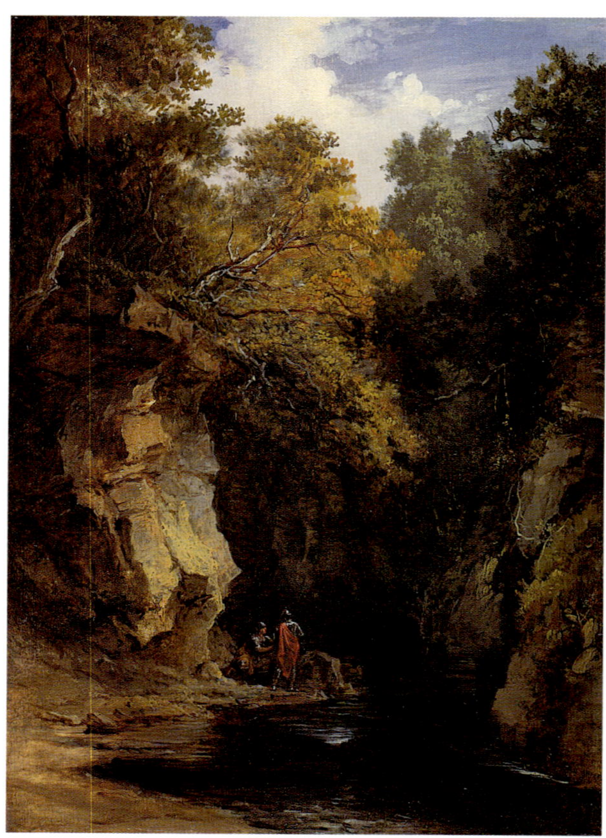

No wonder then that the landscape of Rosslyn, just seven miles from the centre of Edinburgh, became a beauty spot of wide renown. With its wooded glen and ruined craggy Castle towering above, winding river and waterfall below, it offered all that was required by the disciple of the Picturesque. The grandeur of the Italianate landscape, which had long inspired painters, was to be found in a gentler form on Edinburgh's own doorstep.

The painter Alexander Nasmyth (1758–1840) was a formative influence in Edinburgh during the last decades of the eighteenth century. He was well established and highly regarded in the art of portrait painting but his outspoken political views began to alienate him from many of his potential sitters and he found himself drawn to a new and more experimental art. His son James wrote: 'At length he devoted himself to landscape painting. It was a freer and more enjoyable life. Instead of painting the faces of those who were perhaps without character or attractiveness, he painted the fresh and ever-beautiful face of nature.'[9]

Nasmyth, like his predecessors, Jacob More and William Delacour, began to explore his local landscape. All three artists made expeditions to Rosslyn; indeed John Beugo (1759–1841), Edinburgh poet and painter, suggested in his poem 'Esk Water', that Jacob More had found his earliest inspiration in Rosslyn Glen.

One of Nasmyth's earliest known landscapes is *Rosslyn Castle with the Esk*.[10] Another oil of similar date is entitled *Rosslyn Castle with Rosslyn Chapel* [plate 34].[11] *On the Esk* [plate 35] is more romantic in nature, the addition of Highland soldiers in full regalia an allusion to the themes beloved of Scott and Burns.

There was a strong sentiment of patriotism amongst Scottish artists at the turn of the century, many of whom were wary of the recent 'discovery' of Scotland's beauties by their English counterparts and were jealous guardians

PLATE 32
Paul Sandby
*Rosslyn Castle, Midlothian, c.*1780
Yale Center for British Art, Paul Mellon Collection, New Haven

PLATE 33
Julius Caesar Ibbetson
*Rosslyn Castle with Washerwomen and Cattle, c.*1800
McManus Galleries (Dundee City Council Arts)

PLATE 34
Alexander Nasmyth
*Rosslyn Castle with Rosslyn Chapel, c.*1789
Collection of E. Derricott

PLATE 35
Alexander Nasmyth
*On the Esk, c.*1800
The Robertson Collection, Orkney

34

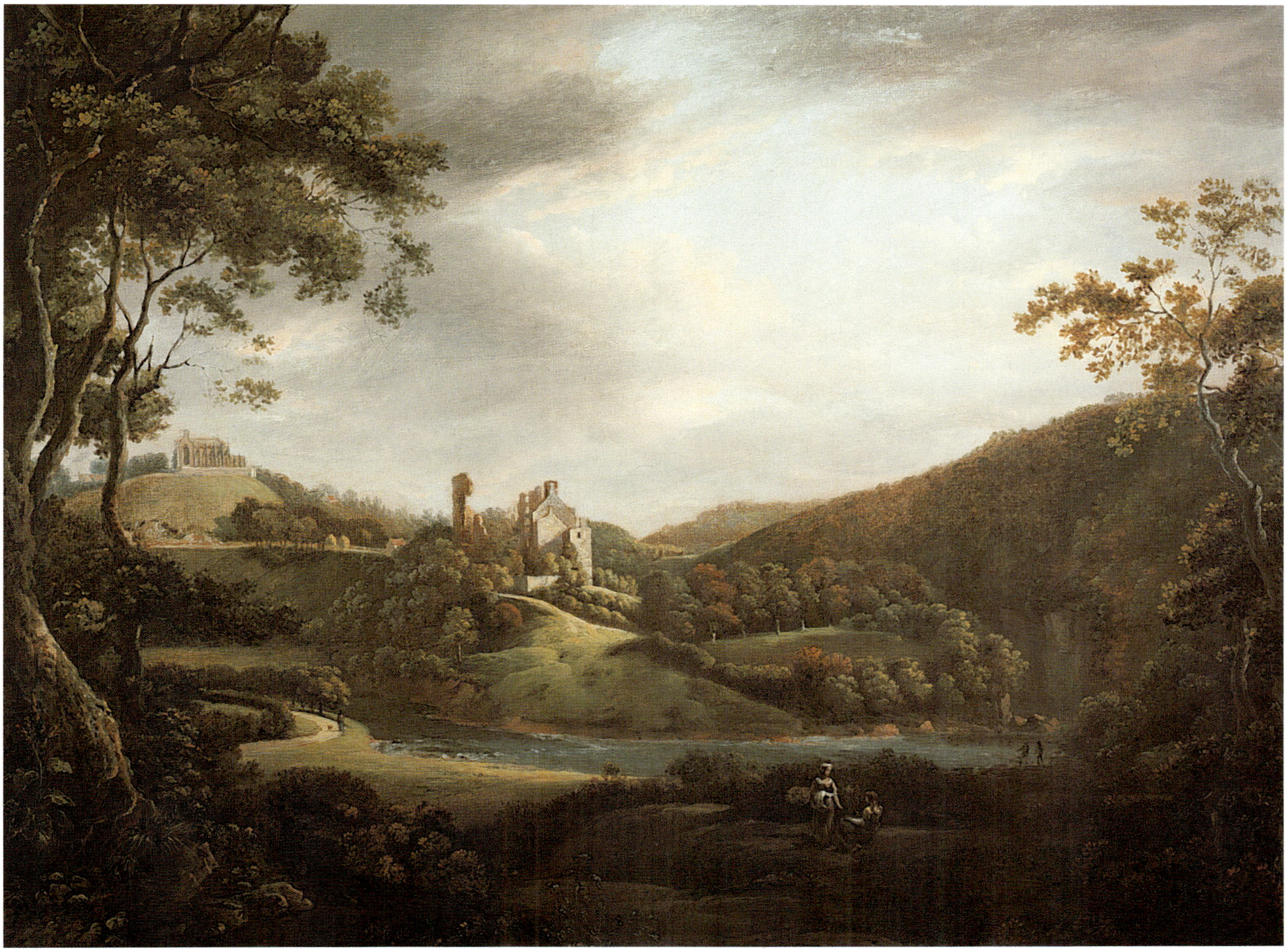

of their own heritage. This is given unmistakable voice in the subtitle of a poem by the Scotsman James Alves, written in 1800: 'The Banks of the Esk, or, a saunter from Roslin to Smeaton, A Poem, Descriptive, Historical and Moral, with an introductory Canto, by way of retaliation upon some English authors who have wantonly abused the people and country of Scotland.' Alves's patriotism knows no bounds as he boldly suggests that the architecture of Rosslyn Chapel rivals that of St Peter's in Rome:

> *From Rome, the nurse of science and of arts*
> *Lo! Architecture all her pow'r imparts,*
> *Steals from each temple ev'ry tempting form*
> *And robs St Peter's,* ROSLIN *to adorn.*[12]

The visiting English for their part were perhaps guilty of treating their northern neighbours with condescension. Joseph Farington's comments on Nasmyth's *Rosslyn Castle* were somewhat dismissive: 'I was surprised at the liberty taken with one of the views of Rosslin. He had certainly exhibited all that is to be found at the place, but I am sure that there is no one point from which he could see all that was represented.' He concluded that his paintings were 'likely enough to please people not conversant with superior art'.[13]

Nasmyth enjoyed a well-documented friendship with Robert Burns (1759–1796). His was the distinction of being chosen by the poet to paint his portrait, an honour not lightly bestowed. As James Nasmyth (1808–1890) wrote, 'Burns had been asked by several artists to sit to them but he had a great dislike to do so – But at the earnest request of "Jean" [Mrs Burns] he consented to sit to be painted by his friend Nasmyth and my father made a present of this the only portrait to Mrs Burns, in whose possession it remained till her death'[14] [plate 36].

A letter from Nasmyth to a friend, William Cribb, records a memorable excursion made by the two to Rosslyn in the early hours of a summer morning in the late 1780s, after a night of revelry in town:

My Dear Sir
As you wish me to give you some account of a walk to Rosslynn and a breakfast I had with my old aquaintance R. Burns The Much Admired Poet of Nature and of Scotland it is as follows. One morning in the early part of the summer of 1787 we met at my house at 5 o'clock, the morning was fine and we walked out to that Romantic Spot it was the first time my friend had been there I had the pleasure of taking him down the Rocky and well-wooded banks of the Esk … This one of the days of my life that I look back to with intense pleasure.[15]

Their arrival at Rosslyn Castle at dawn was recorded in Nasmyth's pencil sketch, now in the collection of the National Gallery of Scotland, on which his son James based his oil painting [plate 37]. The poet is seated on a rock, pen in hand, whilst the painter stands beneath the bridge to admire the glory of the morning sunrise.

The expedition culminated in a welcome Scottish breakfast at the Roslin Inn: 'Tea Eggs & Some Whisky … the charge was very moderate in our opinion…'.[16] Burns, inspired by the hospitality of the landlady, Annie Wilson, wrote the following verse, described variously as having been scratched onto a pewter plate or scribbled on the back of the bill for breakfast:

'At Roslin Inn'
My blessings on ye, honest wife!
I ne'er was here before;
Ye've wealth o' gear for spoon and knife:
Heart could not wish for more.
Heav'n keep you clear o' sturt and strife,
Till far ayont fourscore,
And by the Lord o' death and life,
I'll ne'er gae by your door![17]

During the 1790s Nasmyth set up a drawing academy at his Edinburgh residence in York Place, which was well attended by many other young Scottish painters. He was clearly a charismatic teacher who inspired his pupils. The Revd John Thomson (1778–1840), Hugh William Williams (1773–1829) and David Roberts (1796–1864) are all recorded as having taken early instruction from Nasmyth.[18] The extent to which the tuition was formal is not well documented, but Roberts later wrote: '… if love and admiration for his works, unwearied industry in copying them and afterwards doing my best to imitate them, could make a pupil, I was one in the truest sense of the word'.[19]

'Grecian' Williams who 'from his long residence in Scotland considers that he is a Scotchman'[20] enjoyed a relationship with Nasmyth based on a curious combination of mutual support and rivalry. Perhaps better known for his views of Greek subjects, as his sobriquet suggests, Williams's contribution to the emergence of landscape painting in Scotland at the turn of the century is considerable.

It has been said of the two painters: 'If Williams was Alexander Nasmyth's pupil in 1790, he very soon began to overtake him in originality of view. Even allowing for the difference in age, they obviously inspired and influenced each other, to the extent that it is often difficult to know who was imitating whom.'[21] Certainly their respective views of Rosslyn Castle [plates 34, 39] invite comparison. The view, the degree of detail and the mood are all similar and the difference in handling can primarily be attributed to the use of different media – Nasmyth's oil and Williams's watercolour. Williams, Nasmyth's junior by fifteen years, demonstrates a fluency in watercolour painting which was further developed in his 1805 view of the Castle from the north [plate 40].

Like Nasmyth, Williams knew Rosslyn well and must have enjoyed the hospitality offered at the Roslin Inn, for he arranged a visit for his good friend Dr Anthony Todd Thomson (1778–1849) to Rosslyn and Hawthornden, which is recorded in Thomson's journals:

By nine, we were seated in the little inn at Roslin, eating a true Scotch breakfast. The table groaned beneath hung beef, tongue, cold fowls, hot beef steaks, rolls, toast, jelly and marmalade … After breakfast we proceeded to the chapel of Roslin, which is now shewn by the landlord of the inn … Those of the party who were able to scramble over the rocks proceeded down the best of the river. Nothing can exceed the romantic scenery which the banks present, between Roslin and Hawthornden … After returning to town, we concluded this delightful day by dining with my friend Williams.[22]

Paul Sandby (1731–1809) is often credited with being the first to bring the picturesque places of Scotland to the attention of the English. Between 1747 and 1752 he toured Scotland in his capacity as draughtsman for the Ordnance Survey, making detailed sketches for topographical reference. During the winters when travelling became impracticable, he stayed in Edinburgh, working the drawings into maps and finished topographical views. He became great friends with John Clerk of Eldin (1728–1812), son of Sir John Clerk of Penicuik, whose family

36

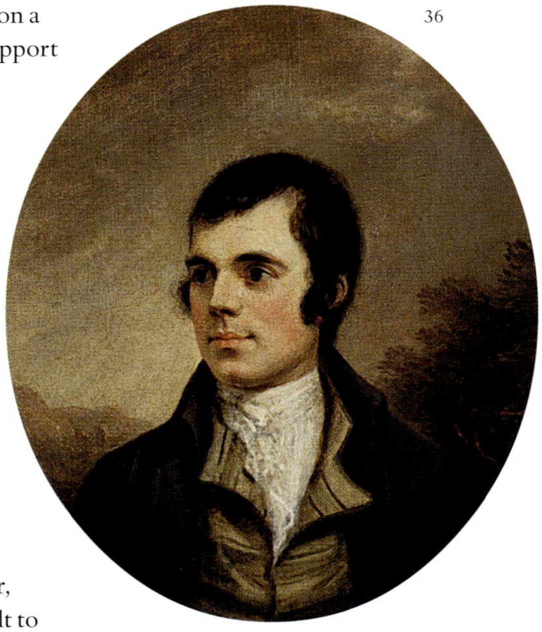

PLATE 36
Alexander Nasmyth
Robert Burns, 1787
Scottish National Portrait Gallery, Edinburgh

PLATE 37
James Nasmyth
Robert Burns and Alexander Nasmyth at Rosslyn Castle
Royal Scottish Academy, Edinburgh

PLATE 38
Revd John Thomson of Duddingston
Rosslyn Castle from the Glen, 1830
Hunterian Art Gallery, University of Glasgow

37

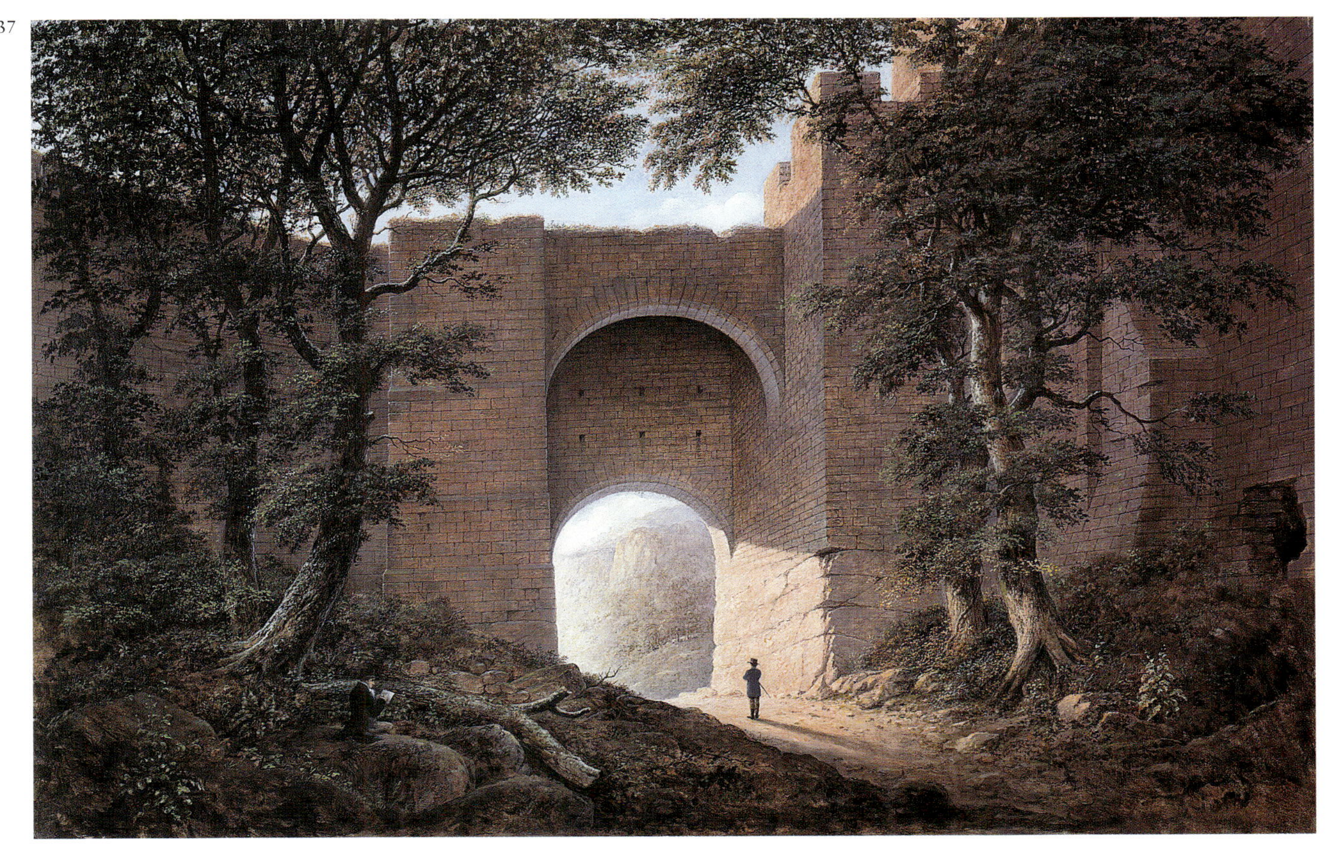

38

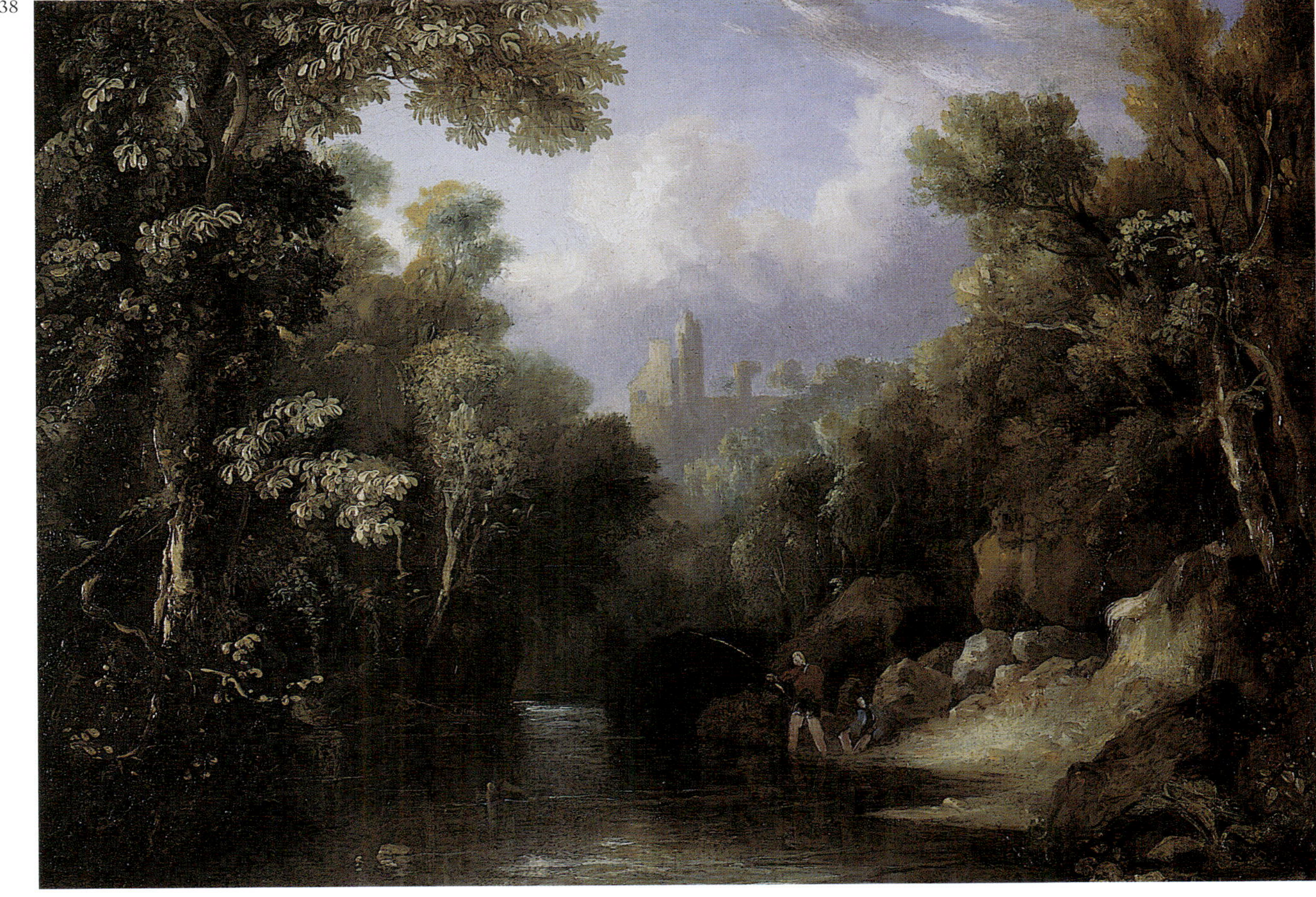

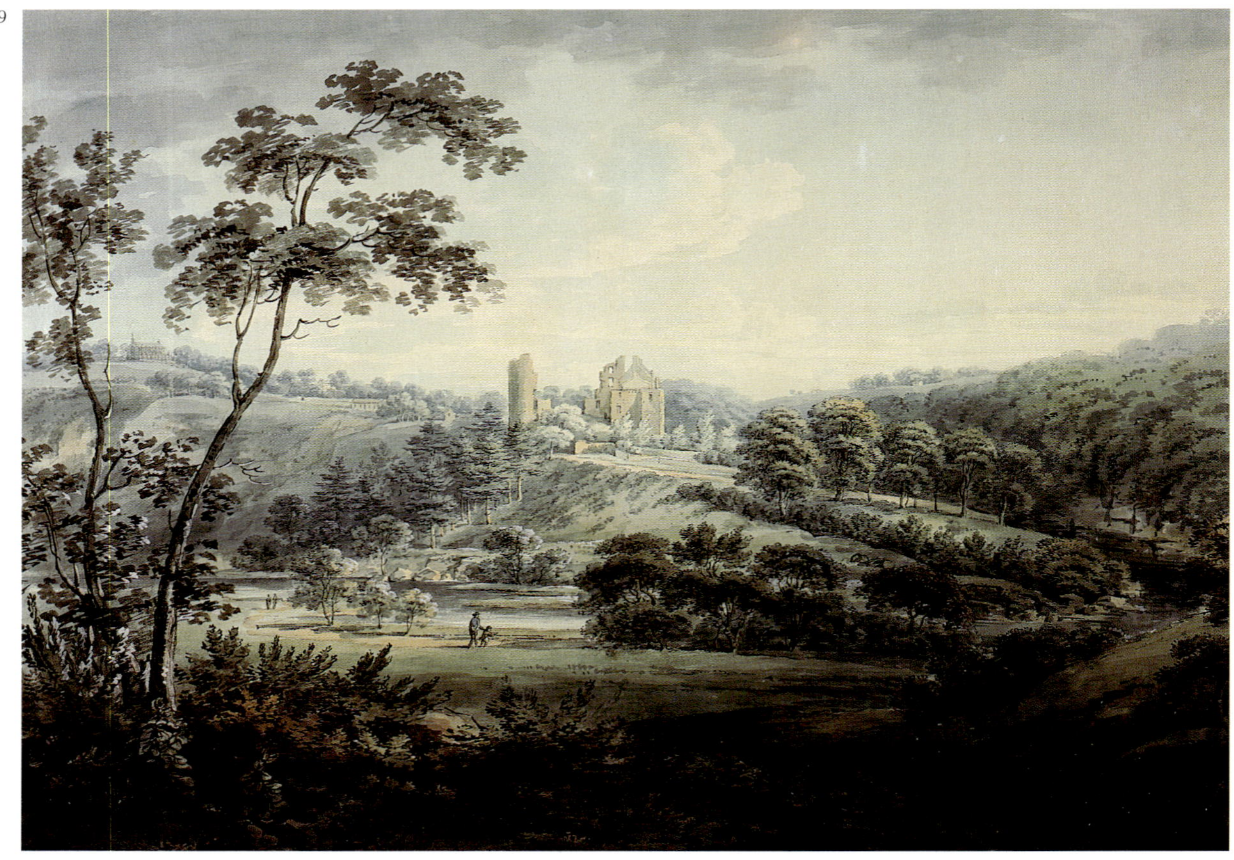

40

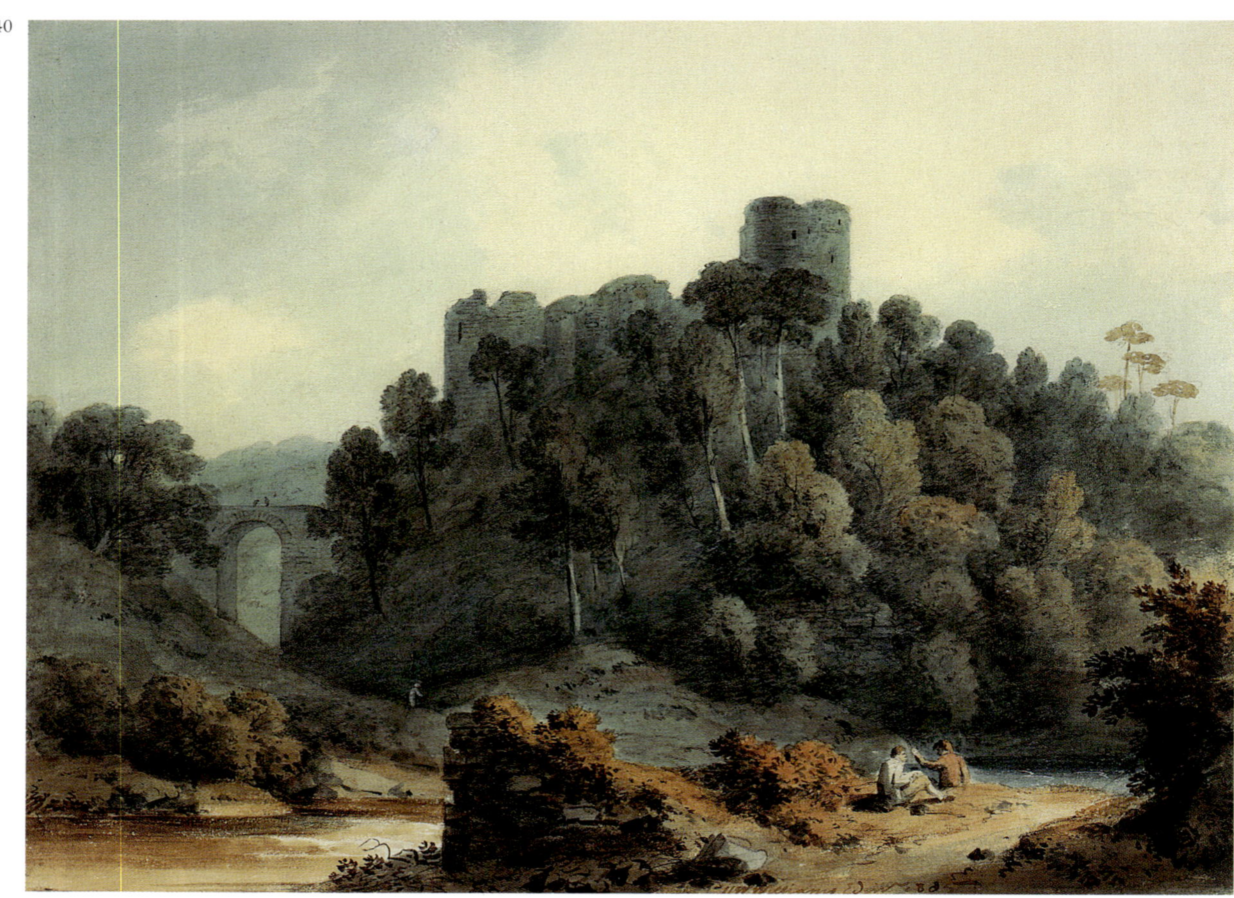

estate was situated just a few miles from Rosslyn. Robert Adam (1728–1794), the architect, was Clerk's brother-in-law and it is probable that they and Sandby made sketching trips together during these years. Clerk can be numbered amongst the earliest Scottish enthusiasts for local landscape and its architecture. He and Sandby learnt the technique of printmaking from an Edinburgh engraver, and Clerk became a skilled amateur etcher, producing numerous meticulous views, including three of Rosslyn Castle.

Sandby himself made countless sketches in the environs of Edinburgh, of which two are known of Rosslyn [plate 6].[23] The detailed watercolour [plate 32] is a work of a completely different genre, bearing stylistic similarity to works of a later date. It is possible that he made another trip to this part of Scotland in the late 1770s and that this watercolour was executed as a commission for one of the subjects, who have been identified as Lady Frances Scott and Lady Elliot.[24]

Another early English visitor to Rosslyn with a style of watercolour akin to that of Sandby was Thomas Hearne (1744–1817). Sir George Beaumont said of him, '... a man of purer integrity does not exist – as an artist – where shall we find a more faithful disciple of nature?'[25] His pen and wash drawing is topographically accurate, showing the ruined archway over the bridge at the time of his visit in 1778 [plate 9]. Hearne made sketching tours of Scotland with Beaumont and Joseph Farington (1747–1821) during the winter of 1776–7 and again in 1777–8, the date of his drawing of Rosslyn Castle [plate 41].

A similar companionship existed between James Boswell (1740–1795) and Samuel Johnson (1709–1784) who toured the Hebrides together in 1773. Boswell was intent on paying a visit to the landscape of his illustrious predecessor, William Drummond of Hawthornden. His diary entry for 20 November 1773 records that he was even willing to incur the displeasure of his host, Sir John Dalrymple of Cranston, by arriving late and missing lunch:

I resolved that, on our way to Sir John's, we should make a little circuit by Roslin Castle and Hawthornden ... I would by no means lose the pleasure of seeing my friend at Hawthornden, – of seeing Sam Johnson *at the very spot where* Ben Johnson *visited the learned and poetical Drummond. We surveyed Roslin-castle, the romantick scene around it, and the beautiful Gothick chapel, and dined and drank tea at the inn. It was very late before we reached the seat of Sir John Dalrymple, who certainly with some reason was not in very good humour.*[26]

The fact that Boswell's excursion of 1773 was prompted by an impulse so different from the tours of his contemporaries Thomas Pennant (1771) and Thomas Hearne (1778), both of whom were interested in providing accurate topographical records of picturesque ruins, demonstrates the appeal of Rosslyn to artists of all kinds.

In 1789 Captain Francis Grose (1731–1791) made an extensive Scottish tour in the company of fellow antiquarian Robert Riddell. The resulting two volumes, *The Antiquities of Scotland*, were published in 1789 and 1791, and included engraved plates of both Rosslyn Chapel and Castle. 'Captain Grose was in town here for a few days, which he occupied in taking sundry views in our neighbourhood, he visited Roslin and Hawthornden with its caves etc etc took sketches...', in the words of George Paton.[27] Their base was Riddell's home, Friars Carse, in Nithsdale, where their closest neighbour was the poet, Robert Burns. Grose and Burns clearly enjoyed a lively friendship and the poet dedicated to him the following humourous lines:

The devil got notice that Grose was a-dying,
So whip! At the summons, old Satan came flying;
But when he approach'd where poor Francis lay moaning,
And saw each bed-post with its burthen a-groaning,
Astonish'd, confounded, cries Satan:– 'By God,
I'd want him ere take such a damnable load!'[28]

English artists tended to point one another to places of interest, thus establishing the well-trodden route for the 'picturesque tour' of the late eighteenth century. Joseph Farington was one of those responsible for moulding the Scottish itinerary of future picturesque travellers. He

41

PLATE 39
Hugh William Williams
Rosslyn Castle, 1795
Private Collection

PLATE 40
Hugh William Williams
Rosslyn Castle from the North, 1805
Private Collection

PLATE 41
Thomas Hearne
Sir George Beaumont and Joseph Farington Sketching a Waterfall, c.1777
Dove Cottage, The Wordsworth Trust

42

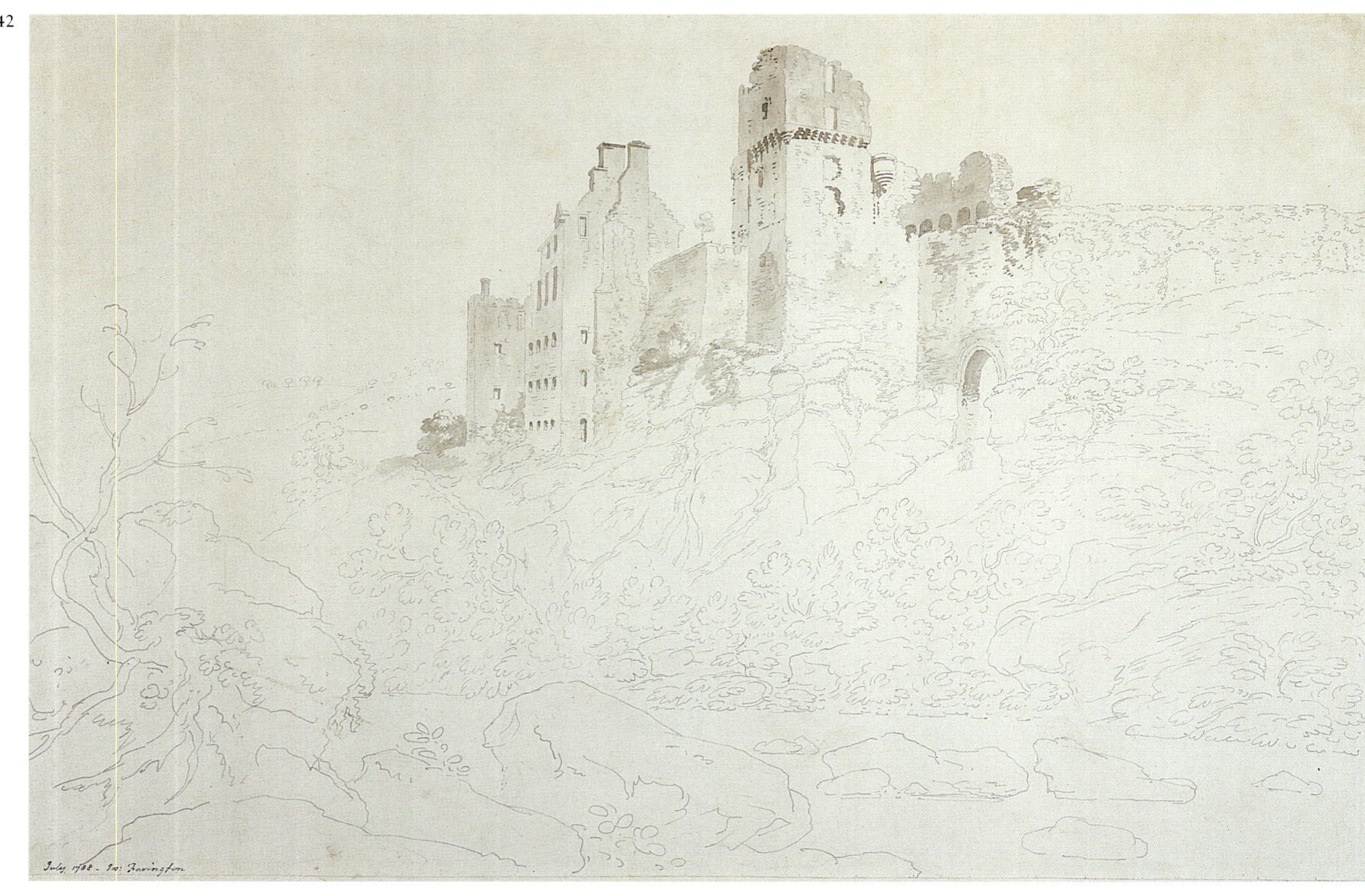

43

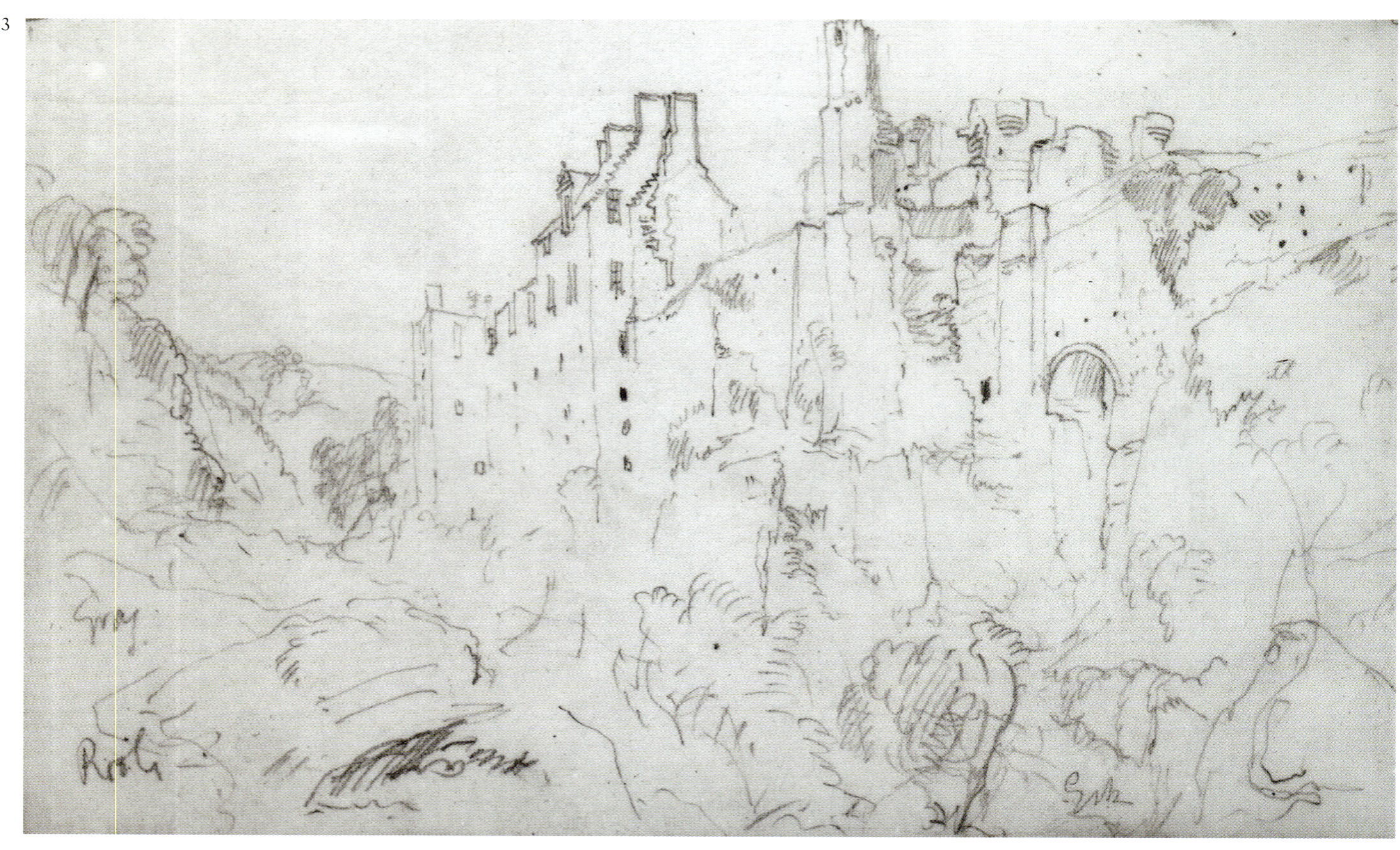

44

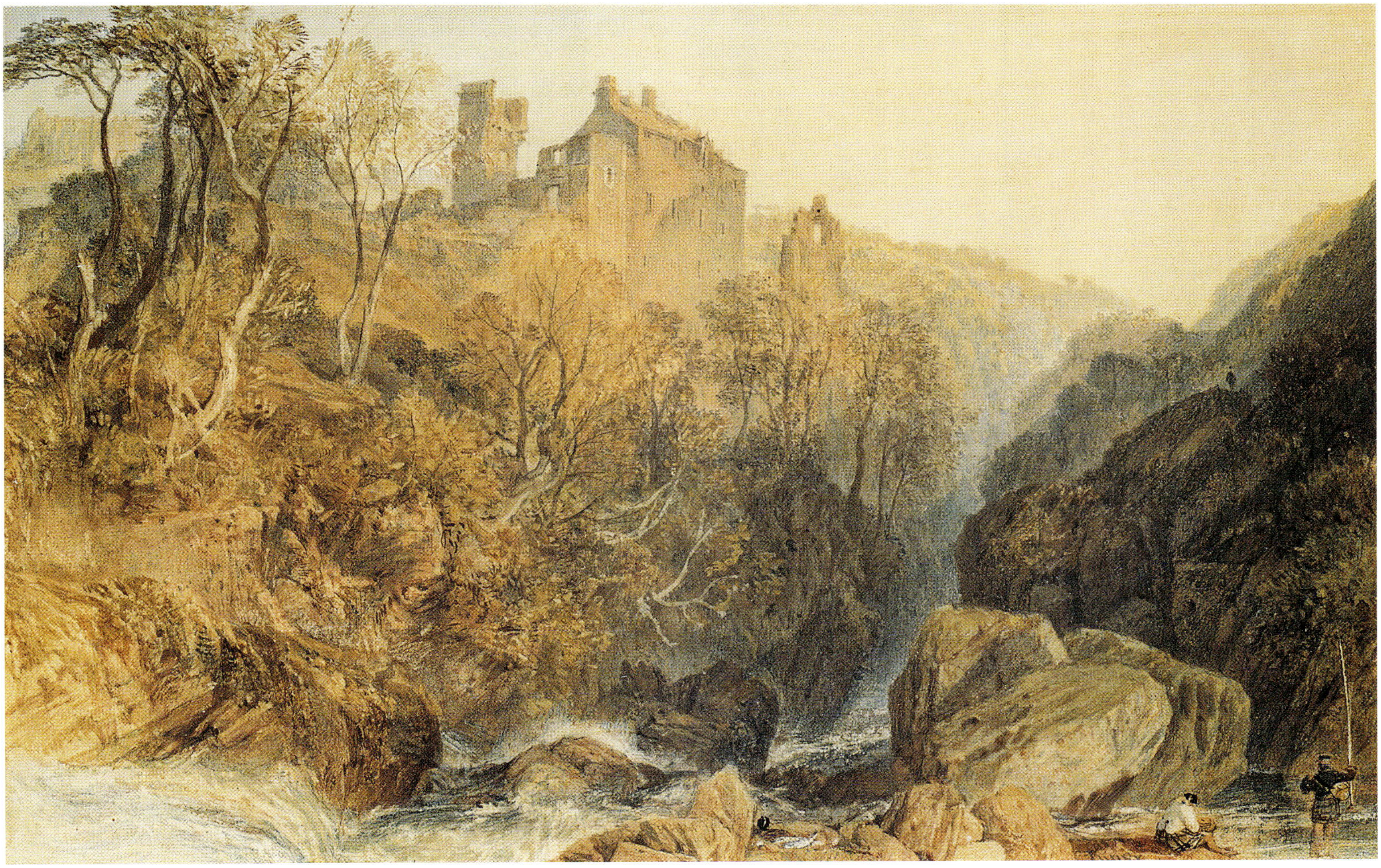

himself made two Scottish tours in 1788 and 1790 and was of the opinion that such a journey should start in Edinburgh, before continuing across the Forth and onwards to the Highlands. He describes Rosslyn Castle in his diaries: 'The castle is a ruin … It is built of the stone of the country, of a deep, dull, reddish cast, but time has so crusted & mossed most of the surface that at present it is of a mild, varied & agreeable tint. It stands upon a rock, at the foot of which runs a stream broken by large stones' [plate 42]. With the rest he was unimpressed: 'In short if I may so express myself Rosslin is a place that has been allowed to run to weed.' The inn he describes as 'a very shabby House, dirty & uncomfortable'. But he also noted that 'There is very picturesque matter about The place'.[29]

Before J.M.W. Turner (1775–1851) set out on his first Scottish trip of 1801 he received directions from Joseph Farington to 'particular picturesque places', which must have included Rosslyn. Both the 1801 'Dunbar' and 'Edinburgh' sketchbooks contain pencil drawings of the Castle ruins, and his 'Scotch Lakes' sketchbook of the same date bears the inscription, 'Edinburgh to Roslyn 6m¼',[30] on the inside back cover, which suggests that it was possibly an excursion that he planned to repeat. It appears that this was a shorter trip than the one projected, but Rosslyn must have remained in his memory, for he was to return in 1818 to make sketches for Sir Walter Scott's forthcoming *The Provincial Antiquities and Picturesque Scenery of Scotland*. The sketches are contained in the 'Scotch Antiquities' sketchbook[31] and one of the views of the Castle from the river below [plate 43] is a study for his watercolour *Rosslyn Castle* [plate 44]. During this trip, Turner went sketching with Revd John Thomson of Duddingston and Hugh William Williams, although the spirit of collaboration does not seem to have been much in evidence: 'Turner took sketches of Roslin, Borthwick and Dunbar castles, but no-one saw them except Walter Scott…'[32]

One English painter who came to spend a considerable time at Rosslyn, in the summer of 1800, was Julius Caesar Ibbetson (1759–1817). He was an artist whose career as a painter was closely linked to his patrons, with whom he frequently travelled giving drawing or painting instruction. His sociable nature and entertaining company ensured that he was in some demand in this role. He numbered the Earls of Bute and Warwick, and Richard Fulke and Charles Greville, brothers of the latter,

PLATE 42
Joseph Farington
Rosslyn Castle, 1788
Private Collection

PLATE 43
Joseph Mallord William Turner
Rosslyn Castle, from the 'Scotch Antiquities' sketchbook, 1818
Tate, London

PLATE 44
Joseph Mallord William Turner
Rosslyn Castle, c.1822
Indianapolis Museum of Art

amongst his patrons. The Grevilles, together with Sir George Beaumont, probably had some part in bringing Ibbetson to Scotland, as it was through them that the painter first had dealings – not altogether successful as it transpired – with the dealer Thomas Vernon in Liverpool.[33] Vernon exhibited some of Ibbetson's paintings in a show in Edinburgh in 1800 and encouraged him to visit the city with him on this occasion. The artist seemed delighted with Edinburgh society, despite a muted welcome from some of his rival painters, but due to an overwhelming flurry of invitations, needed privacy to concentrate on his own work. He retired to the village of Roslin, where he was employed by the Countess of Balcarres to spend several months as tutor to her daughters, the Ladies Elizabeth and Anne Lindsay.

The landscape at Rosslyn clearly appealed to the picturesque sensibilities of Ibbetson, who used the image of the craggy Castle ruin to great effect in several of his oil paintings. The foreground is invariably occupied by a counter balancing subject. His is the distinction of first depicting cows at Rosslyn, a favourite theme in his paintings and one which led Benjamin West to describe him as 'the Berghem of England' [plate 45]. Whether or not this was artistic license on Ibbetson's part it is hard to say. The romantic notions of the Englishman are clearly evident in the delightful groups of washerwomen that grace his pictures [plate 46]. He was teased on this subject by Lady Balcarres: 'It is altogether a beautiful picture, but why have you given all the Scotch lassies shoes and stockings? They wear them sometimes in cold weather – but not in such fine summer weather as is in your picture.'[34]

It appears that Ibbetson's work was much admired in Edinburgh, for the painting Lady Balcarres had teased him about was finally unveiled to universal acclaim. James Clerk, for whom it had been painted wrote that 'George Thomson (whose taste you admit) has given his unqualified approbation.'[35] The influential George Thomson (1757–1851), collector, editor and publisher of Caledonian music and song,[36] had already written to Ibbetson while he was still at Rosslyn, exalting him to the rank of 'Mr Ibbetson, Landscape Painter, Roslin' and asking him to book a room at the Roslin Inn with the good Mrs Annie Wilson, in preparation for a visit to him there: 'You are to bespeak a room & a hot joint for us at Wilson's by 3 o'clock as we intend to be extremely hungry about that time.'[37] Thomson was also to become a buyer of Ibbetson's work: 'I assure you that I do not know another Artist who would make me lay out twenty pieces on a picture … I am quite enchanted with my Claude – Ibbetson.'[38]

Indeed, so at home did the 'Landscape Painter [of] Roslin' feel that his reply to an inquiry from Lady Balcarres concerning his health suggested that he would happily be buried in the Rosslyn graveyard: 'in answer to the affair of digging me up like a potato the doctor advises the *planting* of me in Roslin churchyard, a recipe which he observes He has known effectually to cure most if not all the complaints with which I am afflicted, particularly when covered with one of those heavy stones which make people so comfortable & prevent the world from seeing us make Fools of ourselves, & indeed I am of the doctor's

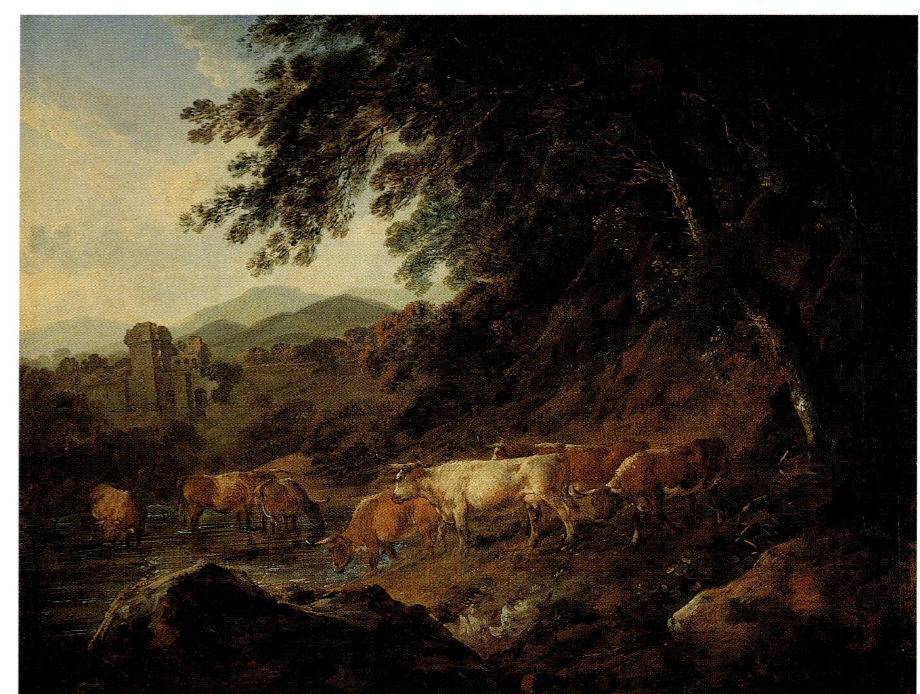
45

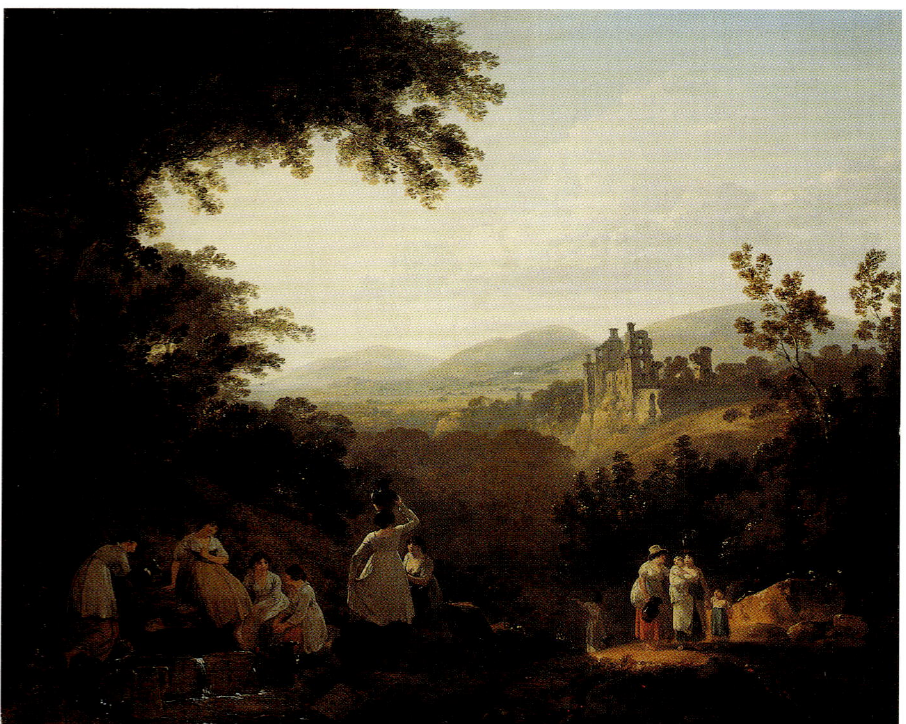
46

PLATE 45
Julius Caesar Ibbetson
Rosslyn Castle with Cows Drinking, *c.*1800
Collection of the Duke of Buccleuch and Queensberry KT

PLATE 46
Julius Caesar Ibbetson
Rosslyn Castle with Washerwomen
Location unknown

PLATE 47
Paul Sandby
Lady Frances Scott and Lady Elliot Drawing with a Camera Obscura, *c.*1780
Yale Center for British Art, Paul Mellon Collection

PLATE 48
Elizabeth Leveson-Gower, Countess of Sutherland
Rosslyn Chapel from *Views in Orkney and on the North-Eastern Coast of Scotland*, 1807
National Gallery of Scotland, Edinburgh

PLATE 49
John Glover
Rosslyn Castle from the River from the Sketchbook of a 'Scotch Tour 1825'
Collection of John G. Fleming

47

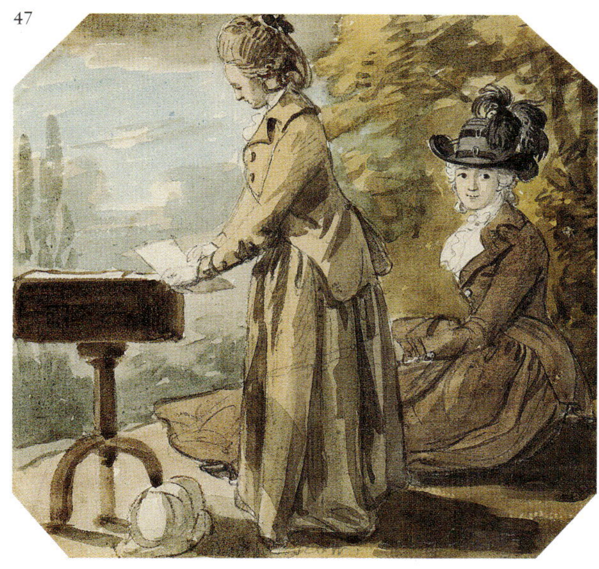

opinion that Roslin church yard is a very healthy bit of ground with a good prospect and other conveniences.'[39]

Ibbetson's short visit to Scotland had proved successful, both in securing him new patronage and in furnishing him with a well-loved subject, which he would continue to use in his paintings. There are at least six known oil paintings of Rosslyn Castle, one of which is dated as late as 1812, and a further three known of Hawthornden.[40]

It was during his stay at Rosslyn that Ibbetson conceived his treatise *An Accidence or Gamut of Painting in Oil and Watercolours*, which he dedicated to his pupil Lady Elizabeth Lindsay.[41] The relish with which lady amateurs had embraced landscape painting was probably in large part due to the joy of drawing from nature, which provided a challenging discipline to complement the established studio classes. Sandby had presumably given drawing lessons to Lady Frances Scott and Lady Elliot at Rosslyn in the late 1770s, as recorded in one of his watercolours [plate 47]. It shows the pupils using a camera obscura, a box with a mirror that reflects a view onto a sheet of thin paper placed over a glass screen, thus enabling the subject to be studied in miniature through a lens.[42] James Nasmyth also made a sketch of his father employing the same tool, suggesting that the camera obscura played a part in the Nasmyth classes.[43]

The teaching at this academy was gradually entrusted to Alexander Nasmyth's daughters, under whose guidance the institution flourished. As James Nasmyth wrote, 'The Nasmyth classes became quite the fashion. In many cases both mothers and daughters might be seen at work together in that delightful painting room … on many a fine summer's day did my sisters make a picnic excursion into the neighbourhood of Edinburgh. They were accompanied by their pupils, sketch-book and pencil in hand.'[44]

Amongst these lady amateurs was Jessy Harden, daughter of an Edinburgh banker, whose delightful journals capture the mood of enthusiasm for the new art of landscape painting amongst Edinburgh's gentry: 'I spent all afternoon at Nasmyth's endeavouring to take a sketch…I find I am very far from expert at the business but I intend to stick to it until I can make some hand of it.'[45] She and her husband, John Harden, were both talented amateurs and regular visitors to Rosslyn: '[My husband] and I set out in the gig yesterday after breakfast & landed at Roslin where we walked about all the forenoon … We dined there and intend to repeat the expedition frequently through the summer.'[46] Not only drawing, but the technically demanding discipline of etching became popular with the more dedicated amateurs. One of these was Elizabeth, Countess of Sutherland (1765–1839),[47] whose volume *Views in Orkney and on the North-eastern Coast of Scotland*, privately printed in 1807, contains three etchings of Rosslyn Chapel [plate 48].

48

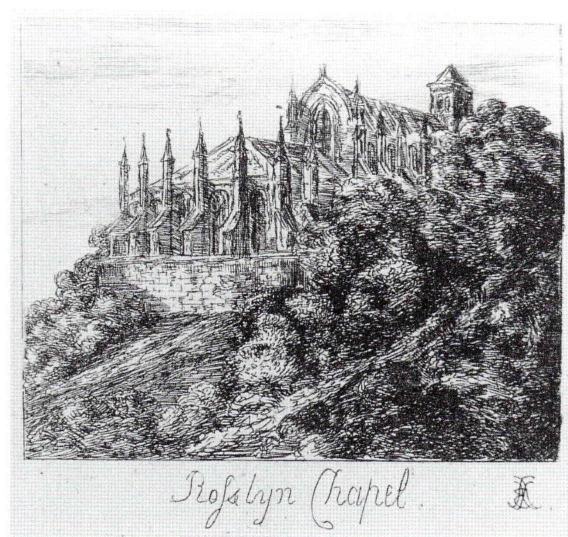

49

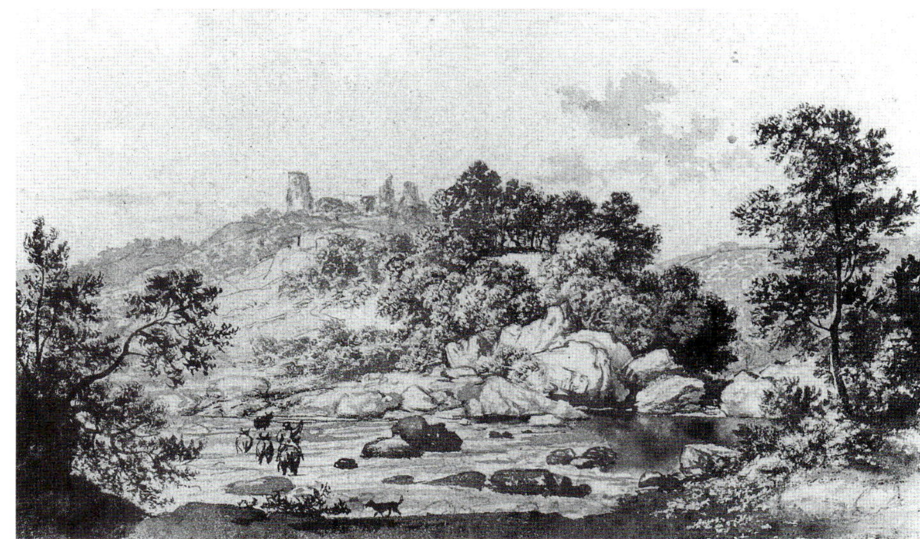

50

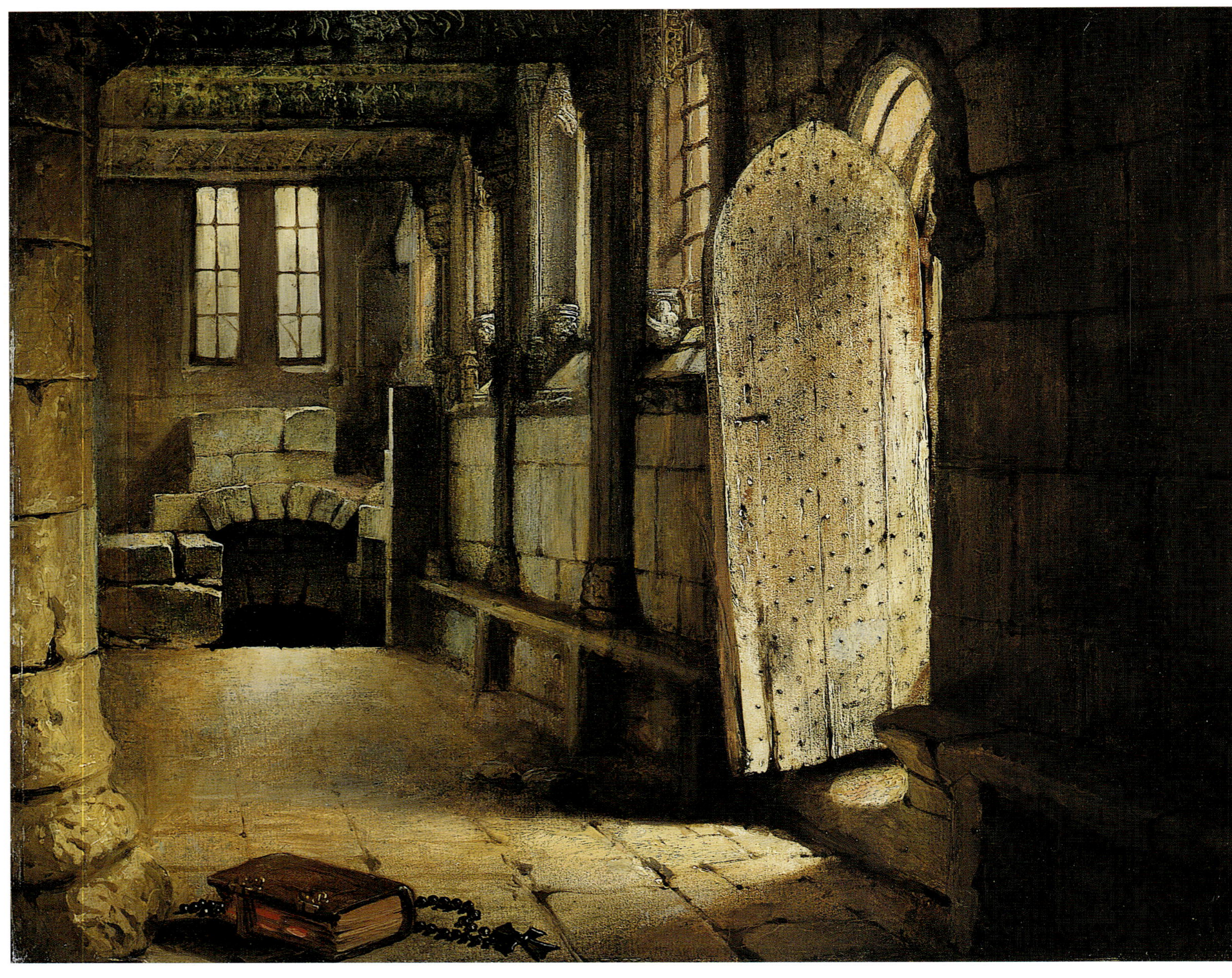

Amateur artists enjoyed a very different status in the eighteenth century from that of today. 'Amateur' meant a lover of the arts and the word did not carry the pejorative overtones of the twentieth century. In fact, at the turn of the eighteenth century, the 'amateur' was highly regarded, as one whose motivation was not merely financial. This is delightfully illustrated by the Revd Edward Bradley (1827–1889), writing under the name of Cuthbert Bede, whose attempts to sketch in the Chapel at Rosslyn were hampered by an inquisitive group, pestering to know 'who I was, and, whether I was an amateur or "only an artist"'.[48]

Amateurs and artists, sketchbook or easel in hand, continued to travel the country seeking subjects well into the nineteenth century. It is to this fashion that such an astonishing number of views of Rosslyn are due. A charming example is one of the views from the sketch-book of a 'Scotch Tour 1825' by John Glover (1767–1849) artist and drawing master [plate 49]. One of the sketches is an interior of Rosslyn Chapel and there are several of the Castle and Chapel from different viewpoints. Glover, with fellow artist Francis Nicholson (1753–1844) [plate 13], had been in great demand as a teacher since the first exhibition of the Old Water-Colour Society in London in 1805. This fashion for retaining a drawing master was one of the great contributions made by the amateur to the development of landscape painting, for many artists relied on patronage and teaching to develop their own talents. Painters would make sketching tours with their patrons or travel to, and from, estates where they had been requested to give lessons. Joseph Farington noted that Glover 'goes from family to family & has 2 guineas a day at each House'.[49] Sir George Beaumont (1753–1827) was the epitome of the generous and talented amateur. Having himself shown great interest in drawing at Eton, where his master was Alexander Cozens (1717–1786), he had continued to practise throughout his life, using his fortunate position to support other artists. On the death of Ibbetson's wife, Sir George and Lady Beaumont took the artist's eldest daughter Mary to live with them. They were also great friends of William Wordsworth (1770–1850) and his sister, Dorothy (1771–1855) when they lived in the Lake District, Lady Beaumont remaining a lifelong correspondent with Dorothy.[50]

The Wordsworths had also visited Rosslyn. Dorothy's detailed journal entries for their Scottish tour in 1803 describe how they visited the Chapel on 17 September, finding it in a state of ruin and locked up, to prevent 'injuries...from idle boys'. She notes how the stone-carved foliage seemed to have become one with the moss and ferns growing inside the Chapel:

The stone both of the roof and walls, is sculptured with leaves and flowers, so delicately wrought that I could have admired them for hours, and the whole of their groundwork is stained by time with the softest colours. Some of those leaves and flowers were tinged perfectly green, and at one part the effect was most exquisite – three or four leaves of a small fern, resembling that which we call Adder's Tongue grew round a cluster of them at the top of a pillar, and the natural product and the artificial were so intermingled that at first it was not easy to distinguish the living plant from the other, they being of an equally determined green, though the fern was of a deeper shade.[51]

Having stayed the night at an inn in Roslin village, the Wordsworths got up early to walk through the glen. Dorothy wrote that she had 'never passed through a more delicious dell than the glen of Roslin'. They walked to the house of their friends Sir Walter Scott and his wife, who were living at nearby Lasswade. So early was their start that they arrived before the Scotts were awake. They breakfasted together and walked back to Rosslyn in the company of their fellow poet.

Although this was Dorothy's only visit, William was to make two further Scottish tours in 1814 and 1831. It is probable that, on the latter trip, he revisited Rosslyn with his daughter Dora, as his sonnet 'Composed at Roslin Chapel during a Storm' is dated the same year. The timeless theme of this poem, suggested by the derelict Chapel, is the same as that of his sister's words, written almost thirty years earlier:

The wind is now thy organist: a clank
(We know not whence) ministers for a bell

51

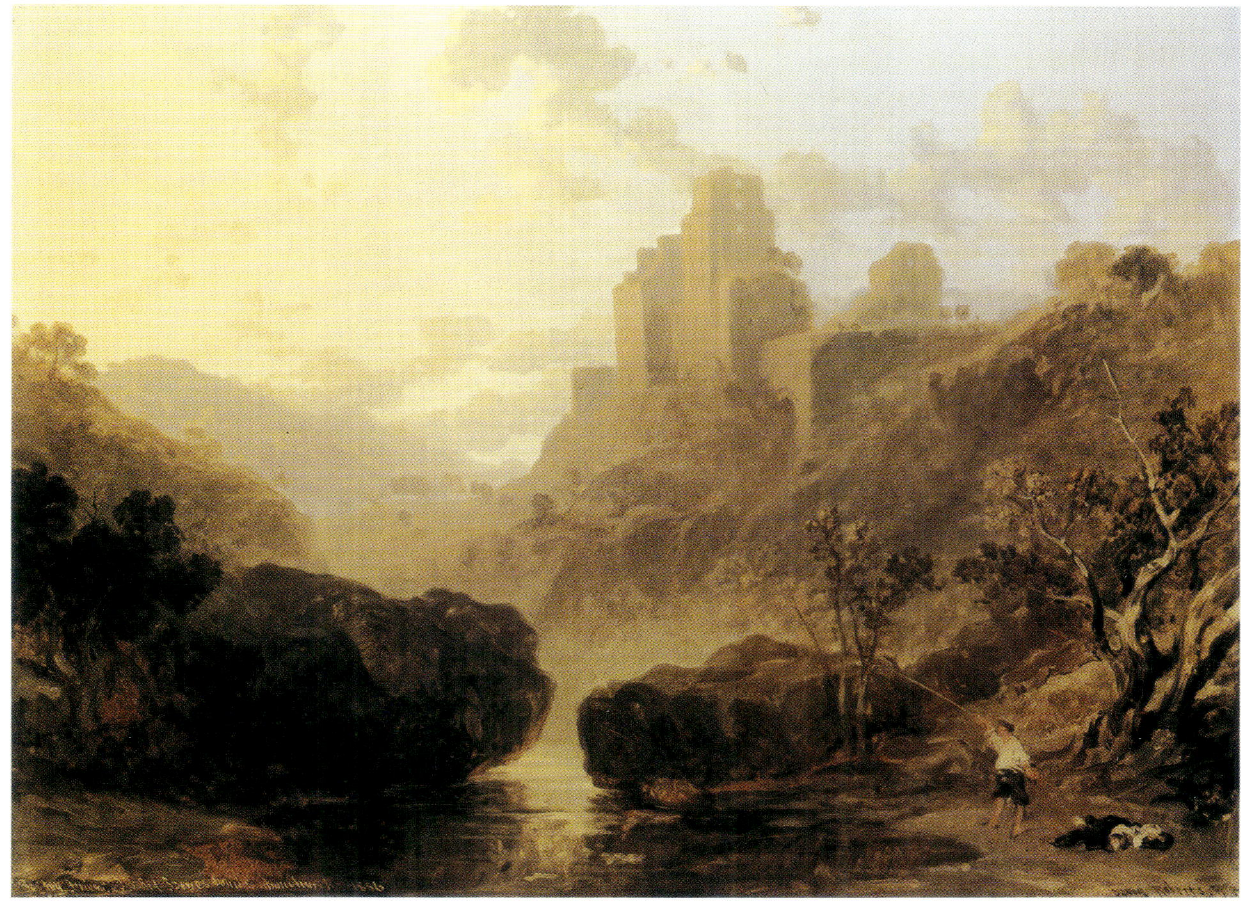

PLATE 50
William Dyce
View of the South Aisle, Rosslyn Chapel, c.1830
Private Collection

PLATE 51
David Roberts
Rosslyn Castle, 1856
Private Collection

52

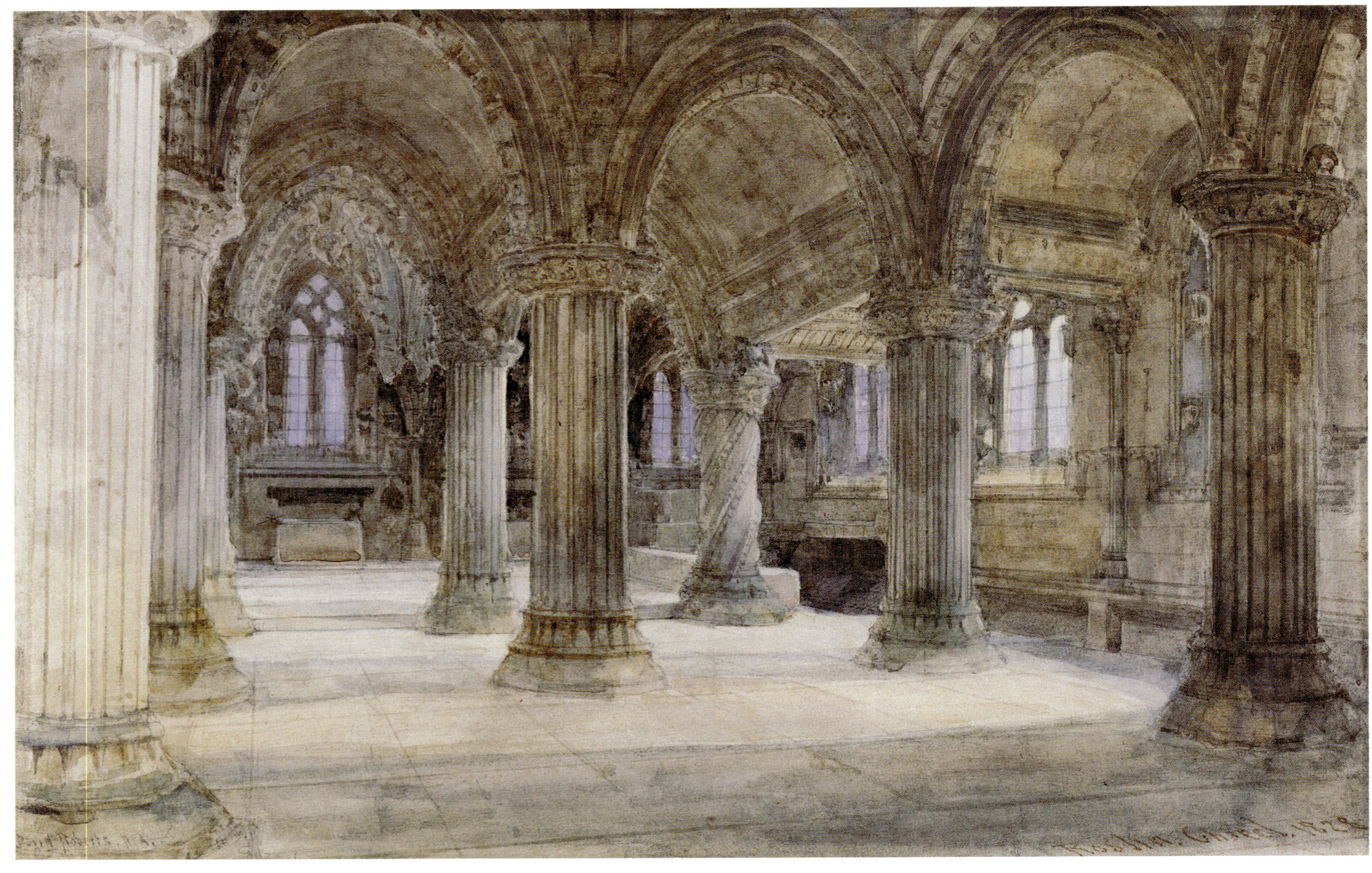

to mark some change of service; as the swell
Of music reached its height, and even when sank
The notes in prelude, Rosslyn! to a blank
Of silence, how it thrilled thy sumptuous roof,
Pillars and arches, – not in vain time-proof,
Though Christian rites be wanting! From what bank
Came those live herbs? By what hand were they sown
Where dew falls not, where raindrops seem unknown?
Yet in the temple they a friendly niche
Share with their sculptured fellows, that, green-grown,
Copy their beauty more and more and preach,
Though mute, of all things blending into one.

It is interesting to speculate whether the artists, William Dyce (1806–1864), and John Adam Houston (1812–1884), had read these lines before they painted their mysterious and 'green-grown' Chapel interiors [plates 50, 61].

David Roberts (1796–1864) was an artist who formed a lifelong attachment to the Chapel and landscape at Rosslyn. Perhaps ultimately better known for his more exotic Eastern subjects, the oil paintings and watercolours of Rosslyn demonstrate the affection that Roberts retained for his native Scotland, and span the most prolific thirty years of his career, from the late 1820s [plate 51]. The earliest watercolour is unadorned with the figures that grace many of his works, and is striking in its simplicity, capturing the atmosphere of the derelict Chapel [plate 52]. In a letter to his daughter, Christine Bicknell, Roberts wrote: 'There is a combination of light & Shade I have never met with in any subject, colour and richness of detail peculiar to itself.'[52] However, the Chapel was not without unforeseen hazards for the painter. By 1842, the year of this letter, it had become a much visited tourist spot and David Roberts laments the temperature and the lack of privacy: 'The cold is insufferable – draughts from all quarters so bad that I had oblidged to leave off today at 3 o'clock … besides which I am pestered with Visitors, who not only know me by name, but all my works …'[53]

In 1842, Queen Victoria also visited both Rosslyn and Hawthornden, and recalled in her Scottish diaries: 'Wednesday September 14. At half-past three o'clock we went out with the Duchess of Buccleuch … to *Rosslyn*. We got out at the chapel, which is in excellent preservation; it was built in the fifteenth century, and the architecture is exceedingly rich … A great crowd had collected about the chapel when we came out of it.' The 4th Earl of Rosslyn

PLATE 52
David Roberts
Rosslyn Chapel, 1828
Collection of Dr and Mrs I.A. Murdoch

PLATE 53
Thomas Stothard
Rosslyn Castle, c.1812
The British Museum, London

was himself to become a poet of some note and in 1887 he wrote a jubilee lyric dedicated to Queen Victoria and published at her command, entitled *Love that lasts Forever*.

The royal seal of approval put Rosslyn firmly on the tourist map. It was now an essential feature of nineteenth-century Scottish travel books and provided a subject for some wonderfully colourful anecdotes and 'historical tales'. Whilst artistic license is happily acknowledged, outrageous invention is quite another thing. Guidebooks to the Chapel have often quoted verses, attributed to Lord Byron (1788–1824), but with no further details of their origin. In fact Byron is not known either to have visited Rosslyn or to have written about it. It appears that, in accordance with a fascinating nineteenth-century habit of poaching the lines of well-respected poets and altering them to fit the intended subject, the verses have been 'borrowed' from *Childe Harold's Pilgrimage*, where their true subject is Rome.[54]

By 1870, the network of visitors to Rosslyn had expanded considerably. A letter to the Earl of Rosslyn from John Thomson, factor of the estate and custodian of the Chapel, dated 27 August, talks of record visitor numbers to the Chapel during this year and of a recent visit by a party of Indian princes.

The country of painter and poet is now enjoyed by countless visitors from all over the world, drawn to a romantic landscape, which to this day retains its mysterious and timeless beauty, still the scene which so enthused Samuel Prout when he wrote:

[Roslin Castle's] romantic situation on the summit of a wooded hill, the hills closing into narrow dells, folding into each other with many turnings, the river between them in some places broken into cascades by immense masses of rock heaped on each other in the wildest manner while in other parts the chasm is deep and the stream silent, beautifully overshadowed by hanging rocks and ancient trees.[55]

53

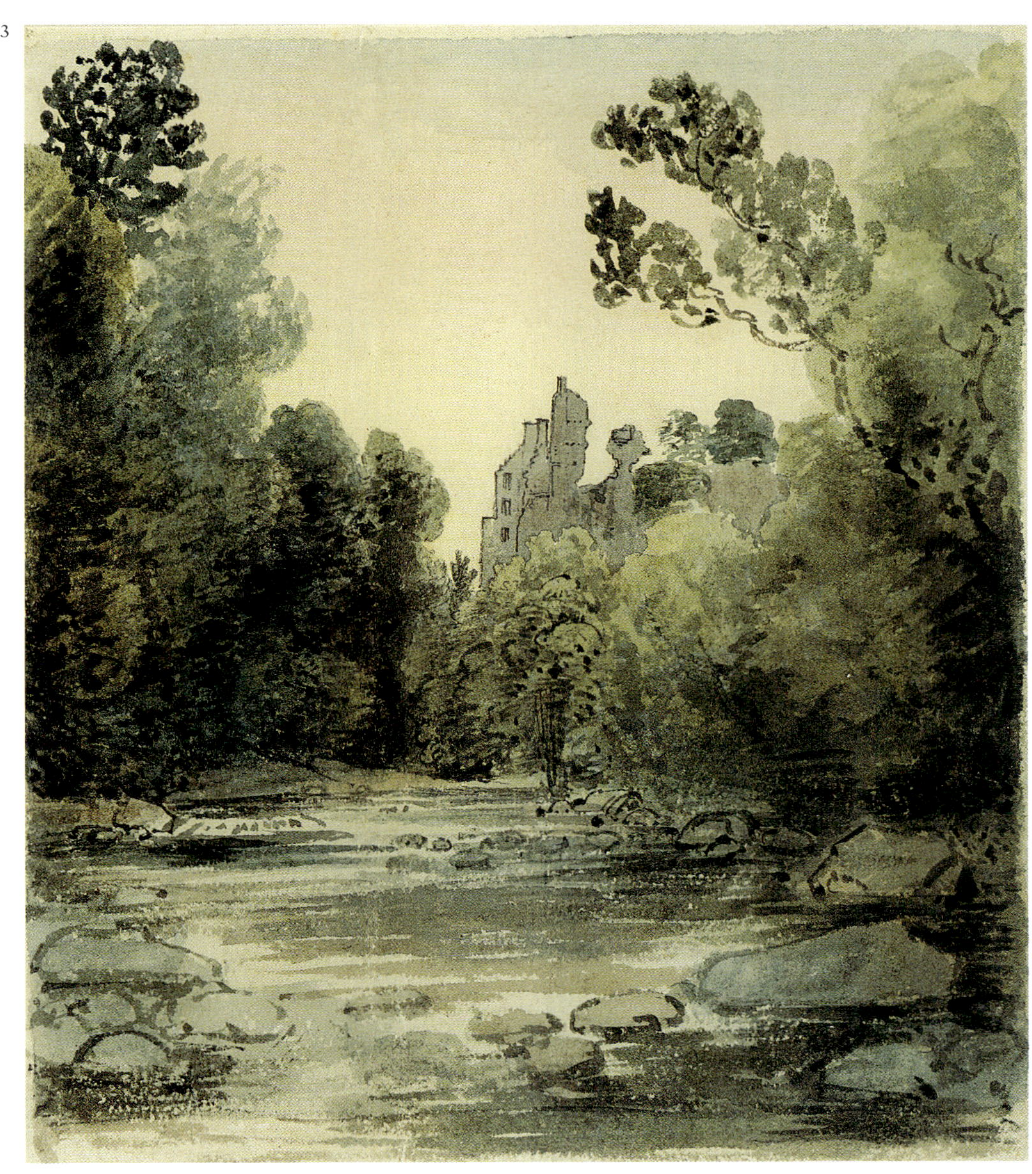

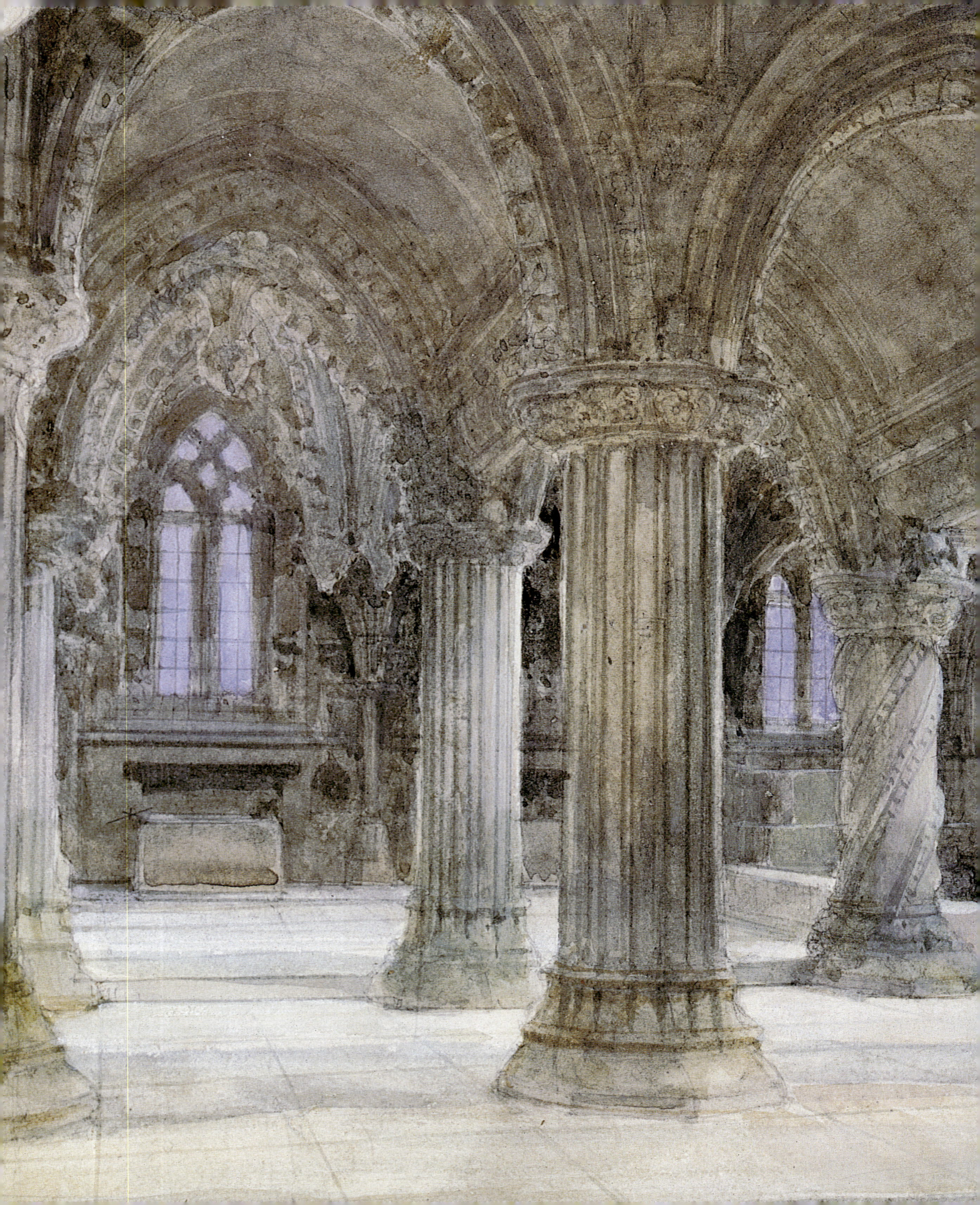

ANGELO MAGGI

The Unmaking of Pictorial Beauty: David Roberts and the Restoration Controversy

In the early and mid-Victorian periods Rosslyn Chapel was extensively restored under the care of James Alexander St Clair Erskine (1802–1866), the 3rd Earl of Rosslyn, whose work precipitated extensive debate, not only on the level of intervention that was appropriate to such an historic structure, but also on contemporary conservation ideas. Lord Rosslyn inherited the title in 1837 and in that year immediately turned his attention to the poor state of repair of the Chapel. His father had previously done little more than the minimum to keep the structure standing. Two architects were to be involved in this work: the exterior, which received Lord's Rosslyn immediate attention, was repaired by William Burn (1789–1870) between 1837 and the mid-1840s, while the thorough restoration of the interior was assigned to Burn's former partner, David Bryce (1803–1876), in 1860.

The restoration of Rosslyn Chapel started in the spring of 1837. On this occasion Samuel Dukinfield Swarbreck (active 1830–1865) published an album of lithographs entitled *Sketches in Scotland* which bears a dedication to the 3rd Earl of Rosslyn [plates 54, 55]. In his notes Swarbreck explains how 'the exterior of the chapel is undergoing a very extensive repair by its owner, … thus securing to after ages these rich remains of Gothic art.'[1] All the requirements for the conservation work were clearly set out by Lord Rosslyn in a letter addressed to Burn in which the architect was 'requested to cause immediate examination of the state of the Chapel of Roslin, and send a report upon the same.'[2] According to his letter the earl planned to remove the high sloping side roof [plate 56] added by John Baxter the elder (d.1770) in the 1730s and replace it with a new lower one over the aisles, 'thereby discovering the whole of the windows and rendering the appearance of the roof more in conformity with the original plan'.[3] The old slate roof was removed but it was a long time before the glazing was completed

54

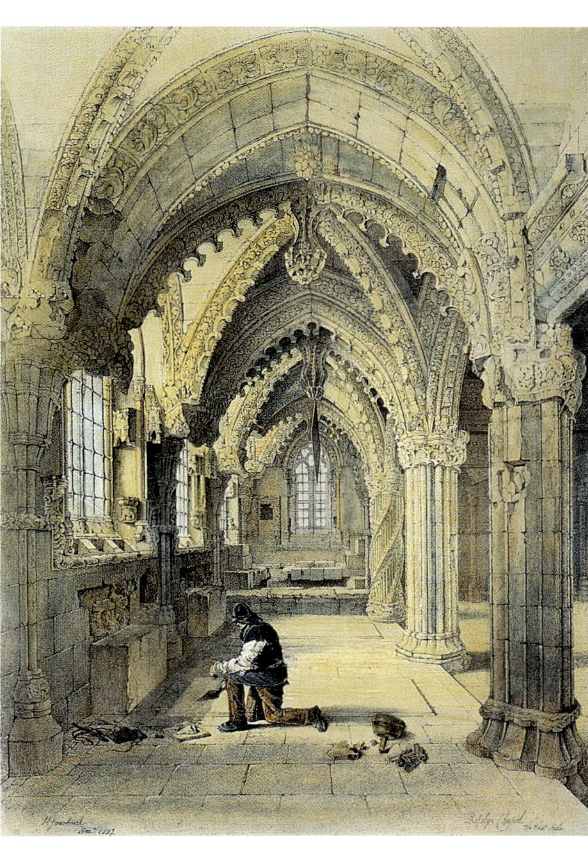

55

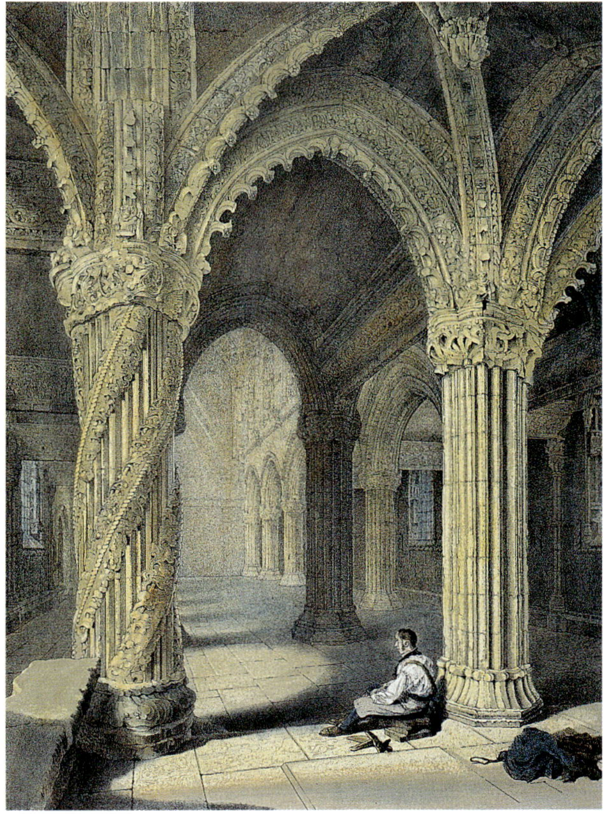

OPPOSITE
Detail from David Roberts *Rosslyn Chapel*, 1828, plate 52

PLATE 54
Samuel Dukinfield Swarbreck
The East Aisle or Lady Chapel, Rosslyn Chapel, 1837
Private Collection

PLATE 55
Samuel Dukinfield Swarbreck
The Interior of Rosslyn Chapel, 1837
Private Collection

56

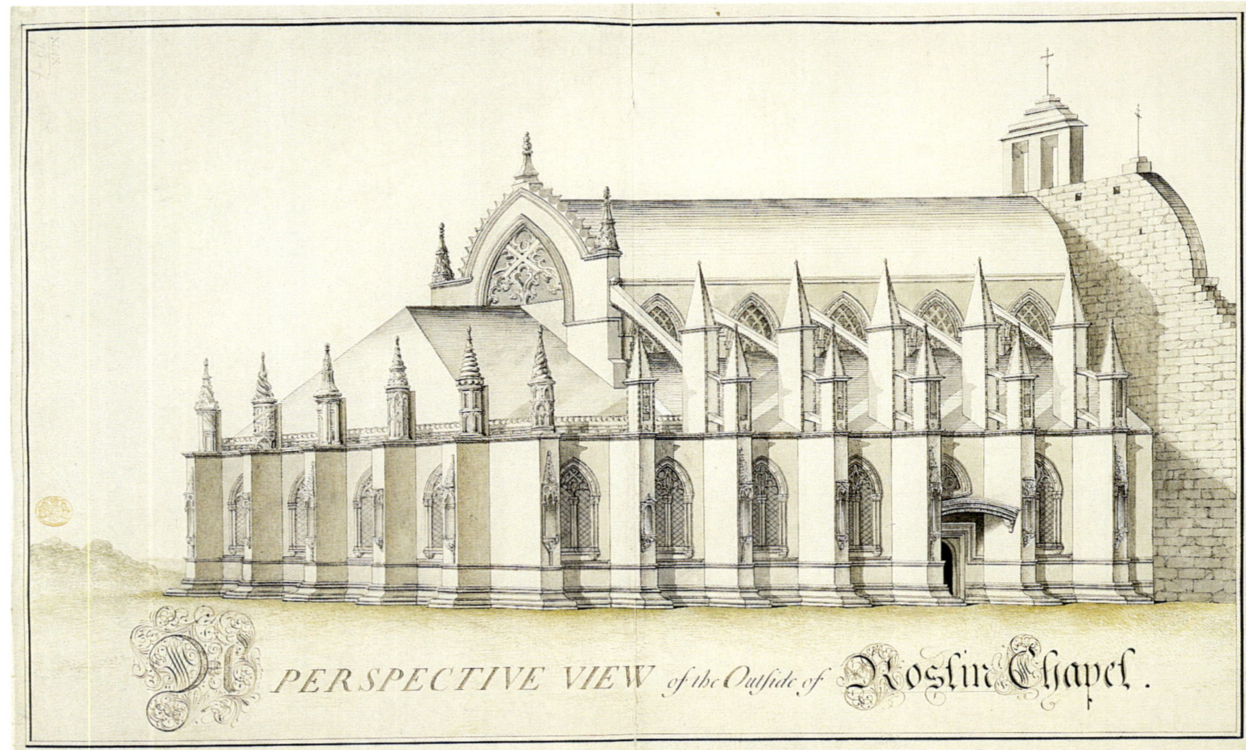

PLATE 56
William Delacour
A Perspective View of the Outside of Rosslyn Chapel, c.1761
British Library Board, London

PLATE 57
Friedrich Schenck after Otto Theodore Leyde
James Alexander St Clair-Erskine, 3rd Earl of Rosslyn 1802–1866, c.1850
Scottish National Portrait Gallery, Edinburgh

PLATE 58
Unknown Photographer
The Architect, William Burn
Royal Commission on the Ancient and Historical Monuments of Scotland, Edinburgh

PLATE 59
Sir Daniel Macnee
David Roberts, 1863
Royal Scottish Academy, Edinburgh

PLATE 60
David Roberts
The Apprentice Pillar, Rosslyn Chapel, 1830
Victoria & Albert Museum, London

and the standing structure made watertight. The reason for this delay is not clear, though the Chapel may have been left open on purpose to let plenty of air into the building to allow the stones to dry out.

While Lord Rosslyn and Burn [plates 57, 58] no doubt believed that they acted in a responsible way in these works of restoration, a major Scottish artist, who at that time was undoubtedly a force to be reckoned with, was horrified by what he found while making a series of oil studies of the Chapel. This was David Roberts (1796–1864).

One characteristic of Roberts [plate 59], by which his popularity was enhanced in early Victorian Scotland, was his intense love of the site, scenery and architecture of Rosslyn [plate 60]. His consequent endeavours were to ensure that these should either be left untouched or, at least, treated with a careful, gentle hand. He either watched with a jealous eye, or could not potentially tolerate the changes proposed by Lord Rosslyn and Burn, by which his beloved Chapel was to be 'beautified'. These feelings set his pen in motion with an intensity indicative of a ruling passion, so that soon after the restoration works started he wrote sarcastic letters to all his friends. 'Awake! Arise! Or be for ever fallen! and save ere too late the Prentice Pillar',[4] he writes in one of the many letters to his friend and biographer, James Ballantine (1808–1877).

In 1842, to mark Roberts's Eastern journey and safe return to Britain, the Royal Scottish Academy gave a

57

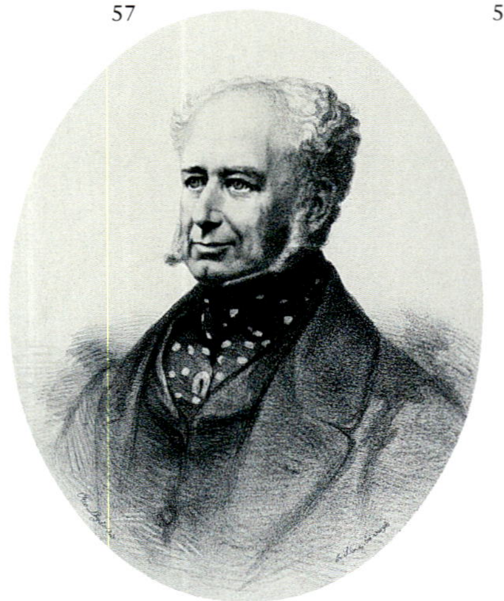

58

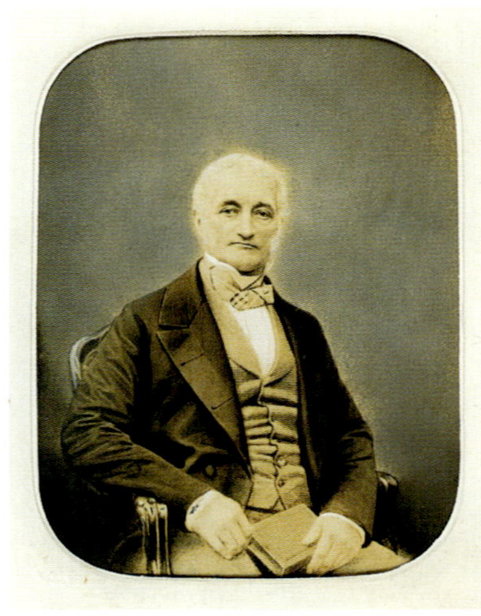

59

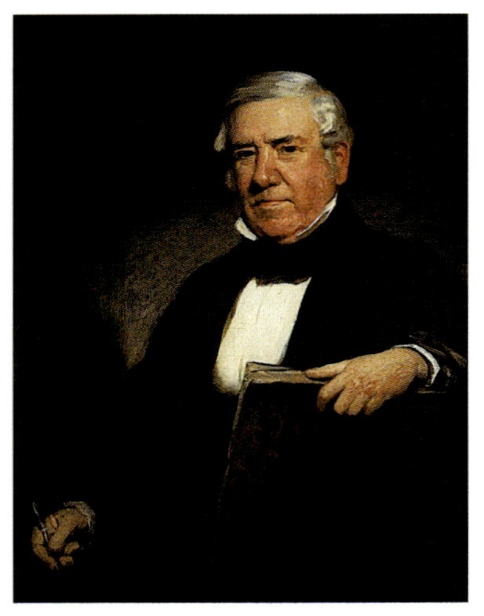

60

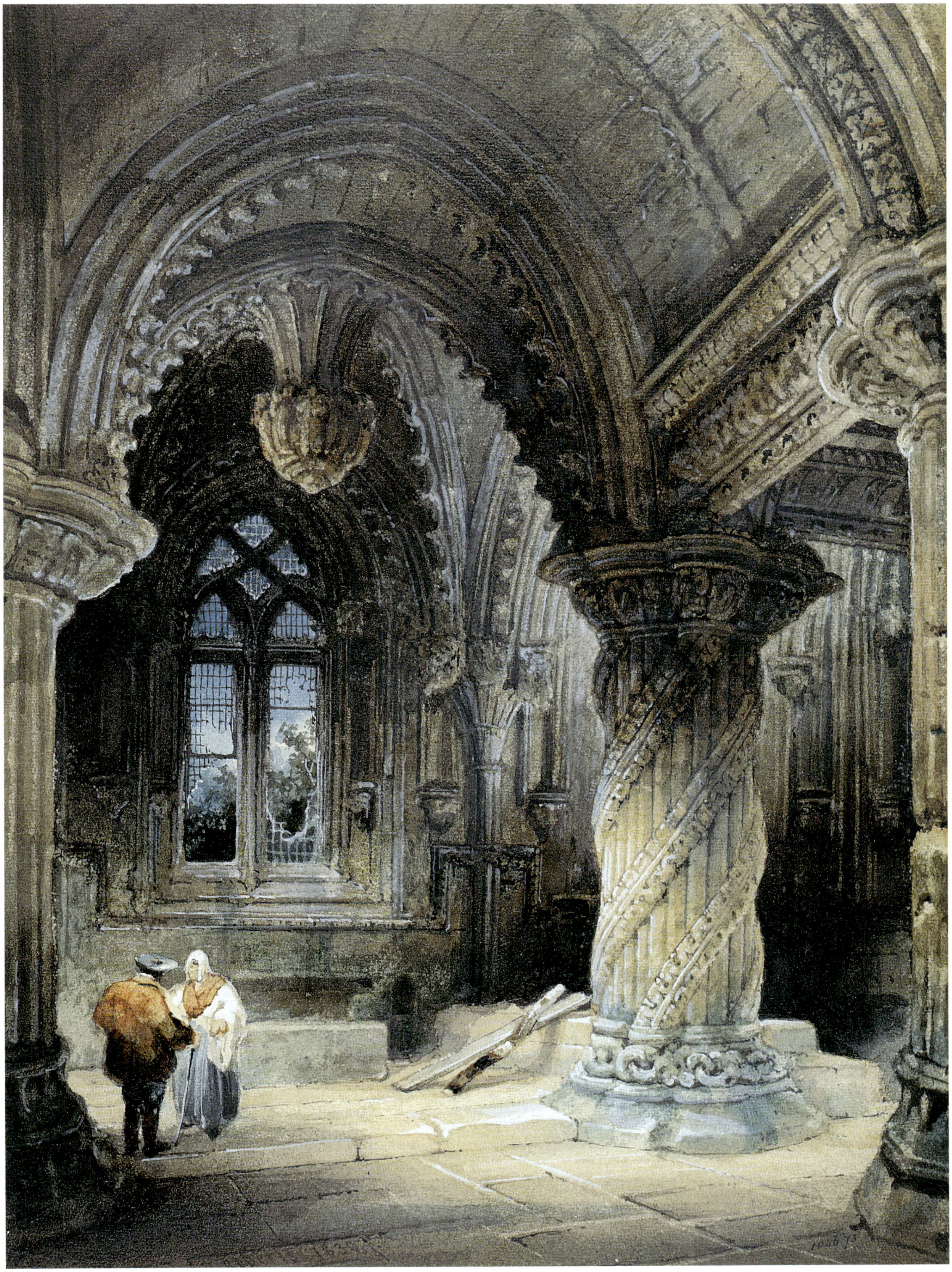

61

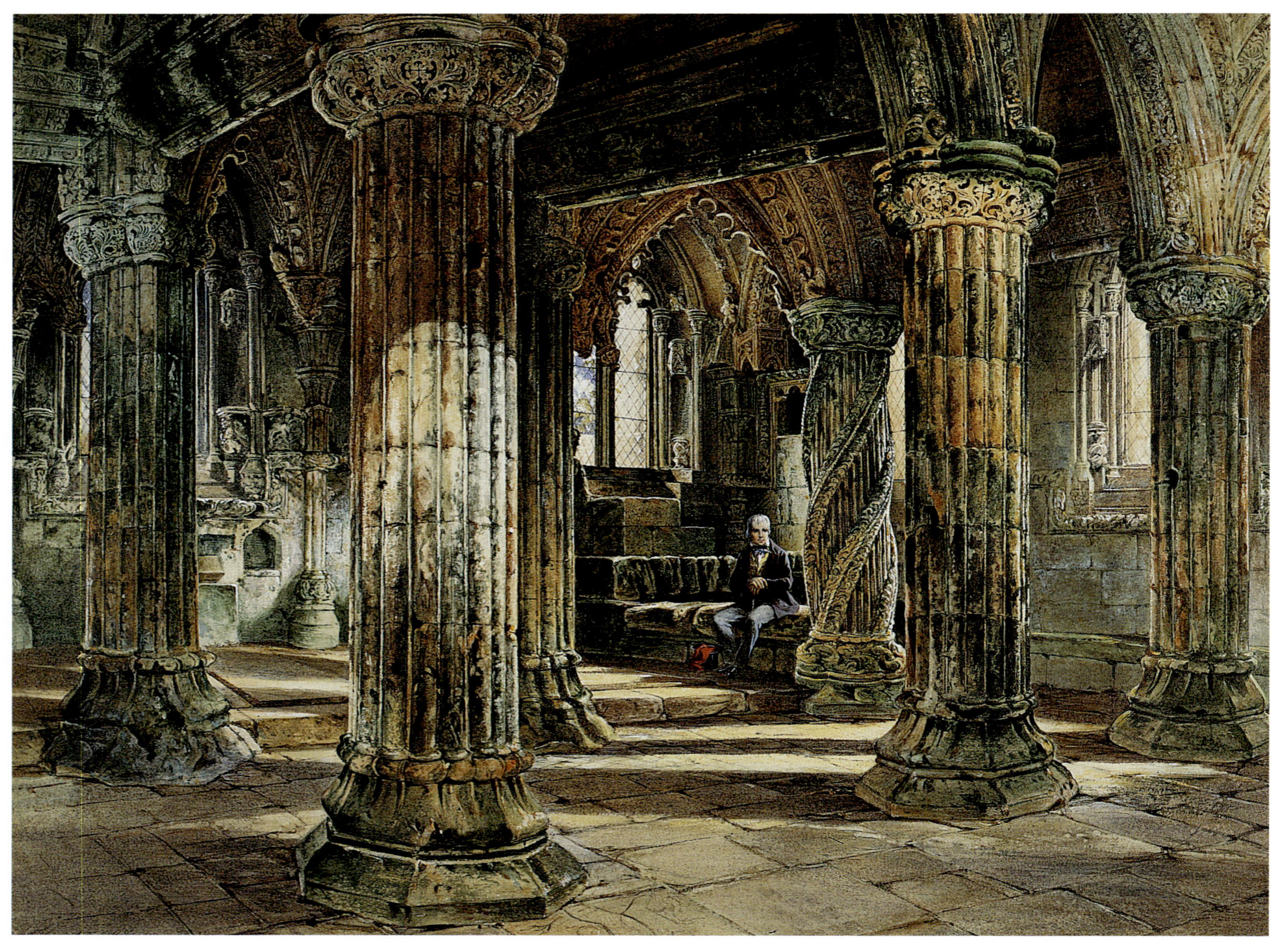

public dinner at which the famous and historically minded Lord Cockburn (1779–1854) presided. It would seem that Roberts used the occasion to raise his concerns about the work that was being carried out at Rosslyn, for a few weeks after meeting him Lord Cockburn records that he received the following letter:

Previously to the recent alteration, the lateral aisles were covered with a temporary and slated wooden roof, which, from its slanting position, covered in a great portion of the windows that light the upper part of the chapel, and served to exclude not only a great current of air, but, together with the then built up state of the great east window, tended in a great measure, by the exclusion of the wind, to the preservation of the interior, by fostering as well as sheltering that green mossy vegetation which had nearly overgrown every part of it; whilst, at the same time, the exclusion of the light itself spread that 'dim religious light', which, even at mid-day, impressed upon the mind those feelings of awe and solemnity so belittling and becoming the long forsaken sanctuary.[5]

One of the most remarkable images representing the actual state of the Chapel at that time is a watercolour by James Adam Houston (1813–1884) who romantically inserted Sir Walter Scott seated near the Apprentice Pillar in the Lady Chapel which is completely covered by lichens and mosses [plate 61].[6] And it is just that decayed state of the building which an anonymous artist recalled in his letter to *The Scotsman* in 1861. He seemed to be scandalised by the fact that the main characteristics of the place – 'the features which render it in the eyes of [my] profession such an object of interest, of study, and of affection'[7] – were lost forever. He continued: 'It is one of the very few ecclesiastical remains in this country to which, with reference to the interior of the building, the term picturesque could be applied.'[8]

PLATE 61
John Adam Houston
Sir Walter Scott in Rosslyn Chapel, 1854
Mr and Mrs P. Wilcockson

PLATE 62
David Roberts
The Entrance to the Crypt, Rosslyn Chapel, 1843
Victoria & Albert Museum, London

62

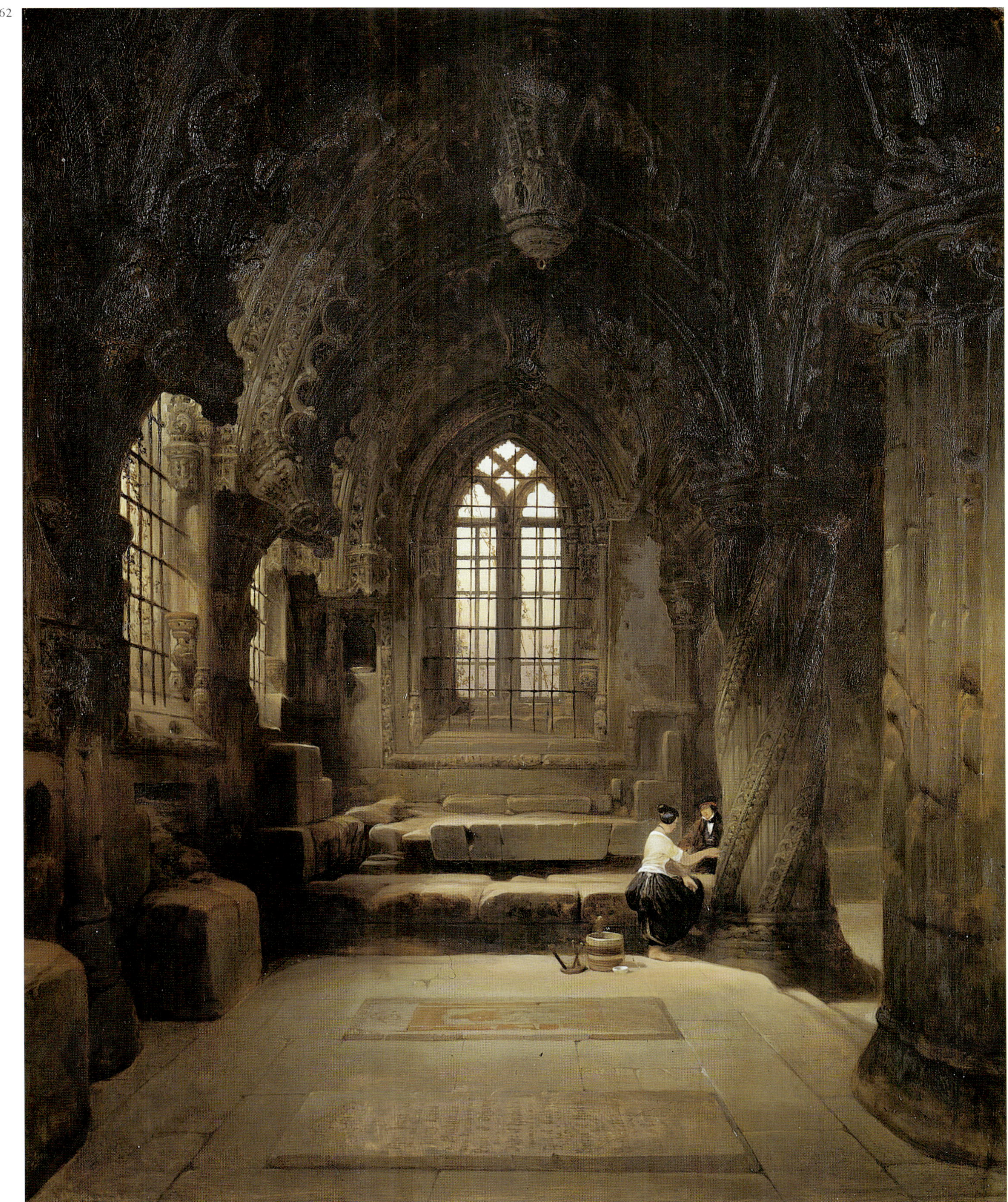

63

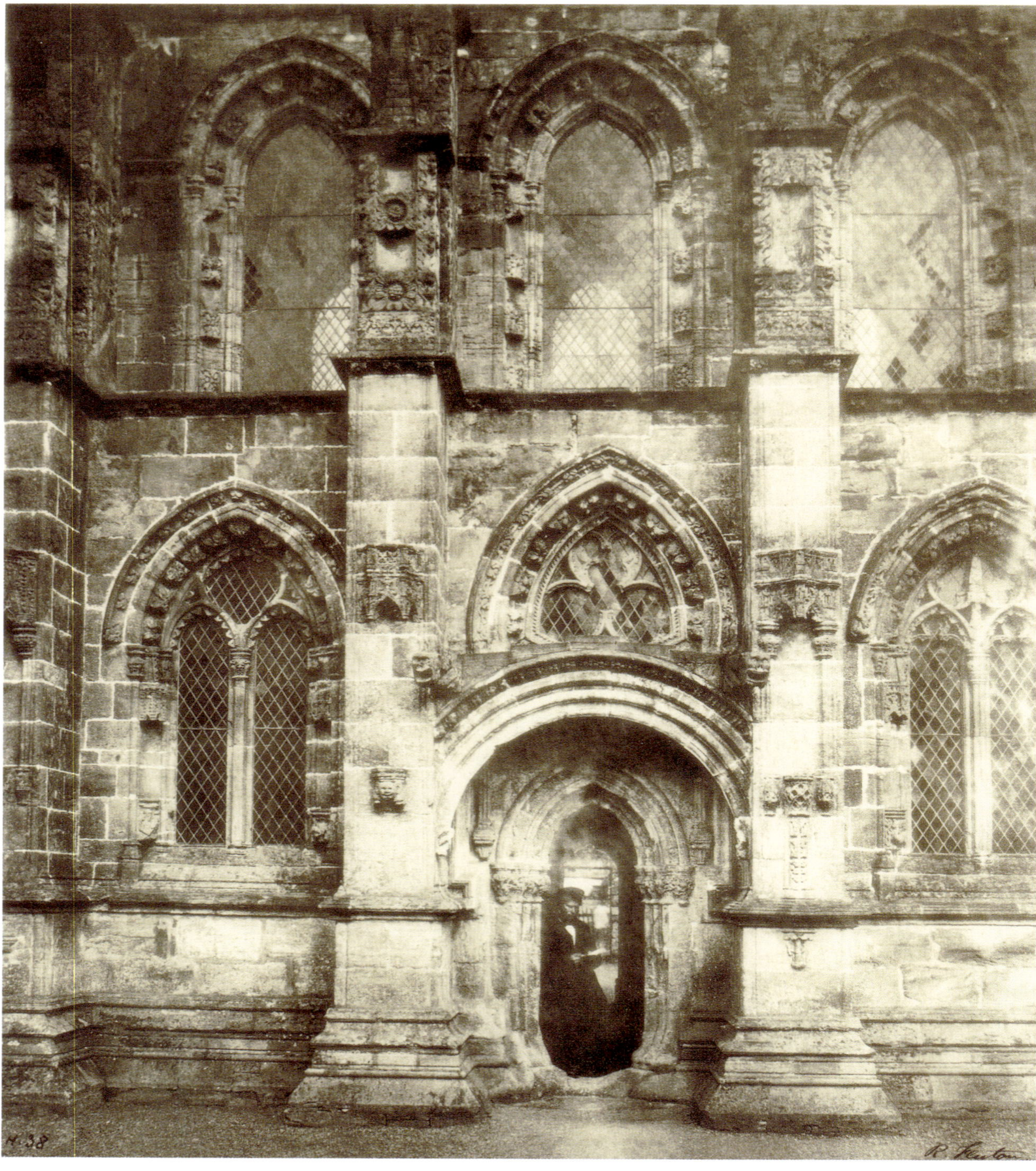

The term Picturesque had a specific meaning that applies to a nostalgic sensibility prevalent in the late eighteenth and early nineteenth centuries. It was John Ruskin who later revolutionised the idea of the picturesque, insisting upon fidelity to Nature, as if this excluded the function of the imagination. Ruskin was both an admirer and a critic of Roberts's work. The fact that the Scottish artist acted as anti-restorer and yet represented the building in a completely 'scraped' state didn't make any sense in Ruskin's mind. He complained that one of the interiors of Rosslyn Chapel 'instead of showing the exquisite crumbling and lichenous texture of the Rosslyn stone, was polished to as vapid smoothness as ever French historical picture [plate 62].'[9] He also stated: 'it is bitterly to be regretted that the accuracy and elegance of [Robert's] work should not be aided by that genuineness of hue and effect which can only be given by uncompromising effort to paint, not a fine picture, but an impressive and known *verity*.'[10]

Only photography could provide truly verifiable

64

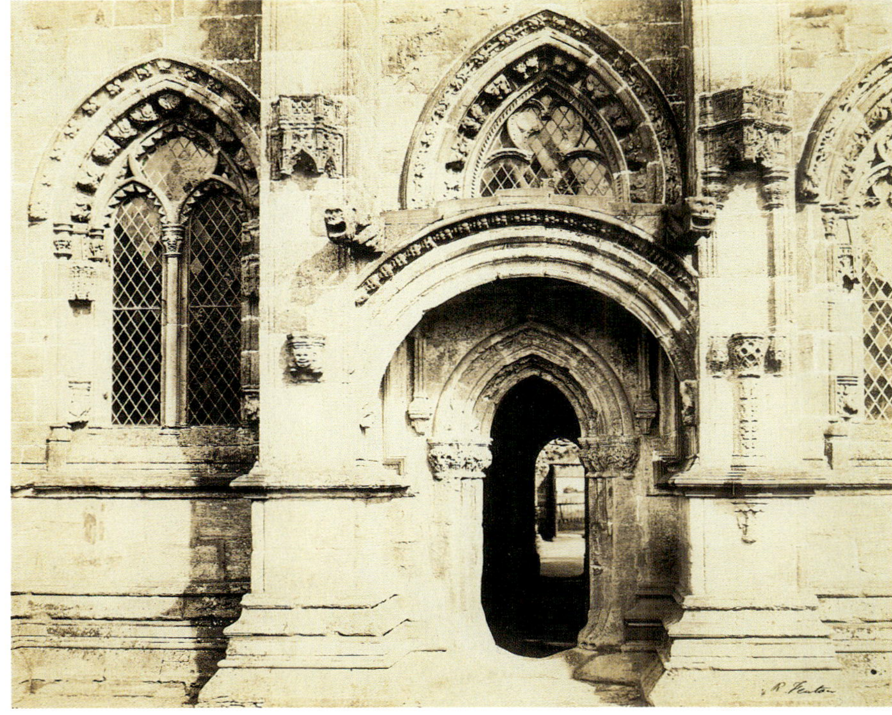

pictorial statements about the shapes and surfaces of things and for this reason it became a medium which competed directly with the realism pursued by many artists of that period. One of the most important figures in the history of nineteenth-century photography who was enchanted by the ancient Scottish monument at Rosslyn was the Englishman, Roger Fenton (1819–1869). On his first trip to Scotland in 1856 he visited and photographed the Chapel between the two phases of the restoration. There are only two examples of Fenton's precious photo-reportage and both represent the Chapel's south porch [plates 63, 64]. One of them in particular is superb – and the use of the figure to emphasise scale is perfect both in positioning and effect. The artistic merit of the picture depends on, and is enhanced by, its sheer technical excellence. Fenton appears to have known Roberts's perspective views of the south porch where the narrow portal allows the eye to enter and bore through the dark interior before reaching the sunlit countryside beyond [plates 65, 66].

The exterior of the Chapel was one of the subjects that David Octavius Hill (1802–1870) and Robert Adamson (1821–1848) experimented with in their early photographic works. The location was a truly romantic setting for the two Scottish photographers. The ornate pinnacles and the charming segmental arch on the south side, well exposed to the noonday sunlight, provided an ideal environment for the calotype process. Invented by William Henry Fox Talbot (1800–1877), the calotype produced a negative from which any number of prints could be made. The image was of cruder quality, but the benefit of multiple printing from a single negative would establish it, and not the daguerreotype, as the basis from which all modern photographic techniques were to evolve.

Capturing with the camera a 'motionless architectural

65

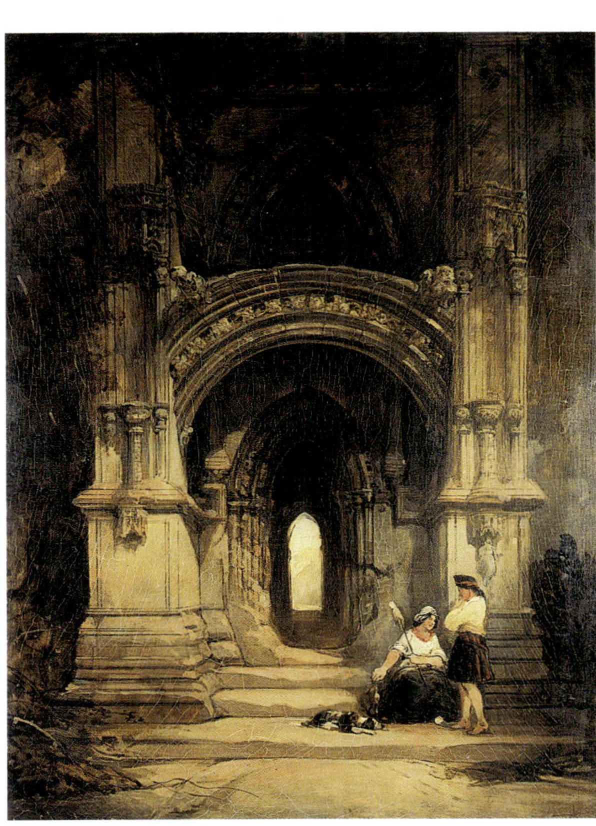

66

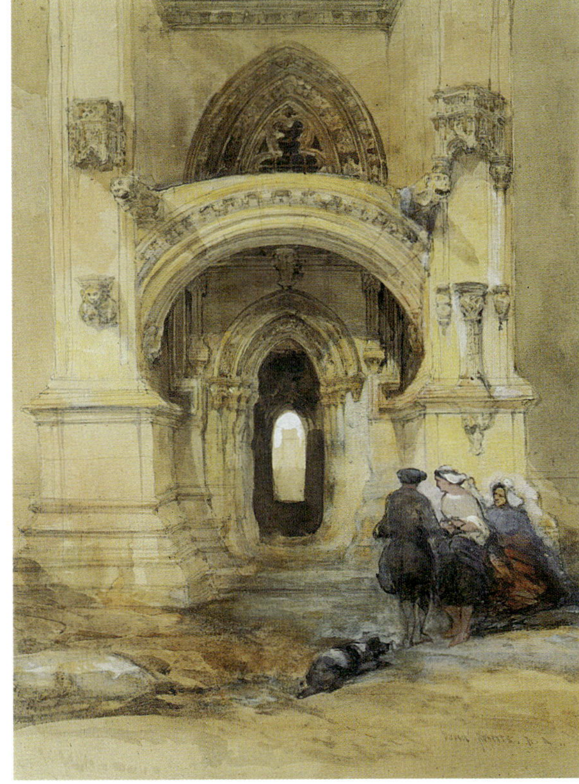

PLATE 63
Roger Fenton
The South Porch, Rosslyn Chapel
Private Collection

PLATE 64
Roger Fenton
The South Porch, Rosslyn Chapel
Victoria & Albert Museum, London

PLATE 65
David Roberts
The South Porch, Rosslyn Chapel, 1845
Blackburn Museum and Art Gallery

PLATE 66
David Roberts
The South Porch, Rosslyn Chapel, c.1842
Private Collection

scene' was easier than dealing with the exposure of a *tableau vivant*. In these early days of the calotype, exposures of many minutes were common, and although Hill gives his images an air of immediacy, like a snapshot, we can see that the figures are carefully posed to ease the physical strain on the subjects. In the Rosslyn Chapel calotypes the architect, William Burn, is romantically leaning against the south entrance [plate 67]; an unknown man is sitting on the edge of the restored east end clerestory window; near the piscina on the north transept the children's arms are either close to their bodies, in the lap or supporting the chin – all devices to cope with the length of exposure. Hill made these arrangements so carefully that the effect seems completely natural, while the Chapel itself becomes part of the pictorial composition. It should also be recognised that essential aspects of the artistic effects of the images are attributable to the manipulation of the technical process by Adamson. It is significant that Hill's later photographic endeavours achieve nothing like the same artistry. The partnership between the two men, a true pooling of talents, ended in January 1848 with Robert Adamson's premature death.[11]

What was often regarded as a weakness of the calotype process by comparison with the daguerreotype was its lack of definition. However, Hill, as a painter, was able to exploit the more generalised effects of the calotype. The graininess and limited tonality inherent in the calotype imposes a unity on the composition, while with the sharpness of the daguerreotype it is easy to lose this sense of the whole by becoming preoccupied with the details. This is quite evident in *The West Wall, Rosslyn Chapel* taken in 1844 [plate 68]. This photograph shows the west wall and part of the north transept, which marks the end of the building. The contrast between the highly finished carving of the wall, the green foreground and the sky is too great for the paper to handle, transforming this image into a surreal, veiled composition in which leaves and grass remain featureless and the architectural details only roughly focused. It is clear that Hill came to regard the calotype as an interpretative rather than a descriptive medium.

According to the photographic historian and photographer Richard Pare, in Hill's photograph there is an expression of space that could not be improved upon by the stunning clarity of the later photographic processes. His 'rhapsodic and romantic interpretation' of this private and contemplative image runs as follows:

The photograph of Roslin Chapel is only nominally a picture of the chapel. Though the building takes up almost half of the

68

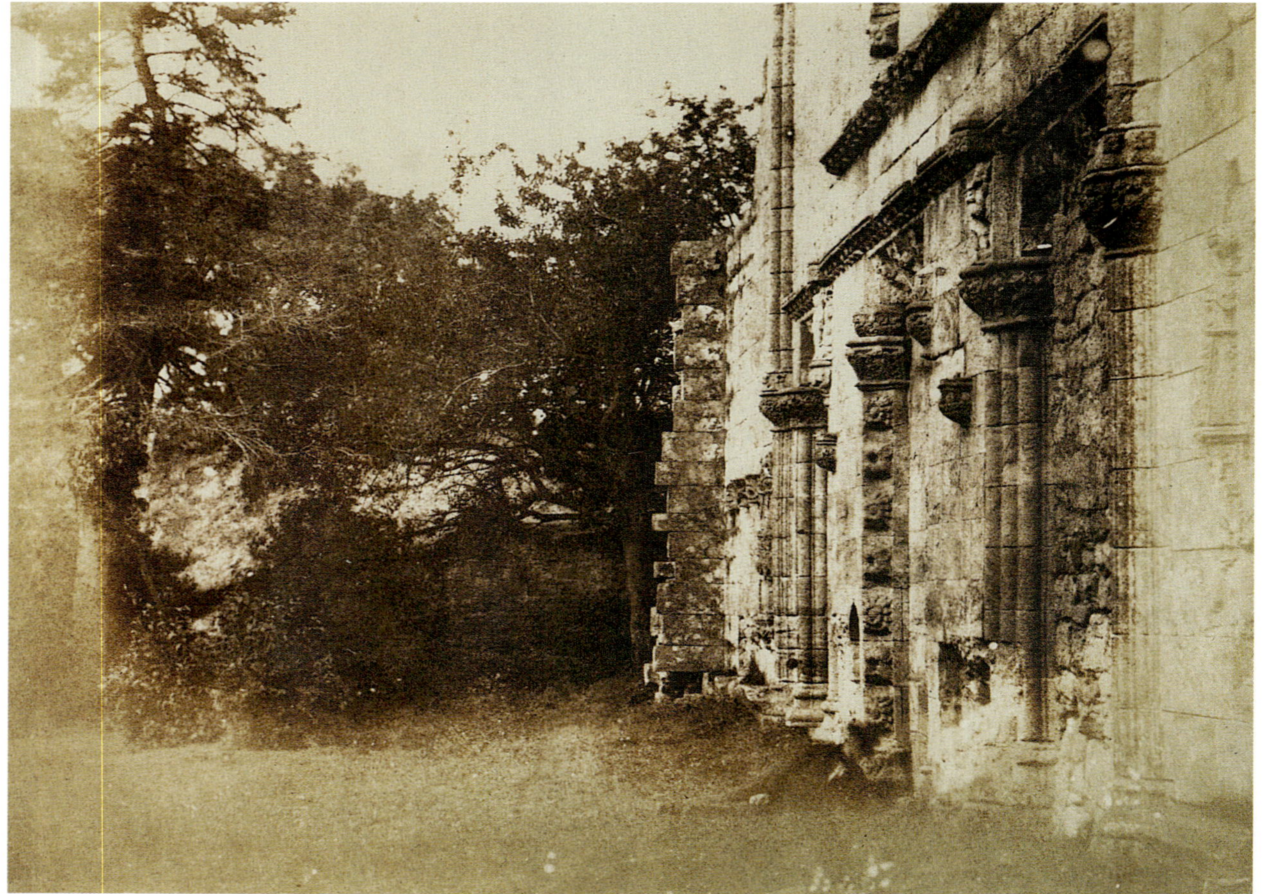

PLATE 67
David Octavius Hill and Robert Adamson
*The Architect, William Burn, at Rosslyn Chapel, c.*1843–8
Scottish National Photography Collection at the Scottish National Portrait Gallery, Edinburgh

PLATE 68
David Octavius Hill and Robert Adamson
*The West Wall, Rosslyn Chapel, c.*1843–8
Scottish National Photography Collection at the Scottish National Portrait Gallery, Edinburgh

67

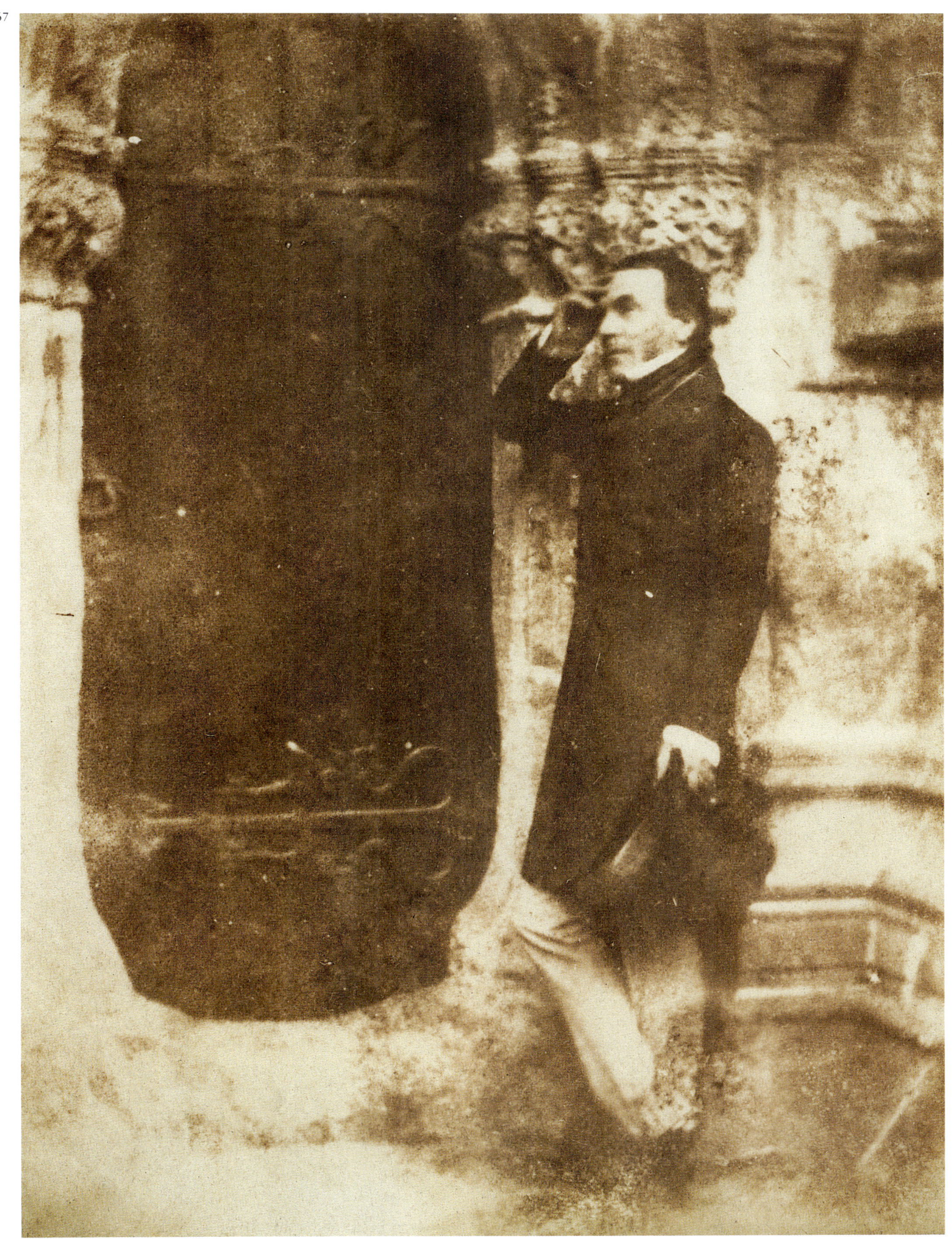

69

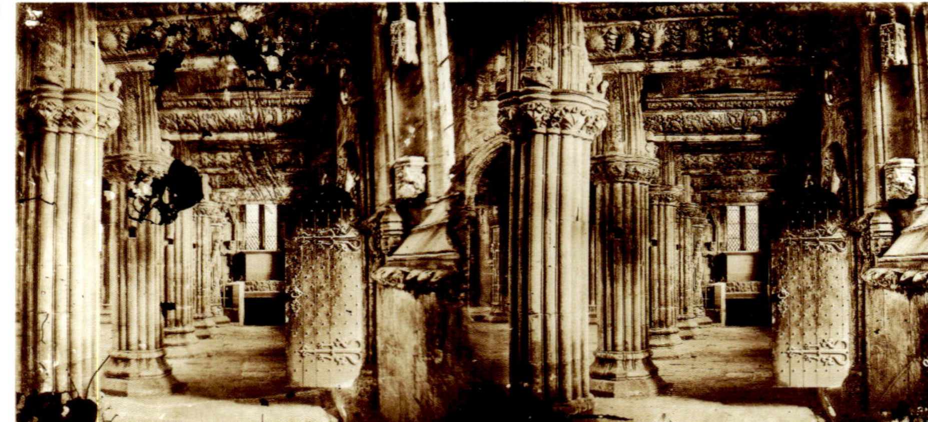

70

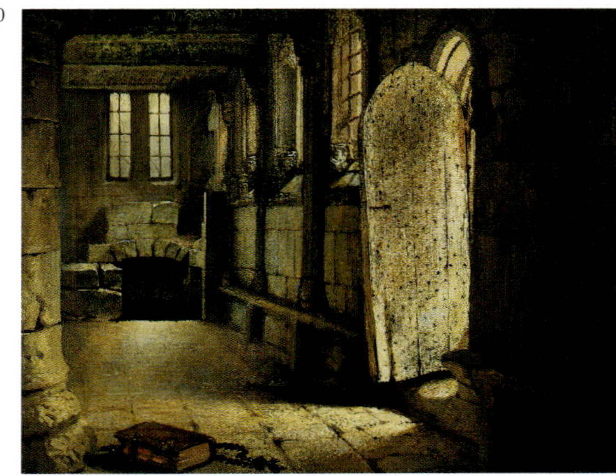

area of the picture space, the extremely oblique vantage point impacts the architectural information to such a degree that the picture is not so much an examination of the ruins of the building as it is a meditation on the nature of the place, its past and its present. We see it enshrouded in creeping ivy and sheltered by an ancient stand of trees.[12]

Talbot, who played a significant role in the discovery of the photographic process, in his celebrated work *The Pencil of Nature* (1844) writes: 'A painter's eye will often be arrested where ordinary people see nothing remarkable. A casual gleam of sunshine, ... or a moss-covered stone may awaken a train of thoughts and feelings, and picturesque imaginings.'[13] We know how a 'gleam of sunshine' in Rosslyn had earlier evoked an artistic response on the part of Joseph Michael Gandy (1771–1843). The kind of diffused shade Gandy managed to reproduce in his works was exactly what many 'pictorial' photographers wanted to capture as well. They were inspired by these artistic compositions in painting. One is an image of the south aisle looking east [plate 69] by the Edinburgh photographer Thomas Vernon Begbie (1840–1915). He shows a row of columns on the left leading to the Apprentice Pillar and the entrance to the crypt. The photographer was deeply impressed by the achievement of the original builders, and in this image he tries to convey the arrangements of the colonnade. Apart from being a technical success, this image closely resembles a painting of 1830 by William Dyce (1806–1864) which shows the same view through the south aisle with the door open, through which an intense 'gleam of sunshine' enters the Chapel [plate 70]. The play of sunlight, which floods through the loosely-swinging door, not only illuminates the sandy interior but fails to touch the mossy dampness of the corners or to illuminate the Bible and the rosary which lie abandoned in the foreground. Dyce's biographer describes this effect as 'an air of questioning, of a narrative incomplete'.[14] Begbie, with a different medium, employs an identical depth of perspective to convey scale, with columns retreating into the centre of the image and adding drama to the visual impact of the battle between light and shade.

As the concept of the artist-photographer became more common, and even though more artists turned to photography, it was still judged a lesser art than painting. Photographs were reckoned to be inferior or little better than engraved views of nature or of works of art. In Scotland this debate on 'Art and Photography' brought to the attention of the public the 'pictorial' photographer William Donaldson Clark (1816–1873), who, in his article 'Photography as a Fine Art', declared 'that there certainly is such a thing as *photographic art*.'[15] His view of *The South Porch, Rosslyn Chapel* [plate 71] can be seen as a distinct form of 'Fine Art'. Unlike many of his contemporaries, Clark was able to create, in a slightly oblique view of the porch, a combination of force and delicacy. That was determined by the fusion of the strong architectural reality of the exterior and the interior darkness sublimated by a patch of light on the moulding base of a pier.

While the status of photography, and its claim to be regarded as an art, was very much the subject of debate, Clark's way of seeing the Chapel was emulated by artists of the time. In fact *The South Porch, Rosslyn Chapel* [plate 72] by the Victorian painter Josiah Wood Whymper (1813–1903) clearly resembles Clark's picture of the porch and the interior effect of light where the pillar appears magically from the darkness. It is interesting to note that, in this case, the photographic image was to form the basis of a work of art. Fifty years later David Young Cameron (1865–1945), while etching the Chapel, made use of the same image chosen by Whymper.[16] He reproduced, in his own style, every single detail photographed by Clark. In his work [plate 73], the narrow portal allows the eye to enter and penetrate through the dark interior before reaching a portion of the window and the base of the pier slightly touched by a beam of light. With this interplay of dark and light Clark and Cameron, photographer and artist, highlight the very tensions of the architecture they describe.

PLATE 69
Thomas Vernon Begbie
The South Aisle, Rosslyn Chapel (stereo photograph), 1860s
The Cavaye Collection of Thomas Begbie Prints, City Art Centre: Edinburgh Museums and Galleries

PLATE 70
William Dyce
View of the South Aisle, Rosslyn Chapel, c.1830
Private Collection

PLATE 71
William Donaldson Clark
The South Porch, Rosslyn Chapel, c.1860
Scottish National Photography Collection at the Scottish National Portrait Gallery, Edinburgh

PLATE 72
Josiah Wood Whymper
The South Porch, Rosslyn Chapel, 1858
Ruskin Foundation, Ruskin Library, University of Lancaster

PLATE 73
Sir David Young Cameron
The South Porch, Rosslyn Chapel, 1899
Hunterian Art Gallery, University of Glasgow

71

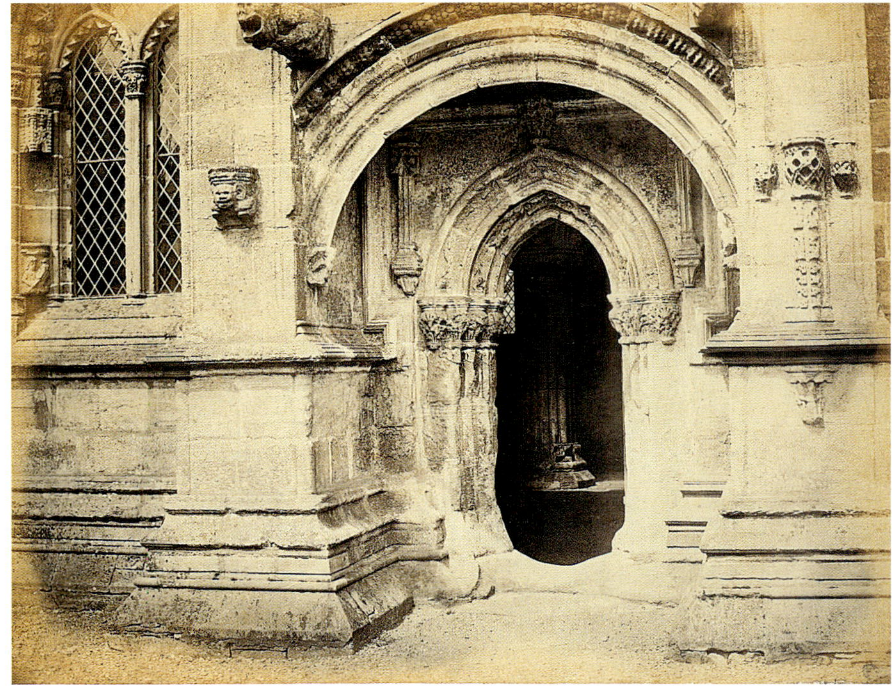

The demand for photographic views was so great that most of the photographers of the 1860s and 1870s were guaranteed to sell whatever they depicted. One of the great figures of commercial photography in Scotland was George Washington Wilson (1823–1893) from Aberdeen.[17] Wilson was particularly concerned to avoid what has been called 'the toy effect', and used longer-focused lenses to achieve 'a much more natural and life-sized effect'.[18] Wilson's contribution to the photographic representation of Rosslyn Chapel is enormous [plates 74, 75]. He started taking photographs of the Chapel in 1859 and from 1861 to 1863 he added to his collection a substantial number of exterior and interior views. It is easy to follow the order in which each shot was taken thanks to the numbering impressed on each glass plate that appears with the location of the view. An important description of his photographic approach to Rosslyn Chapel appears in *The British Journal of Photography*, where the author describes one of Wilson's photographs as 'one of those beautiful illustrations that the archaeologist will delight in'.

72

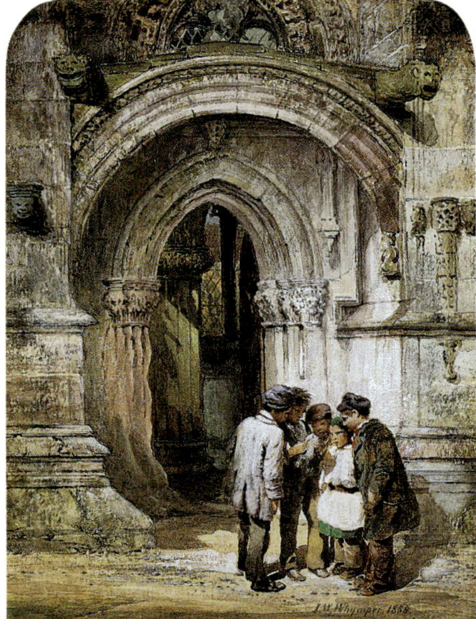

73

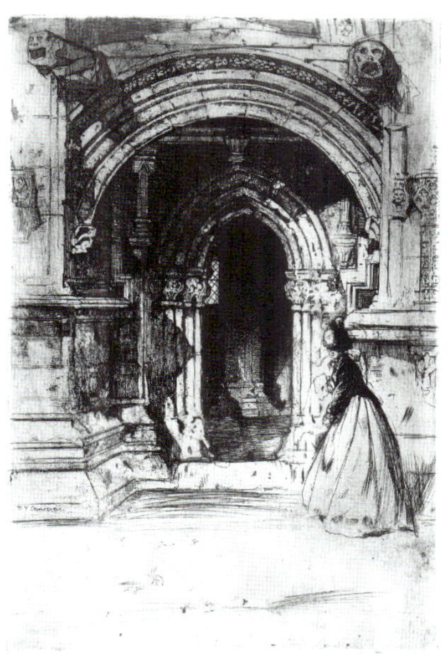

The massive pillars … seem barely able to support the capitals and heavy architraves literally loaded with ornamentation of the most florid character. A gleam of sunshine falling on a huge square block of stone glorifies it; and the general harmony of light and shade, combined with breadth and detail, unite to constitute this a perfect picture which the eye never wearies of gazing on, and which, while we gaze, communicates a sensation of satisfaction and repose that is truly soothing.[19]

Having discussed the contribution of pioneering photographers to the romantic vision of Rosslyn Chapel, it is necessary to turn back to David Roberts's valiant fight for the preservation of his beloved Scottish monument.

Roberts threw himself into opposition against anything that 'far worse, miserable impostors such as Burn'[20] did to threaten the Chapel. One of the most vehement disputes happened in January 1846 at the Royal Institute of British Architects in London, where John Britton gave a lecture on the 'design, construction and architectural characteristics of the Collegiate Church at Roslin.'[21] At the end of the lecture Roberts addressed the meeting in defence of Walter Scott. Britton had criticised certain lines in Scott's *The Lay of the Last Minstrel*, in which there were many 'mistakes' referring to Rosslyn. According to Roberts:

The Lecturer [Britton] *… concluded by stating that however poetical the legend might be – the whole tradition was a tissue of 'falsehoods' – in which he was followed by our distinguished Architect* [Burn] *who instead of throwing some light on the singular construction … told us that he had dug a trench up the centre and lateral Aisles of the Chapel – and having only found one vault with a wooden coffin, he could perfectly confirm all that Mr Britton had said – and that the whole thing was a 'falsehood.'*[22]

Burn's excavation had disproved the story, chiefly spread by Walter Scott, that ten barons of the family were buried in the Chapel or its crypt. Roberts pointed out that the evidence for this story was in Father Hay's account, in which was proved that not only were the barons buried in their armour, but he had explained in minute detail the appearance of the last baron who had been buried in his armour, when his grave or vault was opened.[23]

The debate was, however, just at the beginning. Roberts contended that the east end wall had been pulled

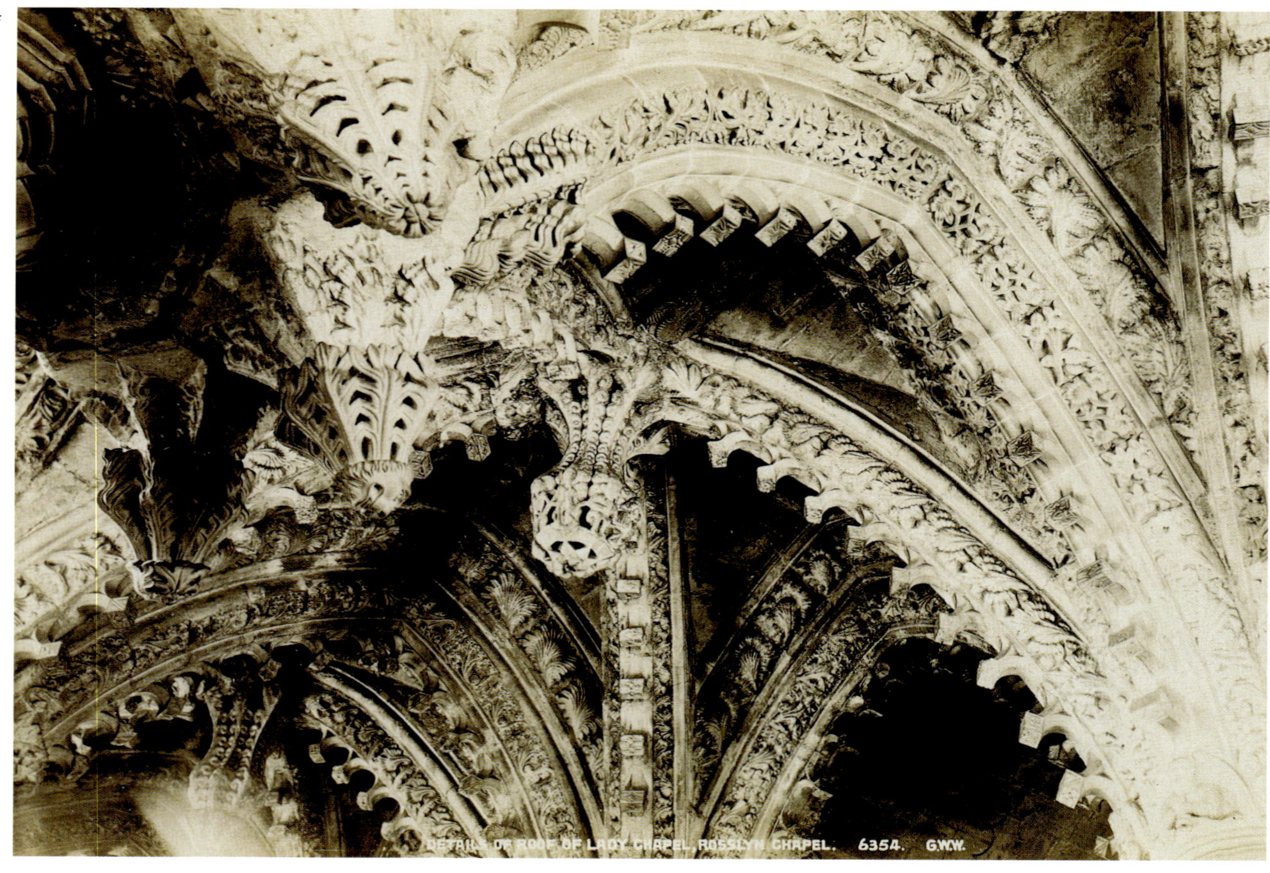

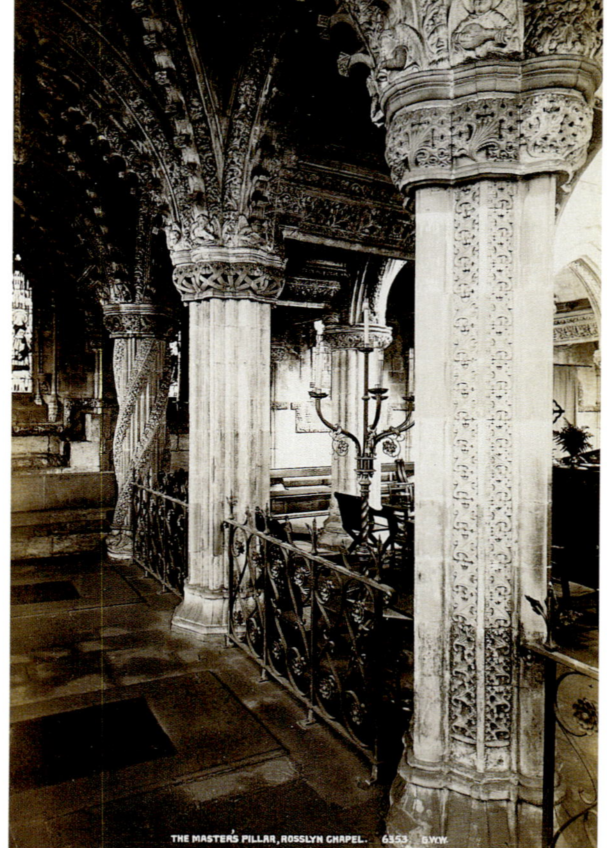

PLATE 74
George Washington Wilson
Detail of the Ceiling of the Lady Chapel, Rosslyn Chapel, c.1880
Private Collection

PLATE 75
George Washington Wilson
The Master's Pillar, Rosslyn Chapel, c.1880
Private Collection

PLATE 76
David Roberts
Section of the Chancel, Rosslyn Chapel, 1846
Private Collection

PLATE 77
David Roberts
Ground Plan of the Chancel, Rosslyn Chapel, 1846
Private Collection

down after the vaulting was finished, and rebuilt three feet further back, and the top of the wall-shafts corbelled out as they now are to meet the groin ribs.[24] For Burn the aisle at the east end, which is considerably wider than the side aisle, was 'part of the original design' and was never intended to have been the same width. Burn considered that 'the altars were probably in the same style as the Chapel and the distance from the pillars to the altars is equal to the width of the aisles.'[25] Roberts did not accept Burn's attack as he alone thought that the Lady Chapel had undergone radical transformations during the past three centuries. In the end he was so dumbfounded 'by the abuse of Sir Walter'[26] and the boldness of Burn's assertions that he left the meeting. In any case, Roberts pointed out a new interpretation of the Chapel's history on the basis of his critical evaluation. He wrote about it to John Britton stating his reasons for coming to the conclusion that an alteration had been made and accompanied the letter with a section and ground plan of the building [plates 76, 77]. These he also sent to Burn, 'affording him the opportunity of retracting what he said'.[27] Britton was thus forced to establish this new archaeological evidence in a succeeding letter to the members of the Architectural Institute in which he emphasised the value of Roberts's ideas.

During the summer of 1846 Roberts entered into an arrangement with James Duffield Harding (1797–1863), William Leighton Leitch (1804–1883) and many other artists to execute forty drawings for a work called *Scotland Delineated*. To enable him to accomplish this task, Roberts travelled to Scotland during September and October, visiting Edinburgh and Rosslyn, and making sketches and copious descriptive notes of all the chief monastic and baronial remains he then saw. Although charming, this work was not a success, coming rather late in a series of similar books; it was also too expensive. The frontispiece of the text, drawn by Roberts himself, represents the south entrance to Rosslyn Chapel and a series of people in Highland costume [plate 78].[28]

It seems that Roberts started the plans for *Scotland Delineated* soon after he took exception to Burn's support for the illustrations in *The Baronial and Ecclesiastical Antiquities of Scotland* (1845–52) by the English architectural illustrator, Robert William Billings (1813–1874). In this connection, in a letter to his friend David Ramsay Hay (1798–1866), Roberts wrote: 'The work you allude as forthcoming on the monastic remains of Scotland I will be glad to see – but wish it had fallen to better hands than the restorer or renovator of St Giles Cathedral and Roslin Chapel – Their overthrow in the days of Knox, was not worse than that their illustration will be in such hands – who is Mr Billings?'[29] A confirmation of the real reason for this publishing enterprise comes from another letter by Roberts to Hay in which the artist states: 'The work on Scotland has fairly started: I have done eight drawings: Melrose, Porch of Roslin Chapel little page, the Castle from Grayfriars, High Church of Glasgow, Roslin Chapel interior, Linlithgow, Falkland Palace, & St Andrews – and if the great Burn, do not look sharp – he may burn his fingers, in authorship – if he may not have done it as an architect. I hope in the description part of Roslin Chapel

76

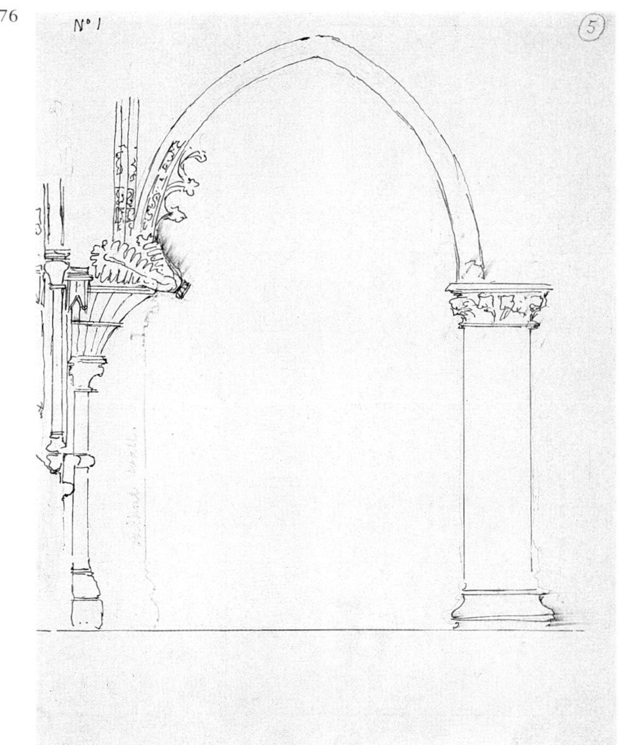

77

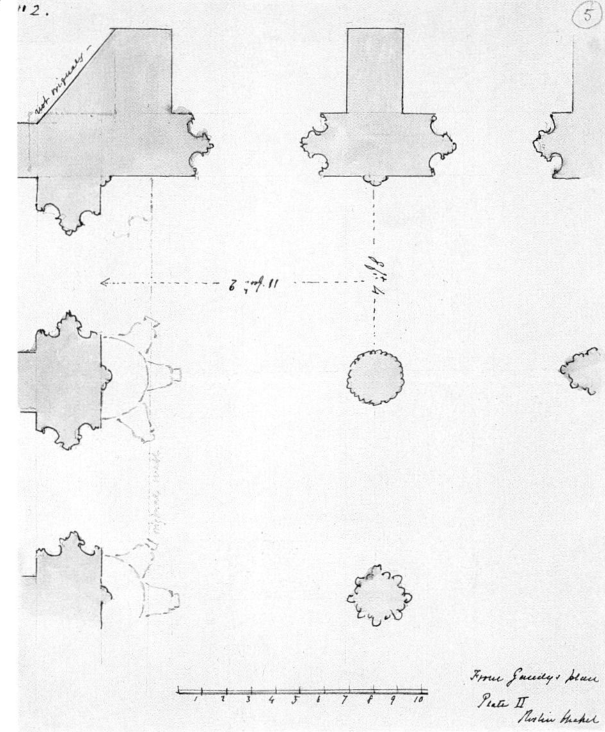

78

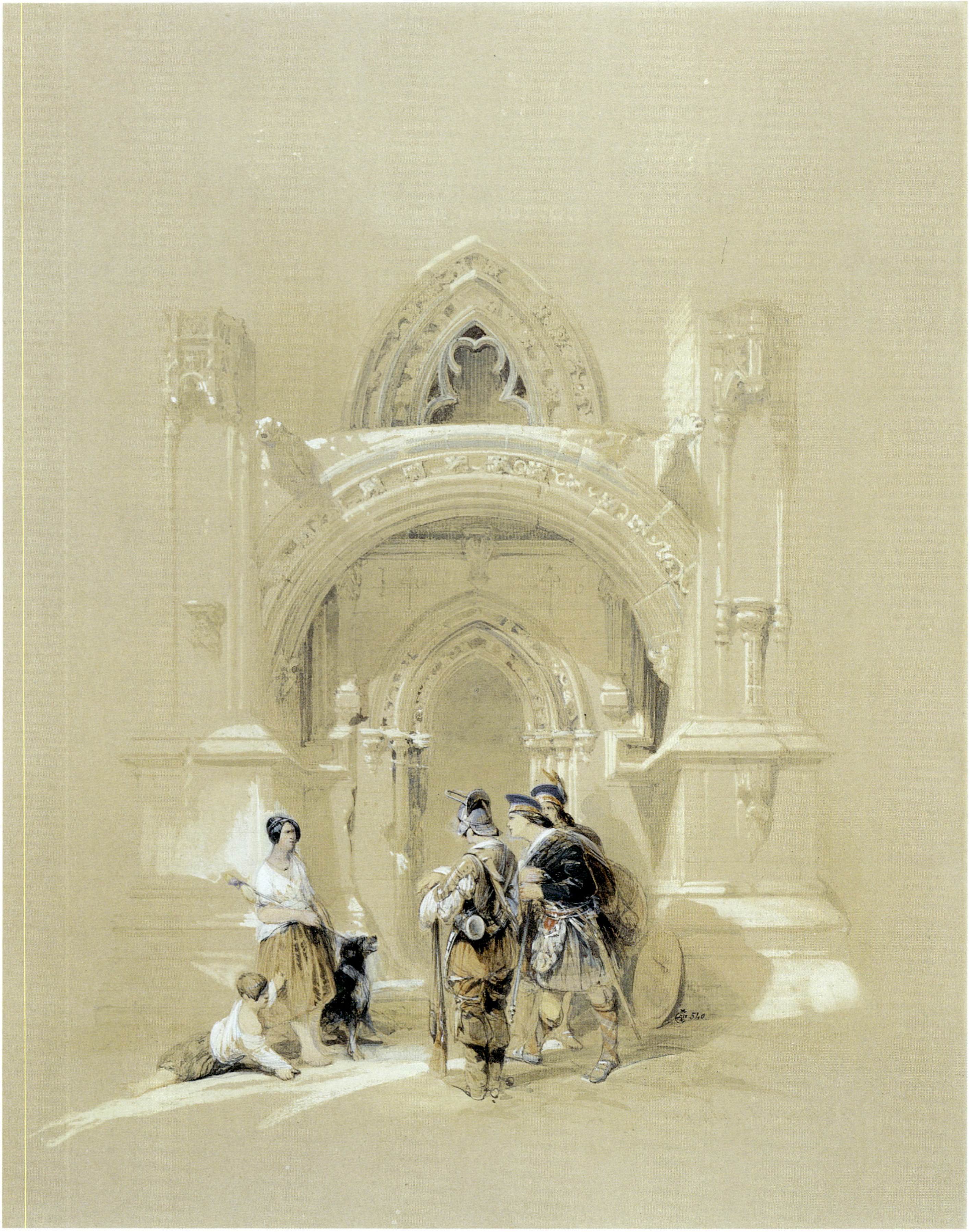

to have an opportunity of pointing out *his* improvements.'[30]

In 1860 responsibility for the works of restoration at Rosslyn passed to David Bryce, who had a lively appreciation of the sculpturesque effects used in many old Scottish buildings. His concern was that the restoration should consolidate the rich decorative detail. Operations commenced initially in order to enclose the family graves and execute some necessary repairs on the east end of the Chapel [plate 79]. One of the most important points in this second phase of restoration was whether the romantic lichen-covered Chapel should be restored to the condition it was in prior to its destruction, or whether it should be preserved in its ruinous state. Time and luxuriant vegetation had lent the Chapel a new beauty, so by the time the restoration was mooted two factions had already formed: lovers of the picturesque and lovers of architecture.[31] Roberts had stated the same arguments, in muted form, eighteen years previously.

It is hard to credit the extent to which one of the most popular Victorian painters could be engaged in a local cause or the intensity with which the different views were expressed. Thanks to Roberts, Rosslyn Chapel became a *cause célèbre* of national significance. In the words pronounced at the Royal Institute of British Architects, in the letters addressed to Lord Cockburn, to Hay and to Ballantine, we can discern a modern sense of historical consciousness. Even though the restoration works had rapidly changed the picturesque character of Rosslyn, provoking a loud outcry in the world of art, Roberts's battle provided a new approach founded on respect for the building's significance as a representation of achievements in the nation's history: it could no longer be judged solely on purely aesthetic criteria. Above all, Roberts had a deep-rooted, undying love for 'the romantic scenery, endeared to him by boyish recollections and associations.'[32] We cannot condemn an artist whose foot had trodden the Near East in search of wonderful and unequalled architectural remains in order to paint them 'on the spot *à la Roslin*.'[33]

79

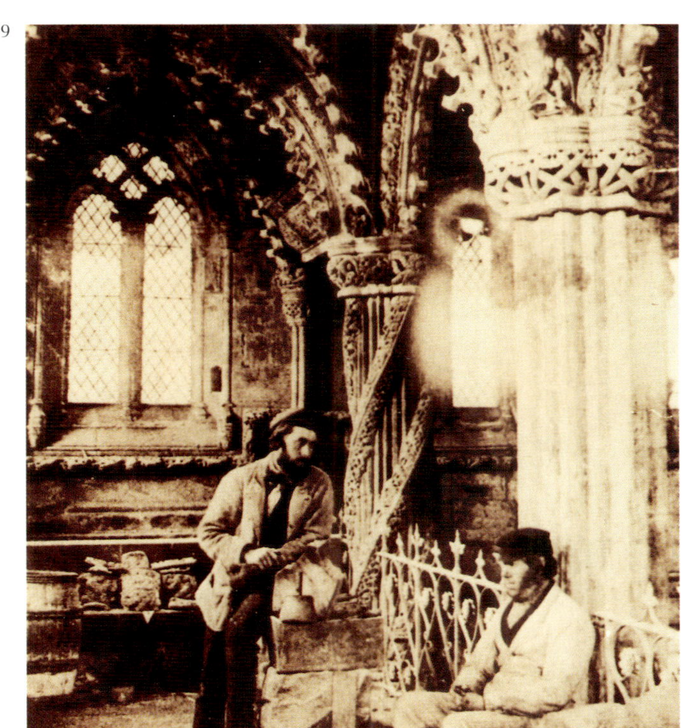

PLATE 78
David Roberts
The South Porch, Rosslyn Chapel, 1845
Victoria & Albert Museum, London

PLATE 79
Unknown Photographer
Sculptor, Lawrence Baxter, and J. Lawrence Tweedie in the Lady Chapel during restoration work, 1862
Royal Commission on the Ancient and Historical Monuments of Scotland, Edinburgh

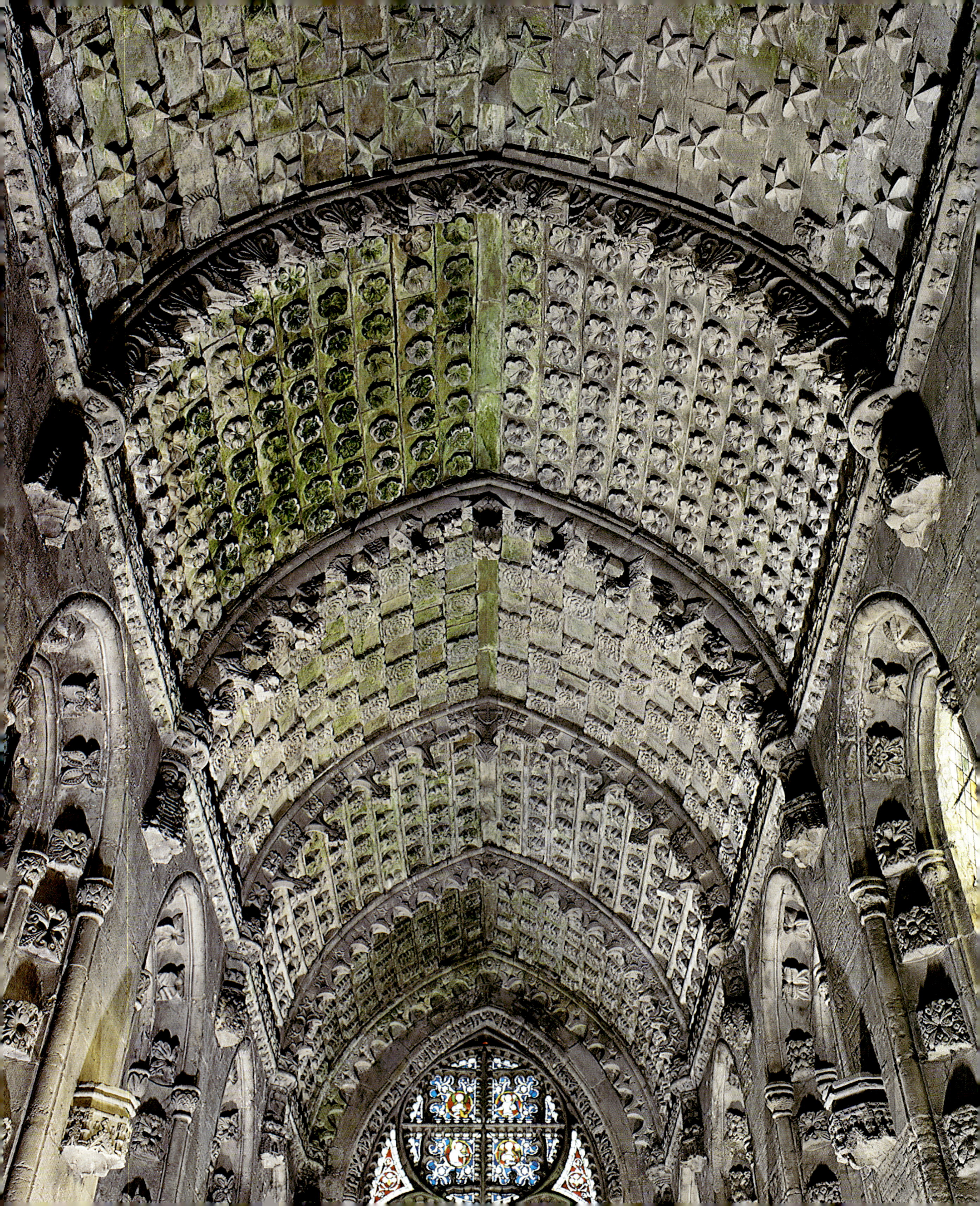

JAMES SIMPSON

The Conservation of Rosslyn: an Unfinished Story of Decline and Recovery

Rosslyn Chapel is a unique and extraordinary building. It has been recognised as such, and as one of the wonders of the Lothians and of Scotland, almost since it was built as the choir of what was to be the most elaborate collegiate church in Scotland, by Sir William St Clair of Rosslyn in the mid-fifteenth century. It has always attracted visitor: pilgrims and travellers and, at least since the eighteenth century, artists, poets and antiquaries. The richness and the late medieval symbolism of its interior sculpture and its undoubted Templar and Masonic associations have inspired a strong sense of mystery and a powerful esoteric interest, which have, in turn, generated a mythology and a literature where fact, interpretation and speculation are intertwined.

The all stone construction of the Chapel, its simplicity belied by the complexity of its carved surfaces, the unusual external appearance of its exposed barrel vault and its setting in relation to the equally spectacular Rosslyn Castle nearby are highly picturesque. Rosslyn Chapel was well known as an ancient, mysterious and romantic sight to be seen in the seventeenth and eighteenth centuries; Baron Clerk took visitors like Dr William Stukeley to see it and oversaw its repair in the 1730s. Its restoration for Episcopalian worship by David Bryce in the 1860s was the cause of considerable controversy at the time, but, whatever may have been lost in this process, its Victorian glass and furnishings can now be seen as an added layer, which has enriched its already complex history and transformed it from the 'monument' it had been since the Reformation back into a working church. The contributions of modern scholars, particularly those of Tom Addyman, Stuart Harrison and Dr Angelo Maggi, continue to add to the body of knowledge and to the fascination of the Chapel.

Rosslyn Chapel was built by the St Clairs and it has remained in the ownership of the St Clairs ever since. When Peter St Clair-Erskine succeeded to the Earldom of Rosslyn in 1977, he and his wife, Helen, were still students at Bristol University; the title carried no great estate with it, just scattered remnants including three parcels of land at Rosslyn, amounting to a few acres in all. On one stood Rosslyn Castle and on another the Chapel and Collegehill, the custodian's house which had once been the inn where Robert Burns, the Wordsworths, Turner, Sir Walter Scott, Queen Victoria and other distinguished visitors had been entertained. None of these buildings was in a particularly good state, but the condition of the Castle was acute. It had been unoccupied since the death of its aged caretaker, Miss Leach, and was being vandalised. The ruins of the great medieval curtain, donjon, and gatehouse were collapsing and the access road was slipping into the North Esk. The site was clearly dangerous and was attracting the attention of the Midlothian Council's building control officer. Remarkably, and in ways which the march of bureaucracy over the last twenty years would make much more difficult today, the road and the ruins were stabilised, the roofed range and its seventeenth- and eighteenth-century interiors repaired and made habitable and the whole site made safe and accessible again. That Rosslyn Castle came through this critical stage in its history so well is due in great measure to the pragmatic and constructive support which the Rosslyn trustees received from the predecessors of the Midlothian Council, Historic Scotland and Scottish Enterprise, through whose 'Community Programme' – amazing as it now seems – much of the ruin stabilisation work was done. That the Castle has thrived and has been enjoyed by so many people since then is owing to the Landmark Trust, which manages it, in its own inimitable way, for holiday letting.

By 1995 the trustees felt able to turn their attention to the Chapel and to Collegehill, which had been unoccupied since the departure in 1994 of the last resident custodian. The establishment of the Heritage Lottery Fund, in 1995, made a sustained programme of conservation work a realistic prospect for the first time. The Rosslyn trustees therefore leased the Chapel itself to a new charitable trust and a local project committee was established with Andrew Russell, a chartered surveyor now also director of Waterfront Edinburgh, as chairman and with Stuart Beattie as project director. The committee saw its first task as being to put the management of the Chapel as a paying 'visitor attraction' – which it had been for nearly a century – onto a proper footing. A new car park was made, the old Stable Range was repaired and much improved visitor accommodation was provided; this put the day to day running of the Chapel onto a financially secure basis and provided the administrative

PLATE 80
The interior of the vault, encrusted with carving and green with algae

infrastructure for the much more important work which was to follow.

When the conservation of the Chapel itself was begun in 1996, it was envisaged that the programme of work might take ten years to complete. It was obvious to all who visited or worshipped in the Chapel that it was green with algae, chronically damp – wet even – and, as a consequence, cold and uncomfortable to be in. Drying the wet masonry and repairing the roof coverings and rainwater disposal and drainage arrangements, to keep it dry in the future, were accepted as the principal objectives. However, it was known that the drying process would be slow and there was real concern that, as the masonry dried and moisture evaporated at the surfaces of the carved stonework, salt crystallisation might cause irreversible damage. Nobody wished to carry responsibility for such a catastrophe and so the work was progressed with considerable caution, prior investigation and theoretical analysis of what was likely to occur. The committee received expert advice from Dr John Dixon, Nicholas Boyes and Stan Johnston. As a first step, a steel canopy, elegantly engineered by John Addison, was erected over the Chapel to enable the slow drying process to begin; it was a bonus that the canopy provided safe access to the upper parts of the Chapel exterior, enabling visitors to see the flying buttresses, the pinnacles and their carvings at close quarters for the first time.

The second phase of work, prompted by the failure of part of the east boundary wall, concentrated on securing the Sacristy, the heavily eroded sandstone of the retaining walls adjacent to it and the rather complex associated drainage arrangements. The Sacristy itself was given a new roof structure, covered with Caithness slates – quarried almost single-handedly by the octogenarian Jack Green MBE – in honour of the St Clair connection, and the long steep stair down to it from the Chapel was repaired and made safer. A detailed record of the Sacristy was made by Tom Addyman. After a somewhat protracted progress, this work is, at the time of writing, very nearly complete.

Work will begin in spring this year on the repair and restoration of Collegehill, which from 2003 will, like the Castle, be managed for holiday letting by the Landmark Trust In the meantime, following completion of a conservation plan, which has dealt with the historical, archaeological and technical conservation and environmental issues in depth, the committee will be planning and assembling the funding for a third phase of work on the Chapel itself. This will deal with the roofs, rainwater and drainage arrangements and the conservation and repair of the high level stonework and the clerestorey windows, in preparation for the removal of the canopy, not later than 2006. Three further phases of work are planned, a fourth dealing principally with the Chapel interior, including heating and lighting, a fifth completing the repair of the low level stonework and windows and, more tentatively, a sixth removing the slurry coating with which the whole interior, including the sculpture, was covered in the 1950s. A full archaeological record will be made as the work progresses.

Securing the future of an extraordinary place like Rosslyn, particularly when it has suffered, as so many sites did in the difficult middle years of the twentieth century, so badly, is a long, painstaking and, at times, frustrating and even painful task. There are those who care deeply, but simply do not appreciate the difficulties, either of raising the funds and satisfying the various requirements of the funders, or of actually doing the job safely, responsibly and well. Many have contributed and

81

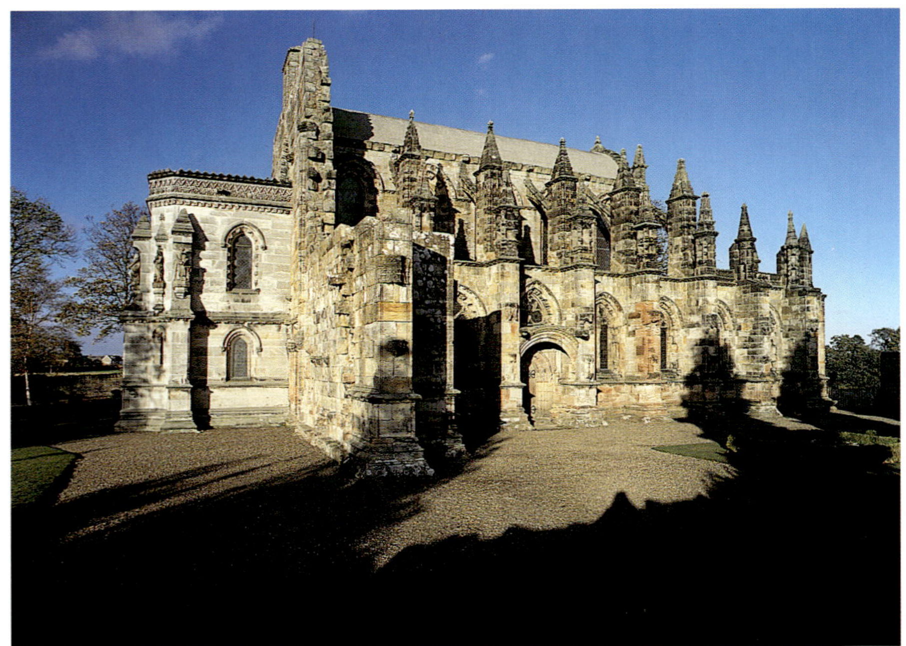

PLATE 81
Rosslyn Chapel from the south, with Andrew Kerr's baptistry of 1887 on the site of the intended crossing

82

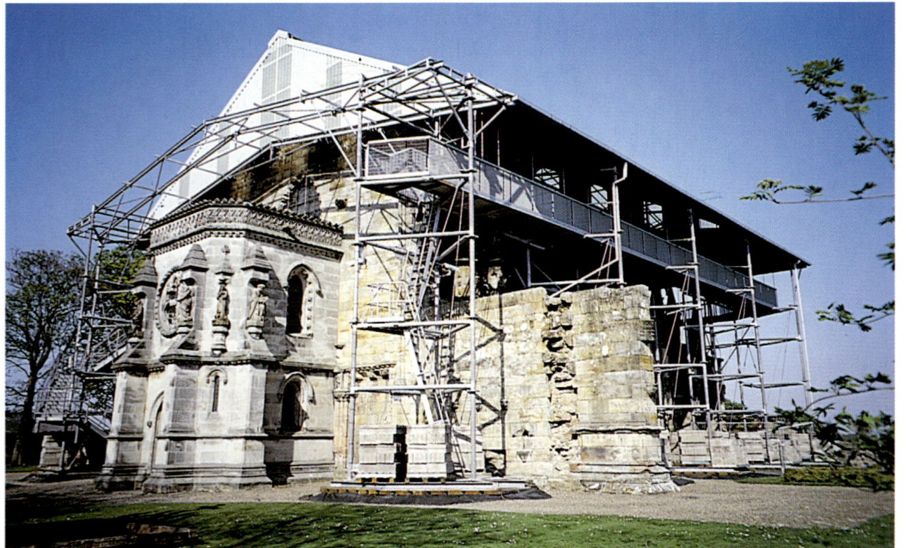

PLATE 82
The steel canopy erected over the Chapel to assist the drying of the masonry

83

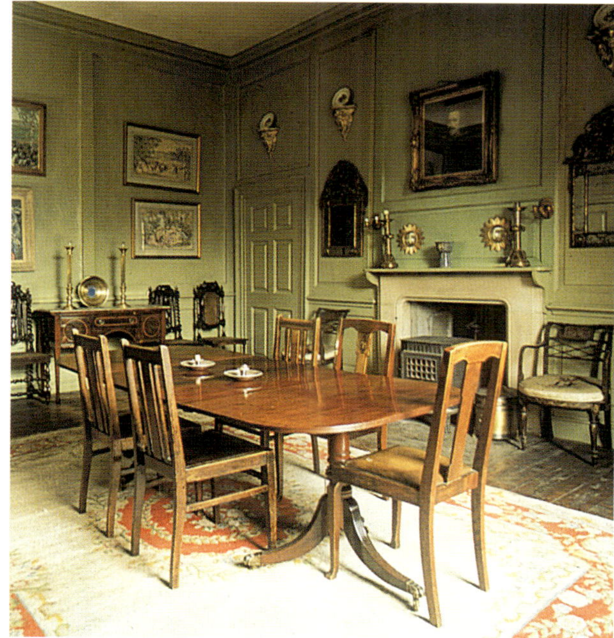

84

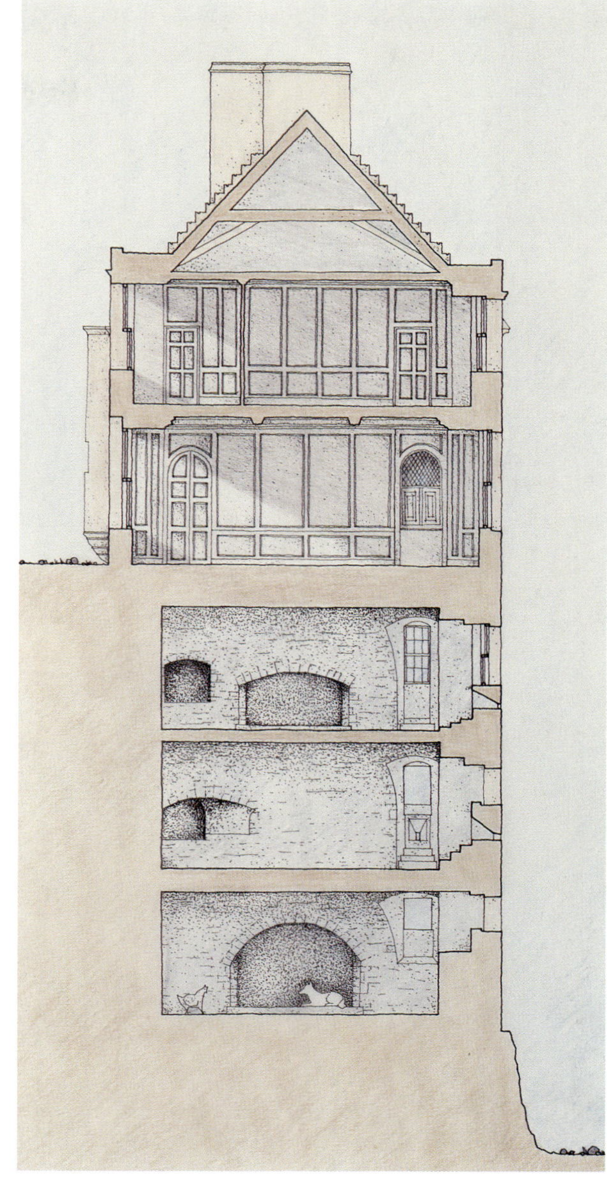

85

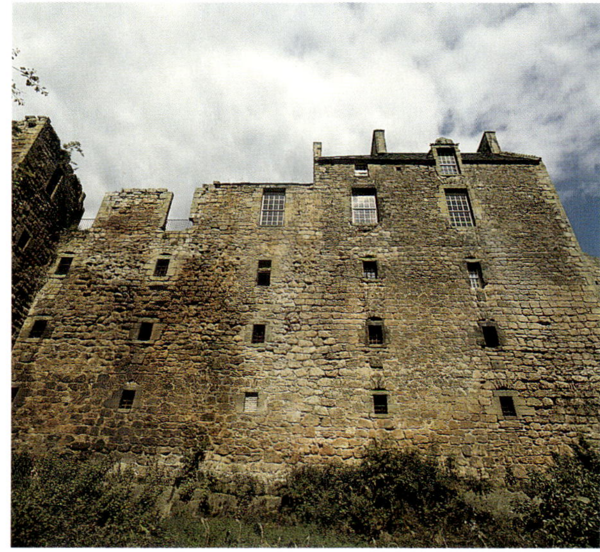

PLATE 83
The mid-eighteenth-century panelled dining room at Rosslyn Castle

PLATE 84
Section of Rosslyn Castle showing how the stone was quarried to form a shelf in the rock, built up with vaults, and the formation of habitable rooms at courtyard level

PLATE 85
Rosslyn Castle from the River Esk

will, all being well, continue to do so. These include the principal funders: Historic Scotland, the Heritage Lottery Fund, the European Regional Development Fund and the Midlothian Council, the first and last of which have given valuable support in other ways. The project committee and its chairman, Andrew Russell, have wrestled with the difficulties in a thoroughly businesslike way and the project director, Stuart Beattie and his staff at the Chapel have managed everything on the spot positively and with extraordinary good humour. In the end, however, the sustaining of the Castle and the Chapel for the benefit of future generations depends on the trustees of the trusts, which share responsibility for holding and managing the site. It depends, particularly, on the Earl of Rosslyn, whose police career – he is presently a commander with the Metropolitan Police – keeps the family in the south, but whose commitment to the long-term future of Rosslyn is total, and on Lady Rosslyn, whose knowledge and enthusiasm is demonstrated by her curatorship, with Dr Angelo Maggi, of this exhibition

It may be 2010 before the programme of conservation and development currently envisaged is completed. Fifty or so years of decline will have been followed by thirty years of making up the deficit. Nor will that be the end of the matter; managing and caring for a site like Rosslyn never ends. It is in the very nature of 'heritage' that responsibilities, as well as rights, are passed on from generation to generation. It will fall to others to carry Rosslyn forward for the benefit, not just of their own, but of future generations in all the centuries to come.

Checklist of Items in the Exhibition

In compiling the checklist of pictures for this exhibition it became apparent that during the eighteenth and nineteenth centuries there was little consistency in the spelling of the name 'Rosslyn'. Indeed, in some cases artists, amongst whom David Roberts is a notable example, have variously inscribed different works with different spellings and used different spellings again in letters. We have, therefore, opted for consistency of spelling throughout, in accordance with the ancient spelling of Rosslyn for the Castle, Chapel and Earldom.

Paintings

SIR WILLIAM ALLAN 1782–1850
The Visit of Queen Victoria and Prince Albert to Hawthornden 1842, 1844
Oil on canvas, 162.5 × 123.8cm
Scottish National Portrait Gallery, Edinburgh

WILLIAM BEATTIE BROWN 1831–1909
Rosslyn, Evening, 1857
Oil on canvas, 60 × 91cm (framed size)
Private Collection

MATHER BROWN 1761–1831
Alexander Wedderburn, Lord Loughborough, later 1st Earl of Rosslyn 1733–1805, c.1791
Oil on canvas, 127 × 101.9cm
Scottish National Portrait Gallery, Edinburgh

GEORGE CATTERMOLE 1800–1868
Rosslyn Chapel, c.1835
Oil on millboard, 27.7 × 22.8cm
Sheffield Galleries and Museums Trust
(illustrated on page 25)

LOUIS-JACQUES-MANDÉ DAGUERRE 1789–1851
The Interior of Rosslyn Chapel, 1824
Oil on canvas, 113 × 97cm
Private Collection
(illustrated on page 31)

WILLIAM DELACOUR D.1767
Self-portrait, c.1765
Oil on panel, 37.5 × 28.6cm
Scottish National Portrait Gallery, Edinburgh

WILLIAM DYCE 1806–1864
View of the South Aisle, Rosslyn Chapel, c. 1830
Oil on panel, 30 × 38cm
Private Collection
(illustrated on pages 46 & 60)

JULIUS CAESAR IBBETSON 1759–1817
Rosslyn Castle with Washerwomen and Cattle, c.1800
Oil on canvas, 45.7 × 61cm
McManus Galleries (Dundee City Council Arts)
(illustrated on page 36)

JULIUS CAESAR IBBETSON 1759–1817
Rosslyn Castle with Cows Drinking, c.1800
Oil on canvas, 64 × 80cm
Collection of the Duke of Buccleuch and Queensberry KT
(illustrated on page 44)

JULIUS CAESAR IBBETSON 1759–1817
North Esk: A Sketching Lesson, c.1800
Oil on canvas, 60 × 45cm
Private Collection

JULIUS CAESAR IBBETSON 1759–1817
A Woodman and his Family Resting near the Ruins of Rosslyn Castle, 1801
Oil on panel, 30.5 × 41cm
Private Collection

SIR DANIEL MACNEE 1806–1882
David Roberts, 1863
Oil on canvas, 91 × 71.5cm
Royal Scottish Academy, Edinburgh
(illustrated on page 52)

WILLIAM MCTAGGART 1835–1910
Rosslyn Castle, 1896
Oil on canvas, 61 × 47.5cm
Fife Council Museums: Kirkcaldy Museum & Art Gallery

ATTRIBUTED TO EDWARD MILLER ACTIVE 1736
Sir William St Clair of Rosslyn, 1736
Oil on canvas, 240 × 143cm (sight)
The Royal Order of Scotland, Edinburgh
(illustrated on page 14)

JACOB MORE 1740–1793
Rosslyn Castle from the South, c.1771
Oil on canvas, 95 × 115cm (framed size)
Collection of the Earl of Wemyss and March KT
(illustrated on page 14)

ALEXANDER NASMYTH 1758–1840
Rosslyn Castle with the Esk, c.1789
Oil on canvas, 61 × 46cm
Private Collection
(illustrated on page 16)

ALEXANDER NASMYTH 1758–1840
On the Esk, c.1800
Oil on panel, 40.6 × 27.9cm
The Robertson Collection, Orkney
(illustrated on page 36)

ALEXANDER NASMYTH 1758–1840
Rosslyn Castle with Rosslyn Chapel, c.1789
Oil on canvas, 70.5 × 92cm
Collection of E. Derricott
(front cover and illustrated on page 37)

ALEXANDER NASMYTH 1758–1840
Robert Burns, 1787
Oil on canvas, 38.4 × 32.4cm
Scottish National Portrait Gallery, Edinburgh
(illustrated on page 38)

JAMES NASMYTH 1808–1890
Robert Burns and Alexander Nasmyth at Rosslyn Castle
Oil on canvas, 60.9 × 91.4cm
Royal Scottish Academy, Edinburgh
(illustrated on page 39)

SIR HENRY RAEBURN 1756–1823
Sir Walter Scott, 1822
Oil on canvas, 76.2 × 63.5cm
Scottish National Portrait Gallery, Edinburgh

DAVID ROBERTS 1796–1864
The Entrance to the Crypt, Rosslyn Chapel, 1843
Oil on panel, 76.3 × 62.3cm
Victoria & Albert Museum, London
(illustrated on page 55)

DAVID ROBERTS 1796–1864
The South Porch, Rosslyn Chapel, 1845
Oil on canvas, 59.7 × 44.5cm
Blackburn Museum and Art Gallery
(illustrated on page 57)

REVD JOHN THOMSON OF DUDDINGSTON 1778–1840
Rosslyn Castle from the Glen, 1830
Oil on panel, 34.2 × 46.3cm
Hunterian Art Gallery, University of Glasgow
(illustrated on page 39)

WILLIAM STEWART WATSON 1800–1870
The Inauguration of Robert Burns as Poet Laureate of the Lodge Canongate, Kilwinning, 1787
Oil on canvas, 83.8 × 132.1cm
Scottish National Portrait Gallery, Edinburgh

Watercolours, Drawings and Sketchbooks

PATRICK WILLIAM ADAM 1854–1929
Rosslyn Chapel, c.1890s
Watercolour on paper, 64 × 55cm (framed size)
Collection of P.A. Campbell Fraser

SAMUEL BOUGH 1822–1878
Rosslyn Castle from the River Esk, 1850
Watercolour on paper, 24 × 34cm
Collection of Patrick Bourne

SAMUEL BOUGH 1822–1878
Midnight Mass at Rosslyn Chapel, c.1862
Watercolour heightened with white gouache over pencil on paper, 28.8 × 40.4cm
Private Collection

WILLIAM DELACOUR D.1767
Prospect of Rosslyn Castle and Chapel from the North-West, 1761
Pen and brown ink with watercolour over pencil on paper, 32.8 × 74.2cm
British Library Board, London
(illustrated on page 15)

WILLIAM DELACOUR D.1767
Prospect of Rosslyn Castle and Chapel from the South-East, 1761
Pen and brown ink with watercolour over pencil on paper, 32.7 × 74.5cm
British Library Board, London
(illustrated on page 15)

WILLIAM DELACOUR D.1767
Plan of Rosslyn Chapel, c.1761
Pen and ink with grey wash over pencil on paper, 34.2 × 49.3cm
British Library Board, London

WILLIAM DELACOUR D.1767
Elevation of the East End of Rosslyn Chapel, c.1761
Pen and ink with grey wash over pencil on paper, 33.3 × 49.5cm
British Library Board, London
(illustrated on page 29)

WILLIAM DELACOUR D.1767
Elevation of the North Side of Rosslyn Chapel, c.1761
Pen and ink with grey and pink washes over pencil on paper, 33.4 × 50cm
British Library Board, London

WILLIAM DELACOUR D.1767
A Perspective View of the Outside of Rosslyn Chapel, c.1761
Pen and ink with grey and green washes heightened with white over pencil on paper, 42 × 68.7cm
British Library Board, London
(illustrated on page 52)

WILLIAM DELACOUR D.1767
A Perspective View of the Inside of Rosslyn Chapel, c.1761
Pen and ink with grey and green washes over pencil on paper, 38 × 48cm
British Library Board, London
(illustrated on page 29)

WILLIAM DELACOUR D.1767
Section of Rosslyn Chapel from East to West, c.1761
Pen and ink with grey and pink washes over pencil on paper, 33.6 × 55.7cm
British Library Board, London

WILLIAM DELACOUR D.1767
Section of Rosslyn Chapel from North to South, c.1761
Pen and ink with grey, pink and brown washes over pencil on paper, 33.8 × 50cm
British Library Board, London
(illustrated on page 29)

WILLIAM DUNN ACTIVE 1816
Inside View of the Chapel at Rosslyn, 1816
Watercolour on paper or fine card, 15.1 × 20.5cm
Scottish Library, Edinburgh City Libraries and Information Services

JOSEPH FARINGTON 1747–1821
Rosslyn Castle, 1788
Pencil and grey wash on paper, laid down on original wash mount, 40 × 60cm
Private Collection
(illustrated on page 42)

JOSEPH FARINGTON 1747–1821
Rosslyn Castle, 1789
Pen, pencil and wash on paper, 32.2 × 55.6cm
National Gallery of Scotland, Edinburgh

MYLES BIRKET FOSTER 1825–1899
Hawthornden
Watercolour and bodycolour on paper, 32.5 × 37cm
Private Collection

MYLES BIRKET FOSTER 1825–1899
Rosslyn
Watercolour and bodycolour on paper, 32.5 × 37cm
Private Collection

JOSEPH MICHAEL GANDY 1771–1843
Sketchbook containing Survey Drawings of Rosslyn Chapel, 1806
Pen, grey ink and pencil (31 sheets), each sheet 14 × 22.5cm
Trustees of Sir John Soane's Museum, London
(illustrated on page 23)

JOSEPH MICHAEL GANDY 1771–1843
The Tomb of Merlin, 1815
Watercolour on paper, 76 × 132cm
Library Drawings Collection, Royal Institute of British Architects, London
(illustrated on page 25)

JOHN GLOVER 1767–1849
Sketchbook of a 'Scotch Tour', 1825
Pencil and wash, 14.7 × 23.5cm
Collection of John G. Fleming
(illustrated on page 45)

FRANCIS GROSE 1731–1791
Rosslyn Castle, View from the North-East, 1788
Pen and wash, 16.4 × 24.5cm
National Gallery of Scotland, Edinburgh

THOMAS HEARNE 1744–1817
Rosslyn Castle, 1778
Pencil, pen and ink with watercolour on laid paper, 16.9 × 23.7cm
Art Gallery of Ontario, Toronto
(illustrated on page 16)

JOHN ADAM HOUSTON 1812–1884
Sir Walter Scott in Rosslyn Chapel, 1854
Watercolour and bodycolour on paper, 43 × 57cm (sight)
Collection of Mr and Mrs P. Wilcockson
(illustrated on page 54)

GEORGE MEIKLE KEMP 1794–1844
The Apprentice Pillar, Rosslyn Chapel, 1824
Pen and ink with watercolour over pencil on paper, 13.6 × 11cm
Royal Scottish Academy, Edinburgh
(illustrated on page 25)

JACOB MORE 1740–1793
Rosslyn Castle with River and Figures, c.1771
Pen and pencil on paper, 29.7 × 50.4cm
National Gallery of Scotland, Edinburgh

ALEXANDER NASMYTH 1758–1840
The Artist with Robert Burns at Rosslyn Castle, 1786
Pencil on paper, 15.9 × 21cm
Scottish National Portrait Gallery, Edinburgh

ALEXANDER NASMYTH 1758–1840
Rosslyn Castle, c.1789
Pencil on paper, 11.8 × 15.7cm
National Gallery of Scotland, Edinburgh

FRANCIS NICHOLSON 1753–1844
Rosslyn Castle from the South-West, c.1812
Watercolour over pencil on paper, 32 × 38.5cm (sight)
Private Collection
(illustrated on page 19)

DAVID ROBERTS 1796–1864
Rosslyn Chapel, 1828
Watercolour over pencil on paper, 24.5 × 38cm
Collection of Dr and Mrs I.A. Murdoch
(illustrated on page 48)

DAVID ROBERTS 1796–1864
The Apprentice Pillar, Rosslyn Chapel, 1830
Watercolour on paper, 31.4 × 22.9cm
Victoria & Albert Museum, London
(illustrated on page 53)

DAVID ROBERTS 1796–1864
The Interior of Rosslyn Chapel, 1842
Pencil and watercolour heightened with white on light brown paper, 25.3 × 35cm
National Gallery of Scotland, Edinburgh
(illustrated on page 13)

DAVID ROBERTS 1796–1864
The South Porch, Rosslyn Chapel, 1845
Watercolour on paper, 47 × 35.9cm
Victoria & Albert Museum, London
(illustrated on page 64)

DAVID ROBERTS 1796–1864
Rosslyn, c.1840s
Watercolour over pencil on paper, 14.7 × 27.6cm
Collection of Mr Andrew Widdowson

DAVID ROBERTS 1796–1864
The South Porch, Rosslyn Chapel, c.1842
Watercolour and bodycolour over pencil on paper, 64 × 52cm (sight)
Private Collection
(illustrated on page 57)

Photographs and Prints

THOMAS ROSS 1839–1930
Rosslyn from the East, 1914
Grey and blue washes over pencil on paper, 25.5 × 22.5cm
National Library of Scotland, Edinburgh
(illustrated on page 33)

JOHN RUSKIN 1819–1900
Rosslyn Chapel, 1838
Pencil on paper, 52.8 × 36.6cm
Ruskin Foundation, Ruskin Library, University of Lancaster
(illustrated on page 27)

PAUL SANDBY 1731–1809
Lady Frances Scott and Lady Elliot Drawing with a Camera Obscura, c.1780
Watercolour over pencil on paper, 12.7 × 13cm
Yale Center for British Art, Paul Mellon Collection, New Haven
(illustrated on page 45)

ATTRIBUTED TO PAUL SANDBY 1731–1809
Bridge and Ruins of Rosslyn Castle, c.1750
Pen and wash, 24 × 38.7cm
National Gallery of Scotland, Edinburgh

GEORGE SHEPHERD FL.1800–1830 AFTER JOSEPH MICHAEL GANDY 1771–1843
The Apprentice Pillar, Rosslyn Chapel, 1809
Watercolour on paper, 44.4 × 63.8cm
Victoria & Albert Museum, London
(illustrated on page 22)

THOMAS STOTHARD 1755–1834
Rosslyn Castle, c.1812
Watercolour over pencil on paper, 23.6 × 20.4cm
The British Museum, London
(illustrated on page 49)

JOSEPH MALLORD WILLIAM TURNER 1775–1851
'Scotch Antiquities' sketchbook, 1818
Tate, London
(illustrated on page 42)

JOSIAH WOOD WHYMPER 1813–1903
The South Porch, Rosslyn Chapel, 1858
Watercolour and bodycolour on paper, 25.5 × 19.5cm
Ruskin Foundation, Ruskin Library, University of Lancaster
(illustrated on page 61)

HUGH WILLIAM WILLIAMS 1773–1829
Rosslyn Castle, 1795
Watercolour on paper, 62.3 × 45.2cm
Private Collection
(illustrated on page 40)

HUGH WILLIAM WILLIAMS 1773–1829
Rosslyn Castle from the North, 1805
Watercolour over black chalk on paper, 29 × 39cm (sight)
Private Collection
(illustrated on page 40)

JOHN WILSON 1774–1855
View of Rosslyn Castle from the River, 1808
Watercolour on paper, 48.8 × 34.6cm
National Gallery of Scotland, Edinburgh

ANDREW BELL 1726–1810
A Perspective View of the Inside of Rosslyn Chapel, 1761
Line engraving after his own drawing, 25.8 × 20.7cm (paper size)
Scottish Library, Edinburgh City Libraries and Information Services
(illustrated on page 28)

J. BURNETT AFTER JOSEPH MICHAEL GANDY 1771–1843
Elevation of Part of the South Side, Rosslyn Chapel, 1812
Engraving, 20.3 × 14.7
Private Collection
(illustrated on page 23)

J. BURNETT AFTER JOSEPH MICHAEL GANDY 1771–1843
Rosslyn Chapel, 1812
Engraving, 15 × 21.2cm
Private Collection

WILLIAM BYRNE 1743–1805 AND S. MIDDIMAN 1750–1831 AFTER THOMAS HEARNE 1744–1817
Rosslyn Castle, 1779
Engraving, 18.4 × 25.3cm
Private Collection

SIR DAVID YOUNG CAMERON 1865–1945
The South Porch, Rosslyn Chapel, 1899
Etching, 28.2 × 18.7
Hunterian Art Gallery, University of Glasgow
(illustrated on page 61)

WILLIAM DONALDSON CLARK 1816–1873
The Apprentice Pillar, Rosslyn Chapel, c.1860
Albumen print, 22.2 × 27.2cm
Scottish National Photography Collection at the Scottish National Portrait Gallery, Edinburgh

WILLIAM DONALDSON CLARK 1816–1873
The South Porch, Rosslyn Chapel, c.1860
Albumen print, 21.9 × 27.7cm
Scottish National Photography Collection at the Scottish National Portrait Gallery, Edinburgh
(illustrated on page 61)

JOHN CLERK OF ELDIN 1728–1812
Rosslyn Castle
First plate
Etching and drypoint, 9 × 10.6cm
National Gallery of Scotland, Edinburgh

JOHN CLERK OF ELDIN 1728–1812
Rosslyn Castle
Second plate
Etching and drypoint, 9 × 10.8cm
National Gallery of Scotland, Edinburgh

JOHN CLERK OF ELDIN 1728–1812
Rosslyn Castle
Second Plate
Etching and drypoint, 9 × 10.8cm
National Gallery of Scotland, Edinburgh

ROGER FENTON 1819–1869
The South Porch, Rosslyn Chapel, c.1860s
Albumen print, 35 × 42.5cm
Victoria & Albert Museum, London
(illustrated on page 57)

THOMAS HIGHAM 1796–1844
AFTER GEORGE CATTERMOLE 1800–1868
Rosslyn Chapel, 1835
Line engraving, 19.1 × 12cm (paper size)
Scottish Library, Edinburgh City Libraries and Information Services

DAVID OCTAVIUS HILL 1802–1870
AND ROBERT ADAMSON 1821–1848
The West Wall, Rosslyn Chapel, c.1843–8
Calotype, 14.8 × 19.8cm
Scottish National Photography Collection at the Scottish National Portrait Gallery, Edinburgh
(illustrated on page 58)

DAVID OCTAVIUS HILL 1802–1870
AND ROBERT ADAMSON 1821–1848
Part of the South Side, Rosslyn Chapel, c.1843–8
Calotype, 15.6 × 11.8cm
Scottish National Photography Collection at the Scottish National Portrait Gallery, Edinburgh

DAVID OCTAVIUS HILL 1802–1870
AND ROBERT ADAMSON 1821–1848
Part of the East End, Rosslyn Chapel, c.1843–8
Calotype, 15.3 × 11.4cm
Scottish National Photography Collection at the Scottish National Portrait Gallery, Edinburgh

DAVID OCTAVIUS HILL 1802–1870
AND ROBERT ADAMSON 1821–1848
Group of Figures at Rosslyn Chapel: West Wall with Piscina, c.1843–8
Calotype, 18.1 × 14cm
Scottish National Photography Collection at the Scottish National Portrait Gallery, Edinburgh

DAVID OCTAVIUS HILL 1802–1870
AND ROBERT ADAMSON 1821–1848
Great East End Window with Figure, Rosslyn Chapel, c.1843–8
Calotype, 17.3 × 13.2cm
Scottish National Photography Collection at the Scottish National Portrait Gallery, Edinburgh

DAVID OCTAVIUS HILL 1802–1870
AND ROBERT ADAMSON 1821–1848
Rosslyn Castle, c.1843–8
Calotype, 11.3 × 15.6cm
Scottish National Photography Collection at the Scottish National Portrait Gallery, Edinburgh

DAVID OCTAVIUS HILL 1802–1870
AND ROBERT ADAMSON 1821–1848
Old Yew Tree at Rosslyn, c.1843–8
Calotype, 15.8 × 11.4cm
Scottish National Photography Collection at the Scottish National Portrait Gallery, Edinburgh

DAVID OCTAVIUS HILL 1802–1870
AND ROBERT ADAMSON 1821–1848
The Architect, William Burn, at Rosslyn Chapel, c.1843–8
Calotype, 15.4 × 11.2cm
Scottish National Photography Collection at the Scottish National Portrait Gallery, Edinburgh
(illustrated on page 59)

JOHN JACKSON 1778–1831 AND HENRY MEYER 1782–1847 AFTER JAMES NORTHCOTE 1746–1831
Alexander Wedderburn, Baron Loughborough, later 1st Earl of Rosslyn 1753–1805, 1812
Stipple engraving, 45.7 × 35.6cm
Scottish National Portrait Gallery, Edinburgh

THOMAS KITCHIN ACTIVE 18TH CENTURY AFTER CAPTAIN ANDREW ARMSTRONG 1700–1794 AND MOSTYN ARMSTRONG D.1791
A New and Correct Map of the Three Lothians, 1773
Engraving (six joined sheets), 88.6 × 155.5cm
British Library Board, London

FRIEDRICH SCHENCK 1828–1901 AFTER OTTO THEODORE LEYDE 1835–1897
James Alexander St Clair-Erskine, 3rd Earl of Rosslyn 1802–1866, c.1850
Lithograph, 51 × 37cm
Scottish National Portrait Gallery, Edinburgh
(illustrated on page 52)

CAPTAIN JOHN SLEZER C.1645–1717
The Chapel of Rosslyn, from *Theatrum Scotiae*, 1693
Engraving, 32 × 42cm (sight)
Private Collection
(illustrated on page 12)

SAMUEL DUKINFIELD SWARBRECK ACTIVE 1830–1865
The East Aisle or Lady Chapel, Rosslyn Chapel, 1837
Tinted lithograph, 42.2 × 28cm
Private Collection
(illustrated on page 51)

SAMUEL DUKINFIELD SWARBRECK ACTIVE 1830–1865
The Interior of Rosslyn Chapel, 1837
Tinted lithograph, 41 × 30.5cm
Private Collection
(illustrated on page 51)

SAMUEL DUKINFIELD SWARBRECK ACTIVE 1830–1865
The North Entrance, Rosslyn Chapel, 1837
Tinted lithograph, 42.2 × 28cm
Private Collection

SAMUEL DUKINFIELD SWARBRECK ACTIVE 1830–1865
Rosslyn Castle and Glen, 1837
Tinted lithograph, 41 × 30.5cm
Private Collection
(illustrated on page 17)

GEORGE WASHINGTON WILSON 1823–1893
The Master's Pillar, Rosslyn Chapel, c.1880
Albumen print, 20.6 × 13.6cm
Private Collection
(illustrated on page 62)

GEORGE WASHINGTON WILSON 1823–1893
A Detail of the Ceiling of the Lady Chapel, Rosslyn Chapel, c.1880
Albumen print, 13.2 × 20.3cm
Private Collection
(illustrated on page 62)

Manuscripts

The Rosslyn Missal
Illuminated manuscript by various hands, *c.* late 12th century to early 14th century
The Trustees of the National Library of Scotland, Edinburgh

Letter of Jurisdiction granted by the Freemen Masons in Scotland to Sir William St Clair of Rosslyn, signed by William Schaw, Maistir of Work, *c.*1600
The Grand Lodge of Antient, Free and Accepted Masons of Scotland

Letter of Jurisdiction granted by the Freemen Masons and Hammermen in Scotland to Sir William St Clair of Rosslyn, *c.*1628
The Grand Lodge of Antient, Free and Accepted Masons of Scotland

Hay's Memoirs. Or a collection of several things relating to the most famed families in Scotland. Done by Mr Richard Augustine Hay, *c.*1700
The Trustees of the National Library of Scotland, Edinburgh
(illustrated on page 21)

Letter from George Thomson to Julius Caesar Ibbetson, 28 August 1800
The Trustees of the National Library of Scotland, Edinburgh

Printed Books

[BISHOP ROBERT FORBES]
An Account of the Chapel of Rosslyn (new edition), Edinburgh, 1778
The Grand Lodge of Antient, Free and Accepted Masons of Scotland

JULIUS CAESAR IBBETSON
An Accidence or Gamut of Painting in Oil and Watercolours, London, 1803
Includes a manuscript letter from Ibbetson to the Countess of Balcarres, 1 January 1802
Private Collection

SIR WALTER SCOTT
The Lay of the Last Minstrel, London, 1805
The Trustees of the National Library of Scotland, Edinburgh

ANONYMOUS
The Mirror of Literature, Amusement and Instruction, Vol.VII, London, 1826; includes a woodcut illustration, *View of Rosslyn Chapel at the Diorama*, after Daguerre
British Library Board, London
(illustrated on page 26)

JAMES MAIDMENT (ED.)
Genealogie of the Sainteclaires of Rosslyn, Edinburgh, 1835
The Trustees of the National Library of Scotland, Edinburgh

E.T. COOK AND A. WEDDERBURN (EDS.)
The Works of John Ruskin, Library Edition, Vol.XXXV, London, 1908
The Trustees of the National Library of Scotland, Edinburgh

Notes

The Living Tradition
pages 11–19

1 James Jackson, *The Chivalry of Scotland in the days of King Robert Bruce, including The Royal Hunt of Roslin*, Edinburgh, 1848, p.iii: hereafter Jackson.

2 'The name was anciently Rosslyn, or Roslyn, and this orthography is still retained by the noble possessors of the property. It is said to signify a *rocky eminence* and a *waterfall* and the natural appearances of the locality favour this derivation. That portion of the Esk, indeed, which runs over a rocky and sloping channel in the immediate vicinity is still designated "The Lynn"'. J. Brydone, *Brydone's Guide to Roslin, Hawthornden &c, by the North British and Peebles Railways*, Edinburgh, 1858, p.16.

3 John Dickson, *Roslin Castle, The St Clairs and their History*, 1897, p.7: hereafter Dickson.

4 Richard Augustine Hay, *Genealogie of the Sainteclaires of Rosslyn*, Edinburgh, 1835, p.6: hereafter Hay.

5 Walter Scott, *The Lay of the Last Minstrel*, Canto Sixth, verse XXIII, *The Poetical Works of Sir Walter Scott* (ed. J. Logie Robertson), London, 1913, p.45.

6 Dickson, p.35.

7 Jackson, p.34.

8 Hay, p.20.

9 Dickson, p.36.

10 Hay, p.26.

11 Hay, p.28.

12 Dickson, p.36.

13 Robert Chambers, *Domestic Annals of Scotland*, Edinburgh, 1858, vol.1, p.536.

14 '*The Green Man*, a theme common to many English churches, has been proved by the researches of Lord and Lady Raglan to be a form of the legendary Robin Hood, who, as we are now aware, was no outlaw, but the spirit or god of the woodland.' Lewis Spence, *Mystical Roslin*, p.27.

15 Dickson, p.36. There is a legend relating that the 'treasure', reputedly hidden in the vaults beneath the courtyard at the Castle, refers in fact to these manuscripts. James Jackson, in his *Historical Tales of Roslin Castle*, Edinburgh, 1837, p.12, gives an entertaining, if somewhat improbable, account of the finding of this literary prize by an Italian count in 1834.

16 Hay, p.151.

17 Although Ibbetson's oil paintings of Rosslyn are variously dated, one as late as 1812, we only have records of a visit to Rosslyn in the summer of 1800.

18 Stanks: 'A Pond or Pool, also a ditch or dyke of slowly moving water or a moat. Scottish dialect, from the old French 'estanc'', Oxford English Dictionary.

19 Dr Robert Forbes, Bishop of Caithness, *An Account of the Chapel of Roslin, 1778*, new edition, Edinburgh, 2000, with Preface by Archibald Orr-Ewing, B.A., Grand Master Mason, p.iv.

20 Hay, p.27.

21 Francis Grose, *The Antiquities of Scotland*, London, 1789, vol.1, p.45.

22 Ibid, p.49. The gardener can be identified from family account books as David Wilson, father-in-law of the famous Annie Wilson, landlady of the old Rosslyn Inn, to whom Burns's verses are dedicated.

23 Cuthbert Bede, *A Tour in Tartan-Land*, London, 1873, p.372.

24 Letter from David Roberts to John Britton, 8 January 1846, private collection.

25 Letter from 4th Earl of Rosslyn to Andrew Kerr, architect, 5 October 1880: Rosslyn Muniments, National Archive of Scotland (GD164–2249).

26 William Beattie, *Scotland*, London, 1838, vol.1, p.80.

Rosslyn Chapel: a Pocket Cathedral in an Earthly Paradise
pages 21–33

1 From the manuscript, 'An Account of the Chapel of Roslin containing an Historical and Geographical Description of the ancient and present State of that extraordinary Piece of Architecture', in the National Library of Scotland (MS 21196). The manuscript was first published under the pseudonym 'Philo-Roskelynsis' in January 1761 in *The Edinburgh Magazine*, and reprinted in 1774 and 1778 by James Murray.

2 A considerable historical literature exists for Rosslyn Chapel and Castle. Key works are: T.S. Muir, *Descriptive Notices of the Ancient Churches of Scotland*, Edinburgh, 1848; Francis H. Groome, *Ordnance Gazetteer of Scotland: A Survey of Scottish Topography, Statistical, Biographical and Historical*, Edinburgh, 1885, vol.VI; James Grant, *Old and New Edinburgh*, London, 1882. Where not otherwise noted, information cited in the text is taken from these sources.

3 Richard Augustine Hay, *Genealogie of the Sainteclaires of Rosslyn*, Edinburgh, 1835, p.27. Hay's father died when he was about five years old, and his mother soon afterwards married James St Clair of Rosslyn. The voluminous study made by Hay of the St Clair family charters was completed in 1700, and part of it was published posthumously in 1835. Hay's manuscripts – the principal source for the history of the Chapel – are kept in the National Library of Scotland (Adv. MS.34.1.9.i). The charters and other formal documents related to the Rosslyn family have been re-copied (Adv. MS.32.6.2., fols.3–82).

4 Ibid.

5 Robert Forbes, 'An Account of the Chapel of Roslin & c. Most respectfully inscribed to William St. Clare of Roslin Esq. Representative of the Princely Founder and Endower', *The Edinburgh Magazine*, January 1761, vol.5, p.2.

6 In connection with the story, and perhaps even its recent origin, it is noteworthy that Captain Slezer calls it 'Prince's pillar', as if named in honour of the founder of the Chapel. See John Slezer, *Theatrum Scotiae*, London, 1693, p.63.

7 For a fuller explanation of Gandy's survey of the building, see Angelo Maggi, 'Poetic stones: Roslin Chapel in Gandy's sketchbook and Daguerre's Diorama', *Architectural History, Journal of the Society of Architectural Historians*, September 1999, vol.42, pp.263–83.

8 Annie Wilson is wonderfully described and depicted by a correspondent of *The Gentleman's Magazine*, September 1817, p.209: 'Annie Wilson recites the Latin Epitaphs with apparent facility; but her pronunciation is so harsh and discordant, that to an English ear it is quite unintelligible: – if any thing in the way of interruption comes across her, she commences once more her elegant demonstration, her narrative of the Apprentice's Pillar, with "his head bearing the scar just about the brow that his master made upon it, his mother's head represented as if bewailing the death of her son, and the apprentice's master's head, just before he was hanged", and finishes with her recitation of the Latin Epitaphs.'

9 The eminent physician Dr Anthony Todd Thomson (1778–1849) during his visit to the Chapel in 1823 notes in his journal the same 'divining-rod': 'After Breakfast, we proceeded to the chapel of Roslin, which is now shewn by the landlord of the inn, since the old lady, who for so many years used to repeat the story of its faded glory, had been gathered to her fathers. Mr Wilson, for that is the name of the present shewman, has too much understanding to

believe one half of what he is obliged to detail. He uses a staff to point to the carvings and other features of the Chapel, and told us that it was a present from Sir Walter Scott, having been the rod of office which the worthy baronet filled when the king visited Edinburgh'. Dr A.T. Thomson, *Journal of a Vacation in Parts of England and Scotland 1823* [unpublished: in the possession of a descendant, Dr Ian Gregg].

10 Not everyone was sympathetic to Gandy's visionary interpretation: for instance, the writer of *Monthly Retrospect of the Fine Arts* for that year, stating that 'Gandy's Roslin Chapel in the Exhibition of the Royal Academy of London is beautifully drawn, but too ideal in colouring and finishing for a real view.' National Library of Scotland (Adv.MS.29.4.2, fols.228–9, inscribed 'Collegiate Church of Roslin, 1809').

11 See John Britton, 'An Essay Towards an History and description of Roslin Chapel, Scotland' in *The Architectural Antiquities of Great Britain; represented and illustrated in a series of views, elevations, plans, sections and details of various Ancient English Edifices: with Historical and Descriptive accounts of each*, London, 1812, vol.III, pp.47–56. The other drawings executed by Gandy, that were published by Britton, ranged from an accurate plan of the building to an extremely detailed outline section; from scaled drawings of single architectural elements to beautiful interior perspectives and a detailed view of the pinnacles. Gandy's work became a source of inspiration and documentation for future illustrators. Beyond the plates published by Robert William Billings in *The Baronial and Ecclesiastical Antiquities of Scotland*, Edinburgh, 1845–52, Gandy's influence can be seen in the designs of John Lessels published in *The Transactions of the Architectural Institute of Scotland*, session 1862–3, in which we are presented with a series of architectural details in a portion of the work entitled 'Roslin Chapel, shown in some of its more peculiar characteristics', National Monuments Record of Scotland (RIAS engraving books, I.12). The architect John Lessels (1808–1883), on several occasions in his career as a planner, decided to escape from the rigorous rules of his work in order to enjoy painting at Rosslyn Chapel. He exhibited several oil paintings of the Chapel at the annual exhibitions of the Royal Scottish Academy from 1847 to 1866.

12 John Britton, *Architectural Antiquities*, op.cit., p.47. Britton, with this comment, is informing us that he accompanied Gandy on his visit to Rosslyn. There is no written testimony to prove it.

13 In reference to this, Gandy, in his sketchbook, clarifies the origin of this detail, writing: 'This one [related to the circular finial] remains at North Door': p.21 recto, Sir John Soane's Museum, London.

14 See Thomas Bonnar, *Biographical Sketch of George Meikle Kemp*, Edinburgh, 1892, pp.8, 13–14.

15 See Leitch Ritchie, *Scott and Scotland*, London, 1835, plate V, p.142.

16 The fact that Rosslyn Chapel was divided into two diferent parts, a central choir for the functions and an ambulatory leading to the Lady Chapel, makes much more sense as a late Gothic plan than the open plan which appears today.

17 John Britton, *Architectural Antiquities*, op.cit., p.49.

18 The painting in question is discussed by John Summerson in his article 'Gandy and The Tomb of Merlin', *The Architectural Review*, April 1941, vol.LXXXIX, 532, pp.89–90. See also by the same author, 'The Vision of J.M. Gandy', in *Heavenly Mansions and other essays on architecture*, New York and London, 1963, p.129.

19 For the English translation of Ludovico Ariosto's *Orlando Furioso*, Canto Terzo, XV, see *Orlando Furioso in English heroical verse* by John Harington (printed by G. Miller for I. Parker, London, 1634).

20 See Brian Lukacher, *Joseph Michael Gandy: The Poetical Representation and Mythography of Architecture*, Ph.D., University of Delaware, U.M.I. Research Press, 1987, p.170. By the same author see also, 'Phantasmagoria and emanations: lighting effects in the architectural fantasies of Joseph Michael Gandy', *AA Files*, 4, London, 1983, pp.40–8.

21 Walter Scott, 'Ballad of Rosabelle', *The Lay of the Last Minstrel: with Life and Notes*, Edinburgh, 1809, canto VI, XXIII, p.148.

22 Robert William Billings, *The Baronial and Ecclesiastical Antiquities of Scotland*, Edinburgh, 1845–52, vol.IV, pp.2–3.

23 Ibid.

24 Ibid.

25 John Ruskin, *Praeterita. Outlines of scenes and thoughts perhaps worthy of memory in my past life*, Orpington, 1885, vol.I, p.432. One of Ruskin's Rosslyn sketches is published in the Cook and Wedderburn edition of *The Works of Ruskin*, London, 1908, vol.XXXV, p.233.

26 Samuel Prout visited Rosslyn on Saturday 20 August 1814. From his journal we know that he finds the Chapel exquisite but has not the time to draw it as this would have taken days. Nevertheless, he published a tinted lithograph representing the Apprentice Pillar in his *Sketches at Home and Abroad: Hints on the Acquirement of Freedom of Execution and Breadth of Effect in Landscape Painting*, London, 1844, plate IX. Ruskin owned a copy of Prout's work, now in the Ruskin Foundation, University of Lancaster.

27 Britton, *Architectural Antiquities*, op.cit., p.52.

28 See Angelo Maggi, 'Daguerre e le suggestioni della Rosslyn Chapel', *Fotostorica. Gli Archivi della Fotografia*, n.3/4, April 1999, pp.32–5.

29 See R. Derek Wood, 'The Diorama in Great Britain in the 1820s', *History of Photography*, Autumn 1993, vol.17, n.3, pp.284–95.

30 See Wolfgang Schivelbusch, *Disenchanted Night: the Industrialisation of Light in the Nineteenth Century*, Oxford 1988, p.216.

31 On the diorama techniques see: G. Bapts, *Essai sur l'histoire des Panoramas et des Dioramas*, Paris, 1891; A.T. Gill, 'The London Diorama', *History of Photography*, January 1977, pp.31–3; Richard Daniel Altick, *The Shows of London*, Harvard, 1978, chap.IX; Bernard Comment, *The Panorama*, London, 1999, chap.IV.

32 Helmut and Alison Gernsheim, *L.J.M. Daguerre, The History of the Diorama and the Daguerreotype*, London, 1956, pp.176, 178.

33 *Le Corsaire*, 25 Septembre 1824, quoted in Georges Potonniée, *Daguerre Peintre et Décorateur*, Paris, 1935 (reprint 1989), p.82.

34 See *Blackwood's Edinburgh Magazine*, April 1826, No.CXI, vol.XIX, p.467.

35 'View of Roslyn Chapel, at the Diorama', in *The Mirror of Literature, Amusement, and Instruction*, Saturday 4 March, 1826, CLXXXV, p.132.

36 See Renzo Dubbini, *Geografie dello Sguardo, Visione e paesaggio in età moderna*, Turin, 1994, p.104. According to Dubbini there are 'strong connections between the techniques used by a Diorama and Scott's literary style. Like a Diorama, Scott's literary descriptions are constructed with an optical conception. In them the variation of light is strong, unexpected and often has supernatural overtones. Thus architecture has a fundamental function in establishing the identity of place, in the definition of local character and in fluctuations of weather.'

37 The advertisements for the *Interior of Rosslyn Chapel* at the diorama in Lothian Road were placed regularly in the *Caledonian Mercury* between 18 April 1835 and 24 October 1835, when it is recorded that 'the view of the Interior of Roslin Chapel will positively close on Saturday the 31st October instantly.'

38 *Caledonian Mercury*, 12 February 1825, p.3.

39 Ibid.

40 Bell's *Perspective View of the Chapel* is a geometrically correct perspective construction of the building in the taste of the architectural treatises of the time. The way of designing on a plane surface the representations of the vault and the flooring suggests use of a grid as an aid to the composition. This severe application of the principles of perspective projection of shadows and reflections makes the Chapel higher than actuality. Antiquarians like George Paton (1721–1807) and Richard Gough (1735–1809) collected several copies of this engraving as soon as it was published.

41 The announcement of his appointment to the School of Design is thus given in the *Edinburgh Evening Courant* for July 12 and 14, 1760: 'The commissioners and trustees for improving Fisheries and Manufactures in Scotland do hereby advertise that by an agreement with Mr De la Cour, painter, he has opened a school in this city for persons of both sexes that shall be presented to him by the trustees, whom he is to teach gratis the Art of Drawing for the use of manufactures; ... Mr De la Cour is likewise to teach the art of drawing to all persons that choose to attend his school at one guinea per quarter.' Quoted in D.F. Fraser-Harris, 'William

De la Cour, Painter, Engraver and Teacher of Drawing' in *The Scottish Bookman*, 5 January 1936, vol.1, pp.15, 16.

42 Helmut and Alison Gernsheim, *The History of Photography; from the Camera to the Beginning of the Modern Era*, London, 1969, p.66.

43 The title is *Two Views: Ruins of Holyrood Chapel, A Moonlight Scene painted by M. Daguerre and the Cathedral of Chartes by M. Bouton in the Diorama of London, Regents Park*, G. Shulze, London, 1825, p.4 (British Library 1359.d.6). About the painting by Daguerre, *Holyrood Chapel, A Moonlight Scene* in the Walker Art Gallery of Liverpool, see the catalogue of the Gallery, p.50; see also Stephen Bann, *The Clothing of Clio. A study of the Representation of History in Nineteenth-Century Britain and France*, Cambridge, Mass., 1984, p.56.

44 These are the words that Gernshiem uses to describe Daguerre's oil painting of the Holyrood diorama, in Helmut and Alison Gernsheim, *L.J.M. Daguerre*, op.cit., p.25.

45 The architect Edward Blore (1787–1879) in his plate of the *Interior of Rosslyn Chapel* for Sir Walter Scott's *Provincial Antiquities and Picturesque Scenery of Scotland* will adopt the same point of view. As in Daguerre, the view of the interior is drawn in a way that alters the height of the Chapel. This lack of proportion is actually caused by the presence of a few visitors, who were drawn according to a false perspective. It is interesting to note that Blore's plate was published in June 1826, soon after the diorama was presented in London.

46 David Patterson and Joe Rock, *Thomas Begbie's Edinburgh. A Mid-Victorian Portrait*, Edinburgh, 1992, p.15. The complete collection of the original glass plates by Begbie is kept in the City Art Centre, Edinburgh.

47 See Thomas Ross, 'Rosslyn Chapel, a paper read at Rosslyn', *Scottish Ecclesiological Society Transactions*, 1914–15, pp.238–47. Ross in his text quotes another architect who made the same kind of suppositions of how the crossing was intended to be finished: Thomas Kemp (1833–1853), son of the well known architect of the Scott Monument. The only surviving record of Kemp's *Collegiate Church of St. Matthew's at Rosslyn in its (supposed) finished state* appears in John Thompson, *The Illustrated Guide to Rosslyn Chapel and Castle*, Edinburgh, 1934, p.2.

48 Ibid., p.240.

49 From *The Scotsman*, 9 May 1861, p.3.

Rosslyn: 'That Romantic Spot'
pages 35–49

1 *The Glen of Roslin*, from *Poems suggested by celebrated Scottish localities*: verses iv and x. *The Poetical Works of David Macbeth Moir*, edited by Thomas Aird, Edinburgh and London, 1852, vol.1, p.169.

2 Walter Scott, *The Lay of the Last Minstrel*, 1805, Canto Sixth, verse XXIII.

3 John Thomson, *The Illustrated Guide to Rosslyn Chapel and Castle*, Edinburgh, 1892, p.9.

4 Robert Chambers, *Domestic Annals of Scotland*, Edinburgh, 1858, vol.1, pp.496–8.

5 The only Rosabelle mentioned in Richard Augustin Hay, *The Genealogie of the Sainteclaires of Rosslyn*, Edinburgh, 1835, p.6, is Rosabell Forteith, daughter to the Earl of Strathearn, who married Sir Henry St Clair *c.*1090. She has subsequently been identified as the Rosabelle in *The Lay of the Last Minstrel*: see John Dickson, *Roslin Castle, The St Clairs and their History*, Edinburgh, 1897, p.12. However, this is doubtful, as the Rosabelle in the ballad is clearly the daughter of the St Clairs of Rosslyn, crossing the Forth to be with her 'Ladye-mother', her 'sire' and 'Lord Lindsay's heir', the latter unlikely if she were already Sir Henry's wife. Furthermore, Rosslyn Chapel, 'that chapel proud', was not founded until 1446 and the St Clairs did not own land at Ravensheuch (Ravenscraig) until Sir William St Clair received them from James III in 1471, in exchange for the Earldom of Orkney. It is most likely that the ancient family name was borrowed for its romantic associations, rather than relating to an actual legend.

6 John Ruskin, *Praeterita*, 1853, chapter XII.

7 Prologue to *The Gentle Shepherd*, James Forrest, Edinburgh, 1808.

8 *Roslin Castle with the Answer*, published Edinburgh, 25 April 1776. This ballad also appears in many later Scottish song compilations.

9 James Nasmyth, *An Autobiography* (ed. Samuel Smiles), London, 1883.

10 J.C.B. Cooksey, *Alexander Nasmyth, A Man of the Scottish Renaissance*, London, 1991, p.27, cat.28a. Dr Cooksey refers to a fall of the tower in 1789 which is not supported by the pictorial evidence: see *The Living Tradition*.

11 Ibid, p.112, cat.R3.

12 James Alves, *The Banks of the Esk, or a saunter from Roslin to Smeaton*, Edinburgh, 1800, p.54.

13 Kenneth Garlick and Angus MacIntyre (eds), *The Diary of Joseph Farington 1747–1821*, London, 1978–98, vol.6, entry for 23 September 1801.

14 Unpublished letter from James Nasmyth to Alexander Fraser. Eccles Central Library.

15 Letter from Alexander Nasmyth to William Cribb, 23 August 1829. There is a discrepancy of dates. A note by James Nasmyth on the reverse of his oil painting, plate 37, states clearly that the excursion took place on 13 June 1786.

16 Ibid.

17 *The Poetical Works of Robert Burns* (ed. Raymond Bentham), Boston, 1974, p.184.

18 J.C.B. Cooksey, *Alexander Nasmyth, A Man of the Scottish Renaissance*, London, 1991, chapter 6.

19 Letter from David Roberts to James Nasmyth, 31 October 1864, quoted in Cooksey, op.cit., chapter 6.

20 Dr Anthony Todd Thomson, *Journal of a Vacation in Parts of England and Scotland, 1823* (unpublished: in the possession of a descendant, Dr Ian Gregg).

21 Joseph Rock *The Life and Work of Hugh William Williams*, unpublished PhD diss., University of Edinburgh, 1996, p.47.

22 Dr Anthony Todd Thomson, *Journal of a Vacation in Parts of England and Scotland, 1823* (unpublished: in the possession of a descendant, Dr Ian Gregg).

23 One in a private collection, one in the collection of the National Gallery of Scotland.

24 Bruce Robertson, *Paul Sandby*, London, 1985, no.109.

25 Sir George Beaumont, letter to Dr Thomas Munro, 30 December 1816.

26 James Boswell, *The Journal of a tour to the Hebrides with Samuel Johnson*, London, 1785, p.503.

27 See James Holloway, 'A Travelling Antiquarian', *Country Life*, 15 April 1982, p.1084.

28 Robert Burns, *On Captain Francis Grose* from *The Poetical Works of Burns* (ed. Raymond Bentman), Boston, 1974, p.186.

29 Kenneth Garlick and Angus MacIntyre (eds), *The Diary of Joseph Farington 1747–1821*, London, 1978–98, vol.6, entry for 22 September 1801.

30 Turner Bequest, Tate Gallery, London: 'Dunbar' (TB LIV); 'Edinburgh' (TB LV); 'Scotch Lakes' (TB VLI).

31 Turner Bequest, Tate Gallery, London, 'Scotch Antiquities' sketchbook 1818 (TB CLXVII).

32 S.F.L.S. Schetky, *Ninety Years of Work and Play, Sketches from the Public and Private Career of J.C. Schetky*, Edinburgh, 1877, pp.108–9.

33 Julius Caesar Ibbetson, *An Accidence or Gamut of Painting in Oil*, second edition, with a brief memoir of the author's life, London 1828, p.x.

34 Rotha Mary Clay, *Julius Caesar Ibbetson*, London, 1948, p.68.

35 Letter from James Clerk to Julius Caesar Ibbetson, 1 May 1801: Ibbetson family records. Clay, p.68.

36 It was through George Thomson that the ballad of *Roslin Castle* travelled to Austria, when it was set to music by Franz Joseph Haydn. Thomson confessed that Haydn's music was his 'first love' and he wrote to him in 1799, suggesting he compose tunes for Scottish airs: '… from that time we continued in correspondence till the year 1804, when I received the last of his many compositions'. J. Cuthbert Hadden, *George Thomson, Friend of Burns, his Life and Correspondence*, London, 1898, pp.303–4.

37 Letter from George Thomson to Julius Caesar Ibbetson, 28 August 1800. Crawford Muniments, National Library of Scotland (24/2/26).

38 Letter ftom George Thomson to Julius Caesar Ibbetson, 4 February 1803: Ibbetson family records. James Mitchell, *Julius Caesar Ibbetson*, London, 1999, p.41.

39 Letter from Julius Caesar Ibbetson to the Countess of Balcarres, Crawford Muniments, National Library of Scotland (24/2/13).

40 Rosslyn: Three exhibited; three untraced but previously illustrated as follows:

Christie's, London, 22/11/74, no.93, provenance: Lady Curzon Howe, Clifton Castle.

Sotheby's, London, 20/11/85, no.84, provenance: Ogilvie Collection.

Sotheby's, London, 13/7/88, no.69.

Hawthornden: one in the V&A Museum; two in private collections.

41 'To the Right Honourable Lady Elizabeth Keith Lindsay.

Madam I have presumed to take the liberty of dedicating the following little work ... to your Ladyship ... because the possibility of it was first suggested to me by the Right Honourable the Countess of Balcarres and yourself, during my short residence in your neighbourhood, at Rosslyn, in the summer of 1800, the remembrance of which will always excite in me the most pleasing sensations.' Julius Caesar Ibbetson, dedication from *An Accidence or Gamut of Painting in Oil and Watercolours*, London, 1803.

42 Kim Sloan, *'A Noble Art' Amateur Artists and Drawing Masters c.1600–1800'*, London, 2000, p.174.

43 James Nasmyth's Scrapbook, National Library of Scotland (MSS 3241 and Appendix D9).

44 James Nasmyth, *An Autobiography* (ed. Samuel Smiles), London, 1883, p.57.

45 The Journals of Jessy Allan, 21 July 1802, National Library of Scotland (MS.Acc.2466).

46 Ibid., 12 May 1803.

47 Elizabeth Countess of Sutherland inherited the title, at the age of one, on the death of her parents. She married George Granville Leveson-Gower in 1785 and became Marchioness of Stafford in 1803 when he inherited the title of Marquis. In 1833 her husband was created 1st Duke of Sutherland and Elizabeth thenceforth became known as the Duchess-Countess of Sutherland.

48 Cuthbert Bede, *A Tour in Tartan-Land*, London, 1863, p.394.

49 Kenneth Garlick and Angus MacIntyre (eds), *The Diary of Joseph Farington 1747–1821*, London, 1978–98, vol.6, entry for 20 April 1808.

50 *Memorials of Coleorton, letters to Sir George and Lady Beaumont, of Coleorton, Leicestershire, 1803–1834* (ed. William Knight), Edinburgh, 1887, vol.1, p.XVI.

51 Dorothy Wordsworth, *Recollections of a Tour made in Scotland A.D. 1803* (ed. J.C. Shairp), Edinburgh, 1874.

52 Letter from David Roberts to Christine Bicknell, 1 October 1842. National Library of Scotland (D. Bicknell).

53 Ibid.

54 '[Oh, Roslin!] Time, War, Flood and Fire,
[Have made your] glories star by star expire.
Chaos of ruins! Who shall trace the void,
O'er the dim fragments cast a lunar light,
And say, 'here was, or is', where all is doubly night?

Alas! [thy] lofty [castle]! And alas!
[Thy] trebly hundred triumphs! and the day
When [Sinclair] made the dagger's edge surpass
The conqueror's sword, in bearing fame away!'

From Lord George Byron, *Childe Harold's Pilgrimage*, London, 1881. I am grateful to Dr Jane Stabler for this information.

55 Richard Lockett, *Samuel Prout*, London, 1985, p.173.

The Unmaking of Pictorial Beauty: David Roberts and the Restoration Controversy *pages 51–65*

1 Samuel Dukinfield Swarbreck, *Sketches in Scotland Drawn from Nature and on Stone*, London, 1837, caption to Plate 1: 'North Entrance to Rosslyn Chapel'.

2 Letter from James Alexander St Clair Erskine to William Burn, dated 1836, National Archives of Scotland (GD 164/1013).

3 Ibid. The evidence that John Baxter the elder was the architect for this roof is contained in the Clerk of Penicuik papers, National Archives of Scotland (GD 18/5010/6). Sir John Clerk of Penicuik (1676–1755), one of the most significant and endearing personalities among the early eighteenth-century antiquaries in Scotland, pursued his interest of preserving Rosslyn Chapel, encouraging General James St Clair and acting as patron to the repair works between 1738 and 1742: 'Either about the Chapel, or House, it never entered in to my thoughts. Since You was so kind as take the trouble to direct the repairing of the Chappell, I have all alonge left that to you, to do in it as you had a mind, and indeed every thing about it.'

4 James Ballantine, *The Life of David Roberts, R.A.*, Edinburgh, 1886, p.201.

5 David Roberts wrote personally to the editor of *The Scotsman* (Wednesday, 6 December 1843, p.3) to ensure publication of his letters to Lord Cockburn regarding the state of Rosslyn Chapel. The name of Lord Cockburn is never mentioned in the paper. Evidence that the 'eminent and learned personage in Scotland' to which these letters were addressed was Cockburn, is contained in Roberts's letter to his Scottish friend David Ramsay Hay, London, 27 November 1843, National Library of Scotland (MS.3521, fols.166–7).

6 The painting in question, titled *Roslin*, was on display at the Royal Scottish Academy in 1855. Houston also exhibited in the same gallery, one year earlier, another painting titled *Roslin Glen*; for this see James Daforne, 'John Alexander Houston', *The Art Journal*, March 1869, p.69.

7 *The Scotsman*, 7 May 1861, p.3.

8 Ibid.

9 John Ruskin, *Modern Painters*, London, 1898, vol.1, p.127.

10 Ibid.

11 In Sara Stevenson, *David Octavius Hill and Robert Adamson, catalogue of their calotypes taken between 1843 and 1847 in the collection of the Scottish National Portrait Gallery*, Edinburgh, 1981, pp.210–11. Landscape calotypes of Rosslyn Chapel are in the Scottish National Portrait Gallery, nos.15–25, 96.

12 Richard Pare (ed.), *Photography and Architecture (1839–1939)*, Montreal, 1982, p.14.

13 William Henry Fox Talbot, *The Pencil of Nature*, London, 1844, caption to plate VI.

14 Marcia Pointon, *William Dyce, 1806–1864: A Critical Biography*, Oxford, 1979, p.24. Charles Dyce (fl.1840–1880), William's younger brother, painted Rosslyn Chapel in 1847 and, recalling the glory which restoration again brought to mind, dramatised the scene by the inclusion of a monk and a Cromwellian soldier.

15 William Donaldson Clark, 'On Photography as a Fine Art', *The Photographic Journal*, 15 May 1863, pp.286–7.

16 D.Y. Cameron, as a painter and graphic artist, had many links with photographers. One of his closest friends was the professional photographer, James Craig Annan (1864–1946), with whom he travelled to Holland in 1892 and to Italy in 1894. He also wrote an article on his friend's photographic style: 'An Artist's Notes on Mr J. Craig Annan's Pictures now being Exhibited at the Royal Photographic Society', *The Amateur Photographer*, 16 February 1900, p.123.

17 Wilson's Aberdeen factory, in addition to producing hundreds of thousands of prints each year, was perhaps the largest producer of landscape and architectural cartes de visite, which also found their way into the family portrait album with its specially cut slots for this standard print format. The little carte de visite measured only 2½ inches by 4 inches (64 × 100 mm) on its mount and, at prices of only a penny or two, became the most popular photographic format of the time. For a general account of Wilson's work see Roger Taylor, *George Washington Wilson, Artist & Photographer (1823–93)*, Aberdeen, 1981.

18 Sara Stevenson, *Light from the Dark Room*, Edinburgh, 1995, p.46. Much technical information comes from Wilson's own writings in *The British Journal of Photography* where he explains his working methods. Wilson also contributed to the history of photography with *A Practical Guide to the Collodion Process* which was published in 1855. His description is clear and concise and not only covers the manipulative process of coating, excising and developing the plate but also gives advice and recommendations, based upon experience, about cameras. For this see a reprint in R. Taylor, op.cit., pp.177–86.

19 'Notice of recently published stereographs. Scottish Gems', *The British Journal of Photography*, No.109, vol.vii, 1 January 1860, p.7.

20 Letter from Roberts to David Ramsay Hay, London, 30 October 1843, National Library of Scotland (MS.3521, f.164).

21 The only published source of this lecture seems to be a later summary of the event published in *The Builder* with some very peculiar notes made by Samuel Joseph Nicholl (1826–1905), who attended the lecture as a young member of the Institute. The author of the article in *The Builder* simplifies Britton's talk on the Chapel, with a long quote from Father Hay's manuscript, whereas Nicholl traces a more interesting account of the paper read, recording the issues that the debate aroused: 'Roslyn Chapel is a fragment of a building that may be called unique, and if it had been found on the banks of the Nile every detail would have been delineated, and most exaggerated accounts of its beauties published'. Nicholl's manuscript and sketches are kept at the Royal Institute of British Architects Library (RIBA/MS.sp./2/4): see 'On the collegiate church or chapel at Roslyn by John Britton read on 12 January 1846' in 'Notes made by Nicholl, while a member of the RIBA in the session 1845–1846'. See also *Architecture in Manuscript, 1601–1996. Guide to the British Architectural Library*, London, 1996, p.296.

22 Letter from Roberts to David Ramsay Hay, London, 30 January 1846, National Library of Scotland (MS.3522, f.31).

23 In this case Roberts refers to the following passage in Father Hay's manuscript: 'When my goodfather was buried, his corps seemed to be entire at the opening of the cave, but when they came to touch his body it fell into dust: he was laying in his armour, with a red velvet cap on his head on a flat stone: nothing was spoiled except a piece of white furring that went round the cap, and answered to the hinder part of the head. All the predecessors were buried after the same manner in their armour.' Hay, *Genealogie*, op. cit., p.154.

24 Roberts also endeavoured to prove this from the buttresses at the north and south-east angles of the east front being connected with those of the north and south fronts by a splayed wall in an unusual manner. See Andrew Kerr, 'The Collegiate Church or Chapel of Rosslyn, its Builders, Architect, and Construction', *Proceeding of the Society of Antiquaries of Scotland*, May 1877, p.225.

25 Ibid.

26 Letter from Roberts to Hay, London, 30 January 1846, National Library of Scotland (MS.3522, f.32); see note 21.

27 According to Roberts he received a reply only from John Britton: 'I received a very civil but I must say guarded note expressing his regret that in having ventured to differ in my opinion he had given me cause of offence. But offering to forward them to the secretary and together with any farther communications I might wish to make bring them before the Institute at their next meeting – In reply to his I wrote to thank him for his kind offer and accepting it – at the same time stating that after his courtesy …', National Library of Scotland (MS.3522, f.32). John Britton in his letter of apology to Roberts, dated 20 January 1846, wrote: 'Thanks for your communication about Roslyn and for the interest you take in such works. I hope nothing will achieve to prevent my attendance at the next meeting of the Architects Institute where I hope an opportunity will be afforded for me and Mr Burn to enter into some explanation for the purpose of doing justice. Such a discovery is worth fighting for and I regret that you did not came forword on the same evening when the drawings were present – you may be assured that I will take some opportunity of bringing the subject before the Institute', National Library of Scotland (Acc.7967/1, Mf.MS.381, 1846).

28 A preliminary watercolour sketch dated 1845 of this frontispiece is in the V&A Print Room (Mus. No.FA 540).

29 Letter from Roberts to Hay, London, 29 December 1845, National Library of Scotland (MS.3522, f.25).

30 Letter from Roberts to Hay, dated 1846, National Library of Scotland (MS.3522, f.41).

31 This is how an anonymous correspondent in *The Scotsman* somewhat prophetically described the nature of the conflict. See *The Scotsman*, 22 June 1861, p.6.

32 Ballantine, *Life of David Roberts*, op.cit., p.148.

33 Letter from Roberts to Hay, London, 9 September 1845, National Library of Scotland (MS.3522, f.16).

Photographic Credits

AIC Photographic Service, plate 57

Bourne Fine Art, plate 35

Richard Caspole, plate 47

Carlo Catenazzi, plate 9

Prudence Cuming Associates, London, plate 4

Chris Hall, plate 85

Trustees of the National Library of Scotland, plate 14a/b (NLS shelfmark: Adv GM 34. 1. 9. (ii), ff. 131v, 132r), plate 15 (NLS shelfmark: GM, plate 31 GM 692, no.237)

Reproduced by kind permission of the National Trust for Scotland, plate 12

Antonia Reeve, plates 2, 3, 11, 13, 17, 19–20, 22, 34, 36–7, 39, 40, 42, 45, 48–9, 50, 54–5, 59, 61, 67–8, 70–2, 74–6, 80–1

James Simpson, plates 82–3

© Simpson and Brown, plate 84

By courtesy of the Trustees of Sir John Soane's Museum, plate 18

Photograph courtesy of Sotheby's, plate 46

Photograph courtesy of Spink-Leger, London, plate 4,52

Further Reading

Ballantine, James, *The Life of David Roberts R.A.*, Edinburgh, 1866

Baynes, Thomas Mann, *Twenty Views of the City Environs of Edinburgh*, London, 1823

Beattie, William, *Scotland Illustrated in a series of views by T. Allom, W.H. Bartlett and H. McCulloch*, London, 1838, vol.II

Bede, Cuthbert, *A Tour in Tartan-Land*, London, 1873

Billings, Robert William, *The Baronial and Ecclesiastical Antiquities of Scotland*, Edinburgh, 1845–52, vol.VI

Britton, John, 'An Essay Towards an History and description of Roslin Chapel, Scotland', *The Architectural Antiquities of Great Britain; represented and illustrated in series of views, elevations, plans, sections and details of various Ancient English Edifices: with Historical and Descriptive accounts of each*, London, 1812, vol.III, pp.47–60

Calder, Angus (ed.), *Byron and Scotland*, Edinburgh, 1989

Chambers, Robert, and William, *The Gazetteer of Scotland*, Edinburgh, 1833

Clarke, Michael, *The Tempting Prospect: A Social History of English Watercolours*, London, 1981

Clay, Rotha Mary, *Julius Caesar Ibbetson*, London, 1948

Cooksey, J.C.B., *Alexander Nasmyth: A Man of the Scottish Renaissance*, London, 1991

Cooper Robert (ed.), *An Account of Roslin Chapel 1778*, Edinburgh, 2000

Crawford, Barbara E., 'Earl William Sinclair and the Building of Roslin Collegiate Church', *Mediaeval Art and Architecture in the Diocese of St Andrews*, British Archaeological Association conference transactions, n.XIV, Leeds, 1994, pp.99–107

Dickson, John, *Roslin Castle, the St Clairs and their History*, Edinburgh, 1897

Errington, Lindsay, and Holloway, James, *The Discovery of Scotland*, Edinburgh, 1978

Forbes, Robert, 'An Account of the Chapel of Roslin & c. Most respectfully inscribed to William St. Clare of Roslin Esq. Representative of the Princely Founder and Endower', *The Edinburgh Magazine*, January 1761, vol.5

Gower, Elizabeth Leveson, Duchess of Sutherland, *Views in Orkney and on the North-Eastern Coast of Scotland, taken in MDCCCV and etched in MDCCCVII; with some Account of the Orkney Isles extracted from Barry's History*, published by the author in 1807

Grant, James, *Old and New Edinburgh*, London, 1882

Grose, Francis, *The Antiquities of Scotland*, London, 1789, vol.II

Guiterman, Helen, and Llewellyn, Briony (eds.), *David Roberts*, London, 1986

Hadden, Cuthbert, J., *George Thomson, the Friend of Burns, his Life and Correspondance*, London, 1898

Hay, Richard Augustine, *Genealogie of the Sainteclaires of Rosslyn*, Edinburgh, 1835

Historical and Descriptive Account of Rosslyn Chapel and Castle with Engravings, engraved by J. & J. Johnstone, Edinburgh, 1827

Irwin, David and Francina, *Scottish Painters at Home and Abroad 1700–1900*, London, 1975

Jackson, James, *Historical Tales of Roslin Castle*, Edinburgh, 1837

Kerr, Andrew, 'Rosslyn Castle, its Buildings Past and Present', *Proceedings of the Society of Antiquaries of Scotland*, 10 December 1877 (plates XXI–XXIV), Edinburgh, 1878, vol.XII, pp.412–24

Kerr, Andrew, 'The collegiate Church or Chapel of Rosslyn, its Builders, Architect, and Construction', *Proceedings of the Society of Antiquaries of Scotland*, 14 May 1877 (plates XI–XVII), Edinburgh, 1878, vol.XII, pp.218–44

Klonk, Charlotte, *Science and the Perception of Nature*, London, 1996

Knight, William (ed.), *Memorials of Coleorton, Letters to Sir George and Lady Beaumont, 1803–1834*, Edinburgh, 1887

Lawson, John Parker, *Scotland Delineated in a Series of Views by C. Stanfield, W.L. Leitch, T. Creswick, D. Roberts and others*, London, 1847–54

Lockett, Richard, *Samuel Prout*, London, 1985

Macmillan, Duncan, *Painting in Scotland, the Golden Age*, Oxford, 1986

MacGibbon, David, and Ross, Thomas, *The castellated and domestic architecture of Scotland from the twelfth to the eighteenth century*, Edinburgh, 1887–92

MacGibbon, David, and Ross, Thomas, *The ecclesiastical architecture of Scotland from the earliest Christian times to the seventeenth century*, Edinburgh, 1896

Maggi, Angelo, 'Daguerre e le suggestioni della Rosslyn Chapel', *Fotostorica. Gli Archivi della Fotografia*, n.3/4, April 1999, pp.32–5

Maggi, Angelo, 'Poetic stones: Roslin Chapel in Gandy's sketchbook and Daguerre's Diorama', *Architectural History, Journal of the Society of Architectural Historians*, September 1999, vol.42, pp.263–83

Mallalieu, Huon, *The Dictionary of British Watercolour Artists up to 1920*, 3 vols, Woodbridge, 1976–90

Masson, Flora, 'Roslin, Hawthornden, and the Vale of the Esk', *Edinburgh Past and Present its associations and surroundings*, Edinburgh, 1877

Mitchell, James, *Julius Caesar Ibbetson*, London, 1999

McWilliam, Colin, *The Buildings of Scotland, Edinburgh and the Lothians*, London, 1980

Nasmyth, James, *James Nasmyth, Engineer: An Autobiography* (ed. Samuel Smiles), London, 1883

Pennant, Thomas, *A Tour in Scotland*, London, 1790, vol.II

Redgrave, Richard and Samuel, *A Century of British Painters*, Oxford, 1981

Robertson, Bruce, *Paul Sandby*, London, 1985

Rock, Joseph, *The Life and Work of Hugh William Williams set within a Scottish context*, unpublished PhD diss., University of Edinburgh, 1996, p.47

Ross, Thomas, 'Rosslyn Chapel, a paper read at Rosslyn', *Scottish Ecclesiological Society Transactions*, 1914–15, pp.238–47

Rosslyn, Peter, *Rosslyn Chapel*, Rosslyn Chapel Trust, 1997

Scott, Sir Walter, *The Provincial Antiquities and Picturesque Scenery of Scotland with Descriptive Illustrations by Sir Walter Scott*, London, 1826, vol.II

Slezer, John, *Theatrum Scotiae*, London, 1693

Sloan, Kim, *'A Noble Art' Amateur Artists and Drawing Masters c.1600–1800*, London, 2000

Stevenson, David, *The First Freemasons, Scotland's Early Lodges and their Members*, Edinburgh, 2001

Stoddart, John, *Remarks on local Scenery & Manners in Scotland*, vol.I, Edinburgh, 1801

Swan, Jim, and McNeill, Carol, *Dysart, A Royal Burgh*, Dysart, 1997

Swarbreck, Samuel Dukinfield, *Sketches in Scotland Drawn from Nature and on Stone*, London, 1837

Thomas, Jane, *Midlothian. An Illustrated Architectural Guide*, Edinburgh, 1995

Thompson, John, *The Illustrated Guide to Rosslyn Chapel and Castle*, Edinburgh, 1934

Thomson, Katrina, *Turner and Sir Walter Scott, The Provincial Antiquities and Picturesque Scenery of Scotland*, Edinburgh, 1999

Views of Roslin Castle and Chapel from drawings by J.M.W. Turner, E. Blore and Thomson of Duddingstone; with a Descriptive Letter, Edinburgh,1828

Watson John, 'St. Matthew's Collegiate Church, Rosslyn', *The Transactions of Edinburgh Architectural Association*, vol.9, pp.105–15

Wordsworth, Dorothy, *Recollections of a Tour made in Scotland, A.D. 1803* (ed. J.C. Shairp), Edinburgh, 1874